9/95

D1483322

WITHDRAWN

Portrait of Mary Wollstonecraft.
Courtesy of the Board of Trustees of the National Museums and Galleries
on Merseyside (Walker Art Gallery, Liverpool).

Mary Wollstonecraft and the Language of Sensibility

Mary Wollstonecraft and the Language of Sensibility

Syndy McMillen Conger

Rutherford • Madison • Teaneck
Fairleigh Dickinson University Press
London and Toronto: Associated University Presses

Associated University Presses
440 Forsgate Drive
Cranbury, NJ 08512

Associated University Presses
25 Sicilian Avenue
London WC1A 2QH, England

Associated University Presses
P.O. Box 338, Port Credit
Mississauga, Ontario
Canada L5G 4L8

The paper used in this publication meets the requirements
of the American National Standard for Permanence of Paper
for Printed Library Materials Z39.48–1984.

Library of Congress Cataloging-in-Publication Data
Conger, Syndy M.
    Mary Wollstonecraft and the language of sensibility / Syndy
McMillen Conger.
        p.   cm.
    Includes bibliographical references and index.
    ISBN 0-8386-3553-9 (alk. paper)
    1. Wollstonecraft, Mary, 1759–1797--Criticism and interpretation.
2. Feminism and literature--England--History--18th century.
3. Women and literature--England--History--18th century.
4. Sentimentalism in literature.   I. Title.
PR5841.W8Z654 1994
828'.609—dc20   93–33718
                                                                      CIP

Photograph of the author by Patti Sullivan-Howd.

PRINTED IN THE UNITED STATES OF AMERICA

to Jim
and our next twenty-five

Contents

Abbreviations

Works cited throughout this study are identified by the following short titles in the text and notes:

Analytical Review: Analytical Review (1788–97), in *The Works of Mary Wollstonecraft*, vol. 7, edited by Janet Todd and Marilyn Butler, 13–502. 7 vols. New York: New York University Press, 1989.

"Cave of Fancy": "The Cave of Fancy" (1787), in *The Works*, 1.185–206.

Collected Letters: Collected Letters of Mary Wollstonecraft, edited by Ralph M. Wardle. Ithaca: Cornell University Press, 1979.

Education of Daughters: Thoughts on the Education of Daughters, with Reflections on Female Conduct, in the more important Duties of Life (1787), in *The Works*, 4.1–52.

Female Reader: The Female Reader; or Miscellaneous Pieces in Prose and Verse; Selected from the Best Writers, and disposed under proper heads; for the Improvement of Young Women (1789), in *The Works*, 4.53–350.

"French Nation": "Letter on the Present Character of the French Nation" (1798), in *The Works*, 6.439–46.

French Revolution: An Historical and Moral View of the Origin and Progress of the French Revolution and the Effect it has Produced in Europe (1794), in *The Works*, 6.1–235.

Godwin and Mary: Godwin and Mary: Letters of William Godwin and Mary Wollstonecraft, edited by Ralph M. Wardle. Lincoln: University of Nebraska Press, 1966.

"Hints": "Hints (Chiefly designed to have been incorporated in the Second Part of *Vindication of the Rights of Woman*)" (1798), in *The Works*, 5.267–76.

Letters in Sweden: Letters Written During a Short Residence in Sweden, Norway, and Denmark (1796), in *The Works*, 6.237–364.

Maria: The Wrongs of Woman: or, Maria (1798), in *The Works*, 1.75–184.

Memoirs (1798): William Godwin, *Memoirs of Mary Wollstonecraft.* New York: Greenberg; London: Constable, 1927.

Mary: Mary, A Fiction (1788), in *The Works*, 1.1–74.

Original Stories: Original Stories from Real Life with Conversations, calculated to Regulate the Affections and form the Mind to Truth and Goodness (1788), in *The Works*, 4.352–450.

"On Poetry": "On Poetry, and Our Relish for the Beauties of Nature" (1797), in *The Works*, 7.1–11.

Rights of Men: A Vindication of the Rights of Men, in a Letter to the Right Honorable Edmund Burke; Occasioned by his Reflections on the Revolution in France (1790), in *The Works*, 5.1–78.

Rights of Woman: A Vindication of the Rights of Woman: With Strictures on Political and Moral Subjects (1792), in *The Works*, 5.79–266.

Preface

Theoretical Perspectives on the Language of Feeling

The 1990s, the bicentennial decade for five of the best-known works of Mary Wollstonecraft, may well begin a new era in Wollstonecraft criticism. Her collected works are available for the first time and extended studies are beginning to appear; all signs suggest that the author of the *Vindication of the Rights of Woman* (1792) is at last to be herself vindicated.[1] She still wants vindicating, primarily because the contexts in which her life and works are generally seen do not do her justice, even make her seem to fail. Viewed as a daughter of the Enlightenment, her extraordinary irrationality seems paradoxical; viewed as a forerunner of Romanticism, her advocacy of reason and her faith in didactic literature seem anachronistic; and viewed as a feminist, her romantic attachments and her sentimental reveries mystify. This book proposes a context better able to explain, if not resolve, certain problems and paradoxes in her life and works: the language of sensibility and its fictions. In order to describe the operation of that language of sensibility without succumbing immediately to its eighteenth-century vagaries, the Preface views it first in the light of recent helpful studies from four contiguous disciplines: linguistics, psychology, philosophy, and feminist theory.

Prisoner of Language?

> In these respects my very reason obliges me to permit my
> feelings to be my criterion.
> —Letter X, *Letters in Sweden* (*Works*, 6.289)

Most Wollstonecraft studies revolve to some extent around a puzzling contradiction in her life and works, and this project is no exception. It asks: Why would an avowed rationalist repeatedly fall prey to her passions? Whatever the cause, the results are unmistakable: passion distorts both her fictions and her exercises in dispassionate prose, destabilizing the point of view, immobilizing the characters or the argument, coloring the setting and the style, and, at least for some readers, undermining her authority. Feelings also tyrannize her private life: demanding her fealty to a dysfunctional family, surprising her into love with inaccessible or unreliable men, at least twice nearly costing her her life. Wollstonecraft's biographers and interpreters over the years have responded variously to this apparent contradiction. Her contemporaries (interestingly enough, both allies and foes) often see her as a daughter of feeling whose professed allegiance to reason is never matched by rational performance,[2] while more recent critics view her as a thoroughly committed disciple of reason who outgrows her childhood thralldom to the cult of sensibility. In either case, however, the language of sensibility often emerges as an imprisoning, crippling, even a corrupting agent in Wollstonecraft's intellectual life,[3] a tempting assumption to make in the current climate of language skepticism in the profession. From this representation of Wollstonecraft as a prisoner of language, so widespread yet largely unexamined, springs the question behind the present investigation of the texts that she inhabits: could the language of sensibility—so seemingly limited, vague, and powerless—have had such far-reaching psychological effects?[4]

Alternate Language, Alternate Reality

Was not the world a vast prison, and women born slaves?
—*Maria* (*Works*,1.1.88)

Wollstonecraft's innovative metaphoric use of a madhouse in her last novel lends some credence to the claim that her language of sensibility can imprison its speakers. The heroine of *Maria* (whom Wollstonecraft states at the outset is representative of her gender) lives in a world in which the linguistic balance of power is alarmingly lop-sided. When her profligate husband declares her a guilty runaway, then a madwoman, his accusations, though without foundation, have the power to set devastating actions in motion. Authorities arrest and detain her in an insane asylum without so much as a hearing. When she eventually does get to court in order to request a divorce, the judge ignores the facts she presents as evidence of her husband's treachery and dismisses her case with contempt. Instead of justice, he, too, offers her instant condemnation for "pleading her feelings." The *Rights of Woman* presents a similar world, this time in polemical prose: Wollstonecraft identifies the language of sensibility as men's primary agent in the oppression of women.[5] What thesis about her relationship to that language, then, could be more apt? Still, it seems almost too facile, too much the all-too-predictable discovery of a twentieth-century critic about an eighteenth-century author. Besides, Wollstonecraft rarely acts like a prisoner of any kind of discourse, sentimental or rational. She experiments with a variety of persuasively authoritative personae in her works: the concerned governess, the intimate friend, the anti-novelist, the political polemicist, the radical feminist, the concerned mother, the impartial reviewer or historian.[6] And when she speaks the language of sensibility, she generally does so without apology, exuding the confident authority or the sometimes defiant self-assurance of an insider speaking to other insiders—the defensive posture taken, according to M. A. K. Halliday, by discriminated members of any society who have developed their own "anti-language."[7]

An antilanguage, according to Halliday, emerges from an "antisociety," a group which finds or feels itself to be outcast from the society and wishes to construct its own alternative identity and reality. An antilanguage develops in dependent relationship to the dominant language of its culture: frequently relying on its syntax and grammar, yet building its own specialized vocabulary from the words of the mother tongue. It abducts known expressions and tropes them creatively to give them new, highly idiosyncratic meanings, making the new language arbitrary and metaphoric by nature. It is also highly selective, abducting and transforming only those terms it finds useful for its own antisociety, and often multiplying available terms for beliefs, values, attitudes, or activities of special interest to that antisociety; in the words of Halliday, it "selectively relexicalizes" useful terms, and, in addition, "overlexicalizes" in key areas. Its distinguishing features, then, are dependency, arbitrariness, metaphoricity, selectivity, and overlexicalization.

Halliday notes near the end of his article that literature itself often functions as an antilanguage; certainly the eighteenth-century's language of sensibility, with a literature-dependent lexicon, has many antilanguage features. Crafted to articulate emotions, it is necessarily metaphoric—including the terms "emotion," "feeling," and "sensibility"—and highly specialized, overlexicalizing affective areas of experience in idiosyncratic ways and neglecting many others. It also offers its speakers alternate identities or realities; in this case, a kind of communal immersion in the authors, heroes, heroines, language, gestures, and myths of sensibility—an antisociety for disaffected sons and daughters of the Enlightenment bourgeoisie.[8]

Halliday discusses the bonding function of antilanguage so central to the antilanguage of sensibility in terms of Roman Jakobson's widely cited model of the six functions of language:

REFERENTIAL
EMOTIVE   POETIC   CONATIVE
PHATIC
METALINGUAL[9]

In Jakobson's terms, the functions of language most frequently emphasized in the discourse of sensibility are the emotive and the phatic. Neither representation of reality (referential), nor persuasive force (conative), nor crafting of the message (poetic), nor clarification of the code (metalingual) is as important to speakers of sensibility as self-expression and the sustained bonding with others like themselves. This is not to suggest that antilanguages have nothing to do with codes; on the contrary, in some cases they may be secret codes only meant to be understood by the initiated few. Halliday's three extended examples of "secret" antilanguage are especially provocative in the context of this study: two are languages of criminal underclasses (one the Renaissance "pelting") and the third a language of Polish prison inmates.

Speaking of Passion

> Sensibility . . . is only to be felt; it escapes discussion.
> —*Mary* (*Works*, 1.24.60)

Wollstonecraft frequently laments, as she does above, that even the specialized language of sensibility inadequately communicates feeling. This is a common complaint in her century; language skepticism runs deep in the counterculture of sensibility. The professors of sensibility cultivate a backup body language system—now more familiar to many than the primary system—consisting in silence, significant looks and other facial expressions, inarticulate sounds, gestures, postures, and unconsciousness. The resulting double code—part antilanguage, part body language—mirrors the lexical development of the term "sensibility" as a sign referring *either* to body *or* to mind, an ambiguity that persists in modern usage for the term "sense" from which "sensibility" derives.[10] It may also be responsible for the modern notion of "sentiment" as a display of inappropriate or excessive emotion.

Historians of the period have long since acknowledged that sensibility "escaped discussion"; just why that is so has not been so readily apparent. Murray Cohen provides a partial answer in *Sensible Words*; eighteenth-century language is a language in transition: "Seventeenth-century linguists sought to establish an isomorphic relationship between language and nature; in the early eighteenth century, linguists assumed that language reflects the structure of the mind."[11] Still designed to refer to external events or objects, the language is increasingly called upon in the eighteenth century to speak of internal states or subjects; and its resources for doing so are limited.[12] To some extent, then, followers of sensibility may very well sometimes be at a loss for words; but they are also not very self-conscious about the words they have. Specifically, they are not trained to recognize, express, or analyze the kind of silent self-talk that psychologists now know generates emotions.

The cognitive-emotive theory of emotion best explains the variety of emotional responses human subjects give to a single, identical stimulus.[13] Assuming such a theory, for example, philosopher Robert Gordon can isolate the cognitive components and the "sententiality" of emotions, and divide them into two classes on that basis: he demonstrates that some emotions spring from the activation of wishes and knowledge (he calls them "factive"), others from the activation of wishes and beliefs ("epistemic"). In either case, emotions result from certain "sentences" in people's minds, sentences they can, with some training, learn to discover and parse: "I am afraid to ride the subway for fear of being mugged," for example.

In "Cognition and Feeling," psychologist Silvano Arieti isolates three "orders" of emotions, two of which he believes depend heavily on language-related processes for their existence. Only the first-order "protoemotions" humans share with animals, elicited by immediate stimuli, transcend or precede language: tension, appetite, fear, rage, and satisfaction. Second-order "preconceptual" emotions, however, are elicited primarily by the "cognitive symbolic processes" of image formation: anxiety, anger, wishes. Arieti calls for more study of image formation, saying it is intensely motivational and "the basis for all higher mental processes." Third-order "conceptual" emotions are the "chronic" emotional states which can give humans the most trouble: depression, hate, love, joy. These states are almost exclusively stimulated and sustained by language: "The escape from depression," he adds by way of example, "can only occur through cognitive means."[14]

The theories of Gordon and Arieti shed long-needed light on one often noted feature of exemplars of sensibility: their tendency to escalation. Men and women of sensibility (actual or fictional) frequently drive themselves to emotional extremes (or chronic states) like hysteria or melancholy, only to be temporarily stopped by mental or physical exhaustion. The literature of sensibility, which begins with moderate poetic expressions of grief and compassion midcentury, reaches sensational Gothic heights by the century's end, a process Louis Bredvold traces in *The Natural History of Sensibility*. Clearly, in both of these instances the use of the language of sensibility does much more than simply express emotion—it creates it as well. Its metaphors stimulate and sustain image-induced second-order emotions like anxiety and desire; and its sentiments (the "emotionally tinged thoughts" and "rationalized emotions" of the *OED* definition) activate, prolong, and intensify prized emotional states like melancholy, love, and ecstasy.

Such knowledge is faintly discernible to Wollstonecraft. She displays an admirable degree of language consciousness throughout her writing career; she even occasionally links certain kinds of language to certain states of mind. To her, however, as to her contemporaries, emotions remain largely "mysterious forces" that often well up from within, rather unexpectedly, in response to random events. As a result, though she frequently talks herself into emotions, she rarely talks herself out of them; she assumes she is not in command.[15] If Wollstonecraft's bouts of suicidal depression are the result of self-talk, and if that self-talk speaks the antilanguage of sensibility, then perhaps she is both its captive and its victim.

The Power of Metaphors

> To give the shortest definition of sensibility, replied the
> sage, I should say that it is the result of acute senses, finely,
> fashioned nerves, which vibrate at the slightest touch, and
> convey such clear intelligence to the brain, that it does not
> require to be arranged by the judgment.
> —"Cave of Fancy" (*Works* 1.3.201)

The eighteenth-century notion of "sensibility" resembles closely the state of psychosomatic readiness philosopher Gilbert Ryle terms an "inclination": a "propensity" or "dispositional property" "to be in a particular state, or to undergo a particular change, when a particular condition is realised." He draws his examples of "inclination" from the material world: the brittleness of glass, the solubility of sugar. An inclination differs from a "mood," one of Ryle's emotional states that is also a "propensity," in that it is not always necessarily activated. Moods "monopolize" people's minds, become chronic, and can eventually become traits of character. People with "inclinations" are also likely, according to Ryle, to experience states he calls "agitations," certain "commotions" that require the pre-existence either of two inclinations or an inclination and a "factual impediment": "There are some words," he adds, "which signify both inclinations and agitations."[16] Clearly, sensibility as it is used in Wollstonecraft's day is one such word, for it can signify either an inclination, an agitation, or a mood.

Even the cautious Ryle does not escape metaphors in speaking of the mind; on the contrary, he frequently employs what George Lakoff and Mark Johnson identify in *Metaphors We Live By* as the dominant metaphor of mind in Western culture: the mind as a brittle (or fragile) entity. Ryle describes moods as containers easy to get into, more difficult to get out of; he exemplifies his inclinations by analogies to entities (glass, sugar); he explains agitations as resulting from the conflict of entities. Our language of mind and emotion, say Lakoff and Johnson, like language dealing with other "intangibles," is "intrinsically metaphorical."[17]

This once assumed, to pursue the hypothesis that Wollstonecraft is a prisoner of language it becomes necessary to ask whether metaphoric language, with all its connotative richness, can, in any sense of the word, ever imprison people. In fact, at least three recent studies of metaphoric language readily acknowledge its ability to structure reality. Eva Kittay calls attention to its "structure-preserving mapping" for domains either previously unknown or unarticulated. Lakoff and Johnson state the case much more emphatically: metaphors "structure not just our language," they insist, "but our thoughts, our attitudes, our actions."[18] If this is the case, can metaphors, then, *determine* thoughts, attitudes, and actions? Lakoff and Johnson make no such wholesale claim, but they do conjecture that people may not easily choose to lay aside major, culturally sanctioned metaphors like "argument is war," "labor is a resource," "time is money," or, presumably, "the mind is an entity." Even the most skeptical of the three students of metaphor, Michael Kearns, admits that, under certain circumstances, metaphors may control or constrain thoughts, or even hold the mind captive: "That the metaphors *can* control conceptions I accept, but not that they must." Certain metaphors of mind may, he adds, be more "constraining" than others, even though people are, hypothetically at least, always "free to create new figures." The mind-as-entity metaphor that dominates the eighteenth century, he believes, encourages people to think of the mind as an initially empty container slowly filling with past ideas and present impressions: "Pamela's mind is as much a prisoner of the external world as she is a captive of Mr. B."[19]

If these studies stop short of insisting that metaphoric language can determine every thought or move, then, they do nevertheless assume that it can limit as well as structure our understanding. To Lakoff and Johnson, metaphors—indeed, all analogies—"highlight" certain features of a subject and "hide" others.[20] If a couple sees love as a chase, for example, they may not be able to conceive of it as a partnership. Kittay's definition of metaphor explains more precisely just how this highlighting and hiding occurs: "Metaphor is the linguistic realization of a leap of thought from one domain to another in which the spring-board is a structure-preserving mapping." She calls her theory "perspectival" to accent the "distinctively cognitive" activity that metaphor encourages: "Since perspectival implies a subject who observes from a stance, we can say that metaphor provides linguistic realization for the cognitive activity by which a language speaker makes use of one linguistically articulated domain to gain understanding of another experiential or conceptual domain." "Perspectival" also implies one particular stance to the exclusion of others, of course. This "framing" and "mapping" of the domain incognita, plus the preoccupation the speakers or auditors of metaphor must experience in comparing two "domains" to ascertain meaning, must frequently hamper their abilities to see beyond the metaphor at hand.

Kittay's study finally emphasizes the liberating richness of metaphoric language more than any tendency on its part to constrain people's abilities to think or initiate action. Metaphor to her is expressive in a special, very complete way—comparable to dream work:

> Contrary to the main contesting theory of language, language ought to be understood as serving primarily neither a referential function, nor a calculative role, nor yet a communicative end, but as having the capacity to perform all these functions through its inherent capacity as an expressive medium. Language is a mode in which most humans are capable of acting, communicating, expressing their thoughts, feelings, desires, and making an impact on their surroundings. *Literal language, with its referential and logical impetus, is a pruning of this rich expressive medium,* just as conscious thought is a constraint on and a pruning of the rich resources of the unconscious—a constraint which is necessary and productive, but which is a constraint none the less.[21] (Emphasis mine)

Refusing to join recent philosophers who, in the tradition of the Royal Society, condemn metaphors as empty verbal legerdemain, Kittay views them instead as a "whole body" language, full of possibility, and absolutely crucial to the life and health of the communication processes they sustain. Her tribute to metaphoric language approximates, interestingly enough, the attitudes of many eighteenth-century writers about their metaphoric language of sensibility. In their optimistic mode, Wollstonecraft and her contemporaries view sensibility and its language, despite its limitations, similarly as rich, life-sustaining, and integrative. They know that in theory, if not in practice, their "dear sensibility" is a state of being that cuts across the usual mind/body and I/thou divides of the day. Whether, more often than not, its words and behaviors function to widen those divides rather than to bridge them is a question this study raises as frequently as Wollstonecraft raises it herself.[22]

One final special feature of metaphors of mind gives them added psychological influence: their diffidence. They do not, Kearns notes in his study, call attention to themselves. Since there is no literal meaning to test them against (how do we, for example, confirm the existence of the id?), they tend, like dead metaphors, to inspire belief, to encourage the assumption that what is being said is the literal truth. Kearns believes that the mind-as-entity metaphors prevalent in eighteenth-century England inspired philosophers to believe in the factuality of certain metaphoric assertions about the mind: the notion of faculties, for example, or the principle of association.[23] This kind of power to inspire credulity should not be minimized in the study of any metaphors of the mind, ancient or modern. Consider Kittay's unquestioning reliance on Freud's models of the mind and of dream work: his metaphoric description of the relationship between conscious and nonconscious thoughts functions as if it were a factual foundation on which to erect her own provocative theory of metaphoric language.

Metaphor and Myth

> Sensibility is the most exquisite feeling of which the human
> soul is susceptible.   —*Mary* (*Works*, 1.24.59)

When a culture's mythology dies, according to Roland Barthes, popular mythologies spring up to take its place and, like their high culture counterparts, they function as ideologically laden metaphors. They are a derivative metalanguage, designed to present the unknown by means of the known. More specifically, they are designed to rationalize omissions, fissures, or contradictions in a culture's belief system that make it particularly vulnerable to criticism: slavery, colonialism, or modern housewifery. In order to do this, they "abduct" signifiers already laden with meaning from familiar and loved cultural contexts, shaping them into a mosaic of signs so richly suggestive, so alluring, that viewers fail to notice its fragmentation, its anachronistic nature, and its essentially muddled message. For the eclectic clustering of signs necessarily dehistoricizes them— strips them of all references to particular times, places, or persons; and this makes it difficult to trace their origins. They seem free-floating, "natural," and axiomatic, and this timeless quality contributes to their already formidable persuasive power. When analyzed, "the knowledge contained in a mythical concept is confused, made up of yielding, shapeless associations"; but most mythical concepts, Barthes believes, escape critical analysis: their alluring decontextualized signifiers deflect or defy clearheaded analysis, instead charming viewers into passivity, then seducing them into belief:

In passing from history to nature, myth acts economically: it abolishes the complexity of human acts, it gives them the simplicity of essences, it does away with all dialectics . . . ; it organizes a world which is without contradictions because it is without depth, a world wide open and wallowing in the evident, it establishes a blissful clarity: things appear to mean something by themselves.[24]

Although Colin Turbayne's *Metaphors for the Mind* discusses metaphor historically rather than theoretically, he, too, believes that metaphor and myth are intimately allied and that they both encourage blind faith. Turbayne, in fact, suggests that myths spring from metaphors. For him the two stages of a successful metaphor are conscious trope and unconscious myth— "make believe" and "belief"— and these two stages correspond to two habits of the human mind: to "devise conceptual structures and project them on reality," then to "become oblivious to the fictional character of these conceptual structures."[25] To summarize, Kearns, Barthes, and Turbayne suggest at least three ways in which metaphoric language can inspire belief and metaphor can become myth: by means of its diffidence, especially powerful in the case of metaphors of mind (Kearns); by means of intimate alliance with myth (Barthes and Turbayne); and by means of human habits of mind (Turbayne).

Ample evidence exists to suggest that the eighteenth-century language of sensibility frequently operates on this mythic plane, busily rationalizing the neglect of the affective realm, not only encouraging beliefs, but also inspiring certain words, attitudes, behaviors, and deeds on the basis of those beliefs. Philosophers of the day, according to Kearns, act—and write—as if Locke's metaphors of mind are facts. Physicians record a rise in the number of nervous disorders once they begin to write about them and treat them; people act as if the newly inscribed illnesses on the largely fantastical map of human anatomy are factual. Social behavior, too, undergoes a number of modifications attributable to gathering conviction in the century—the dominant belief in the mythic language of sensibility—that proof of fine feeling is the equivalent of proof of human exceptionality. Sentimental religions rise in popularity, people begin to show signs of collective guilt about questionable social institutions like slavery or arbitrary incarceration, their marriages become more affectionate, their travels are sometimes sentimentally motivated, and their friendship seeking, letter writing, and novel reading also become sentimentally tinged with such habits as memento trading, tear tracking, outdoor readings, and public weeping.

Examples of sentimental ritual behavior inspired by the myth abound in the novels being read, too, teaching their readers, even as they offer them stories that elicit feelings, how to act out and attenuate such feelings in their own lives. Examples are Pamela's despondent poetry at the pond, Clarissa's writing on her coffin, Harley's trip to Bedlam in *The Man of Feeling*, Toby's steadfast attentiveness to Walter in his dejection and Le Fever at his death, Yorick's seeking out of the mad Maria, and Werther's incorporation of Ossian into his last conversation with Lotte and incorporation of Lessing's *Emilia Galotti* into his suicide ritual.[26] In the eighteenth century, the language of sensibility has at least a potential triple impact, then: once as metaphor, once as myth and associated rituals, and once as emotive appeal.

Goethe admits as much himself when he refuses, years after writing Europe's "catechism of sensibility," *The Sorrows of Young Werther*, to read it again. The book, he fears, will force him to "once more experience the pathological state in which I produced it." "It is, " he adds, "a mass of explosives."[27] And what are those explosives? Cultivation of refinement and sensitivity, for one. Incessant indulgence in the affective perception of self, others, even objects in nature and culture, for another. Unguarded rebellion against any cultural structures that restrict these activities, for a third. But at the heart of the matter for Goethe and his contemporaries is his successful transfer of the act of suicide from the realm of the culturally taboo to the realm of the mythically sanctioned. It is worth noting, briefly, how he accomplishes this transfer, since, for the suicidal Wollstonecraft as well as for Goethe, the novel is clearly a document of some persuasive power; for the age, it arguably represents the language of sensibility in its most evocative and provocative form.

First, Goethe allows his hero to surround himself on the eve of his suicide with a number of positive cultural signs suggesting that his act of self-annihilation is a sacrament, or at least holds sacramental power: Werther props open on his desk a copy of Lessing's *Emilia Galotti*, a sentimental tragedy about a perfectly chaste, extraordinarily obedient daughter who is willing to die for virtue's sake; he drinks wine (just one glass); he writes a confession of sorts before he dies, in which he imagines God forgiving him and uniting him with Lotte in heaven; he "vests himself" in clothes "blessed" by Lotte's touch: "Is it a sin to love you? . . . Very well! . . . I go to my Father, to your Father. I will bring my sorrows before Him, and He will give me comfort till you come."[28] Goethe also sentimentalizes and familiarizes the death by recording only the reactions of Werther's servants and friends, all of whom are devastated with the sense of their loss, and none of whom disapproves of Werther's actions or draws any moral from them. As narrator, at the same time, Goethe remains unobtrusive, descriptive rather than judgmental, allowing the vivid details of the death scene and burial to speak for them-

selves. His restraint lends them the impact of a gruesome documentary
reality:

> At six in the morning, the servant entered Werther's room with a candle.
> He found his master stretched on the floor, blood about him, and the pistol
> at his side. He called to him, took him in his arms, but there was no answer,
> only a rattling in the throat. The servant ran for a surgeon, for Albert. Char-
> lotte heard the bell; a shudder seized her. She awakened her husband; both
> arose. The servant, in tears, stammered the dreadful news. Charlotte fell
> senseless at Albert's feet. . . .
>   Let me say nothing of Albert's distress or of Charlotte's grief.
>   The old judge hastened to the house upon hearing the news; he kissed
> his dying friend amid a flood of tears. His eldest boys soon followed him
> on foot. In speechless sorrow they threw themselves on their knees by the
> bedside, and kissed his hands and face. The eldest, who was his favorite,
> clung to his lips till he was gone; even then the boy had to be taken away
> by force. At noon Werther died. The presence of the judge, and the arrange-
> ments he had made prevented a disturbance; that night, at the hour of
> eleven, he had the body buried in the place that Werther had chosen.
>   The old man and his sons followed the body to the grave. Albert could
> not. Charlotte's life was in danger. The body was carried by workmen. No
> clergyman attended.[29]

And precisely what is the book's final mythic message? "Muddled," as
Barthes suggests all such messages are, to be sure, so much so that a
number of Goethe's contemporaries read it as a recipe or apology for
suicide, even though Goethe apparently believed at the time that he was
simply describing Werther's sorrows. "Countless suicides were ascribed
to its abhorrent teachings: in Leipzig and Copenhagen its distribution
had to be banned by law. Within a short time after the publication of
the novel, a wave of 'Werther-fever' had swept Europe. In 1784 a young
English lady committed suicide and a copy of a translation of *Werther*
was found under her pillow."[30]

Wollstonecraft frequently presents herself as a courageous demythologizer, defusing such explosive packages, ridiculing sentimental
novels, analyzing the pathologies of sensibility, insisting that Werther
is pathetic, that Sterne is indecent, and Rousseau unforgivably selfish. She is at her best in this role in *Rights of Men* and *Rights of Woman*;
there she courageously exposes men's talk of women as so much prejudice and mystification, and shatters man-made icons of female virtue
like Milton's Eve, Rousseau's Sophie, Dr. Fordyce's daughters, Burke's
Marie Antoinette, and Richardson's Clarissa. Her verbal rebellion,
however, as this study will show, never quite translates into sustained
or successful resistance of many of sensibility's myths or mythmakers; there is much truth to Godwin's claim after her death that until

the end she remained a "female Werther," one of those "persons, endowed with the most exquisite and delicious sensibility, whose minds seem almost of too fine a texture to encounter the vicissitudes of human affairs, to whom pleasure is transport, and disappointment is agony indescribable."[31]

Women and Language

> It would be an endless task to trace the variety of
> meannesses, cares, and sorrows, into which women are
> plunged by the prevailing opinion, that they were created
> rather to feel than reason.
> — *Rights of Woman* (*Works*, 5.4.131)

The truism undoubtedly repeated most often in Wollstonecraft studies—that she is ambivalent about the language of sensibility—is easily verified, though not so easily explained. Sometimes she treats that language as if it were the most important means she has to set herself free; at other times she treats it with profound suspicion, as if it were man's primary engine of mind control and oppression. Sometimes, in other words, language is woman's tool; sometimes it is man's weapon. Her faith in language as a means of liberation may find its basis in her own life: born into a financially and psychologically unstable family, she literally writes herself free. But her doubts about the language may also have their origins in her life, tied to the profound distrust of men that begins with distrust of her own father. In the *Rights of Woman* she chafes especially at the following linguistic habits of men: their frequent regression to "moss-covered opinions"; their reservation of certain "manly" virtues for themselves (reason, for example); and their technique of speaking of and to women as if they were children, then flattering them into submission. The recent debate on women and language, which divides the feminist community, far from rendering Wollstonecraft's equivocation obsolete, turns it instead into prophetic insight.

Some feminists— among the most prominent, Sandra Gilbert, Susan Gubar, and Elaine Showalter—have expressed optimism about women's increasing access to language and the power that will come with that access. They accordingly dismiss any gloomy prognostics about the hopeless phallocentrism of the language and insist that language, and people, can change, and that women should have little trouble taking back the "mother tongue."[32]

Other feminists remain much less sanguine about women's chances of retaking—and revising—the mother tongue. For them the language has been remodeled by the men who abducted it after they ceased to speak Latin; for these feminists its syntax and its vocabulary are irreversibly contaminated by phallocentric thinking. Economical, abstract, disembodied, rational, and linear, male discourse erases the feminine by subsuming it under an alien masculine principle. Its aim is to put woman in her place: "Beware, my friend, of the signifier that would take you back to the authority of the signified!" The depth of the disillusionment of the feminists varies: some believe women must simply abandon the existent language and write their own; others recommend guarded accommodation.[33]

At various points in her writing career, Wollstonecraft can be seen adopting each of these attitudes. She tries frontal attack on Edmund Burke in the *Rights of Men* for his cynical misuse of the language of sensibility, recommends militant takeover of the language in the *Rights of Woman*, assumes a magisterial masculine tone in various instances, and invents her own feminine medium of expression in *Letters in Sweden*. This behavior can be interpreted in a number of ways. Wollstonecraft can be seen, for example, as a conscious strategist, selecting a stance towards the language that will best appeal in each case to her intended audience. Or she can be seen as a linguistic novice, experimenting with various attitudes to discover the best use of the code. The present study sees her as a woman artist living in a man's age searching for an authorial voice womanly enough to be true to herself and attractive to other women, and at the same time manly enough to carry across the widening gender gap.

Women, Language, and Madness

My reason has been too far stretched, and tottered almost on the brink of madness . . .
                          —16 April 1787, *Collected Letters*, 50

Like many of her contemporaries, Wollstonecraft seems to feel and fear, at various junctures in her life, something she calls "madness"; and certainly, some of her contemporaries quickly dismiss her as mad, especially those who are least sympathetic to women's rights or the taking of one's own life. It may be, of course, that, as she states, her "reason" or her "nerves" sometimes fail her; but there is some evidence to suggest that her language fails her— that, to take Sterne's comment about Toby not quite out of context, her life is put in jeopardy by words.

In a pathfinding monograph entitled *Language and Woman's Place* (1975), Robin Lakoff concludes that women in traditional society are frequently caught, linguistically, in a classic double bind. If they speak the way they are expected to speak—deferentially, tentatively, emotively, and repetitiously, in rambling narratives—they are given approval as women, but not as the reasonable human beings they very well may be. They are simply and exclusively accepted as suitable females, "not to be taken seriously, of dim intelligence, frivolous, and incapable of understanding anything important . . . a bit of fluff." If, on the other hand, they speak intelligently, energetically, analytically, with conviction and self-confidence, they are "dead"—"ostracized as unfeminine by both men and women"; and on this basis, again, what they say is not given the credence it deserves. They are, in short, damned if they do and damned if they don't. When children are subjected to such double binds or no-win situations, schizophrenia frequently surfaces, Lakoff adds, and families with a history of schizophrenia tend to live with more than the usual number of no-win situations.[34]

Luce Irigaray's recently translated "Women's Exile. Interview" lends continental support to Lakoff's suggestion. Women, Irigaray speculates, are perpetual outsiders to the language because they themselves are "the foundation of the symbolic order." They have no metalanguage of their own and are heavily reliant on body language; as a result, when they are diagnosed as anxious or schizophrenic (which happens frequently), they find it difficult to articulate these states of mind. For this reason they are also difficult to cure, because therapy presupposes an ease with the language. Irigaray concludes that, in this sense, all women are "in a state of madness; shut up in their bodies, in their silence and their 'home'."[35]

It is difficult for a student of Wollstonecraft to read these lines without thinking of the heroine Maria, with whom this Preface began; indeed, Maria's story almost seems like a narrative version of Irigaray's provocative claims. Like a fugitive from Lévi-Strauss's mythic presentation of women as the means of exchange between men, Maria discovers that her body has been offered to the next buyer once her husband has exhausted her fortune. To punish her for refusing to cooperate, her husband at first literally shuts her up in a prison madhouse where her laments, like those of her fellow prisoners, fall on stone walls and hearts. Yet even when she is finally freed, her story goes largely unread and her complaints are virtually ignored in a court of law because she is a woman. She may talk, but her words remain unheard. Figuratively, then, even once she walks free, she remains in her woman's prison madhouse, "shut up in her body and in her silence." Among Wollstonecraft's projected resolutions of Maria's predicament in this unfinished novel, it should be mentioned, is suicide.

If *Maria* demonstrates most vividly Wollstonecraft's sensitivity to profound doubts about women's access to language, her private letters best dramatize her struggle with woman's linguistic double bind, rendered quite acute in her case by her reliance on the feminized language of sensibility. The Introduction continues the discussion of the language of sensibility on a historical-biographical plane. Chapter 1 then investigates her private correspondence from early adolescence to the end of her life, serving as an overview for the analyses of public documents in subsequent chapters. This private correspondence offers invaluable insights into Wollstonecraft's lifelong struggle with the metaphors, metonyms, and myths—with the fictions—of sensibility.

Acknowledgments

I owe a long-standing debt to the libraries and foundations that helped to make the research for this project possible: the rare book rooms of the University of Iowa and the University of Illinois, the British Library, the Newberry Library and Foundation, the National Endowment for the Humanities, the Fulbright Foundation, and the Western Illinois University Foundation.

I am also deeply indebted to Lord Abinger and Dr. B. C. Barker-Benfield of the Bodleian Library, and to *The Carl and Lily Pforzheimer Foundation, Inc.* and the New York Public Library (both its Office of Special Collections and its Office of the Carl H. Pforzheimer Collection of Shelley and His Circle) for permission to quote material from Wollstonecraft's letters. The following people and presses rendered additional invaluable help in the permission process: Sabina Cuttler, Cornell University Press; Kathleen Joswick, Western Illinois University Library; Chris Rubi, New York University Press; and Susan Schott, University Press of Kansas.

Very special thanks are also due to colleagues and friends who responded to portions of this book in meetings of the American Society for Eighteenth-Century Studies and the Samuel Johnson Society of the Midwest, and to the students of my Sensibility Seminar at the Rheinisch-Westfälische Technische Hochschule in Aachen, Germany, whose continental perspectives on my project in its earliest stages were, and remain, invaluable. There are certain people whose fine scholarship and rare conversation have been such a steady inspiration to me during this project that they must not be banished to footnotes: Stephen Cox, John Dussinger, Chris Fox, Jean Hagstrum, Charles H.

Hinnant, Herbert Lindenberger, Mitzi Myers, Catherine Parke, and Leland Warren.

A debt of gratitude too large to pay goes to the three important *J*'s in life, James F. Conger, my husband, Juva T. McMillen, my mother, and Judi Hardin, my friend. Without the support of these three extraordinary people, I could not have completed this project.

Introduction

Mary Wollstonecraft's Language of Feeling

Disregarding William Godwin's characterization of Mary Wollstonecraft as a "female Werther," modern criticism often presents her as an adult convert to faith in reason. Some of this criticism apparently intends to offer Wollstonecraft compensation for two centuries of character assassination and neglect, some of it works to make a political point—that Wollstonecraft is a perfectly reasonable advocate of women's rights.[1] While such readings are certainly understandable, at the same time they obscure the personal conflicts that arise from Wollstonecraft's continuing fascination with the language and values of sensibility. In the decade of the nineties, when the dangers of sensibility become increasingly clear to both its enemies and its friends, Wollstonecraft continues to cultivate it, yet to struggle to correct both its theoretical and practical vulnerabilities as an ethic. She resists its extremes, she rejects its rhetoric, but she never grows out of it. In one sense she struggles unsuccessfully to mediate this troubling ideology to her contemporaries, for she never resolves all the contradictions the ethic causes in her thinking and her life. In another sense, however, her struggle is fruitful, impelling her to creative experimentation as a thinker and a writer, and, in the process, offering the twentieth century the chance to see dramatized a significant confrontation between the century's new language of the heart and its ethic of rights as modified to accommodate the concerns of Enlightenment feminism.

By the time Wollstonecraft begins writing her first novel in 1787, the literary mode of sensibility has reached the apex of its popularity: the works of Richardson, Sterne, Rousseau, and Goethe have swept Western Europe and England, inspiring attacks, tributes, translations, and imitations by the dozens. These authors change the dominant mood of literature for the rest of their century from satiric to sentimental; they divert creative energies from older genres to new ones; and they champion, and quite successfully, the cause of the "lower faculties": passion, the senses, the imagination. If they do not see, as a result, the immediate beginning of a new literary era, since older attitudes, ideas, and forms by no means suddenly disappear, they at least witness a series of major shifts of interest, shifts that language has to stretch to articulate.

Wollstonecraft, like most young women of letters of her day, is highly conversant in the new language of feeling. Her early letters show her preferring its terms, indeed, show her modeling herself on those terms; they structure her views and define her goals. Her later works exemplify, in contrast, sensibility's power over her as a negative influence; they show her, to a greater or lesser extent, trying to extricate herself from the early models. The reason for her gradual shift in attitude from enthusiastic reception to creative resistance most certainly lies as much in the language as in herself. By the time she is ready to use it, on the eve of the composition of her first novel, *Mary*, in the late 1780s, it is an uneasy mixture of nonverbal and verbal signs fraught with paradoxes, omissions, and ambiguities, and laden, too, with the sometimes incompatible obsessions of its leading practitioners. In Williams's apt phrase, it has become a "very difficult" language.[2]

The Introduction seeks to describe the language of sensibility at this particular historical moment at the dawn of Wollstonecraft's adult career. The tragic or pathetic fictions of sensibility which most frequently attract Wollstonecraft's comments are Richardson's *Clarissa*, Sterne's *Sentimental Journey*, Rousseau's *Nouvelle Héloïse*, and Goethe's *The Sorrows of Young Werther*. For her and many other women writers in the decade of the 1780s, however, Goethe is the dominant cult figure; during that period his *Werther* is frequently reprinted, newly translated, celebrated in popular culture, and written about by dozens of poets and educators, including Wollstonecraft, whose letters and reviews verify her familiarity both with the novel and the controversy whirling around it. For some of Goethe's contemporaries, it is the long-awaited declaration of the rights of the heart; for others, it is a most reprehensible apology for any crimes committed in the name of passion, crimes varying in magnitude from the mere rhetorical rejection of the values of both the aristocracy and the bourgeoisie to much more alarming kinds of anti-social behavior like adultery and suicide.[3] Both Wollstonecraft's fictions—and, for that matter, her life—invite the same responses, the same controversy.

Spontaneous Feeling and Indirect Expression

> Albert is not the man to satisfy the wishes of such a heart.
> He lacks a certain sensibility; he lacks—put it any way you
> like—their hearts do not beat in unison . . . Sometimes a
> happy prospect seems to open before me; but alas! it is
> only for a moment; and then, when I am lost in dreams, I
> cannot help saying to myself, "What if Albert should
> die?—Yes, she would become—and I should be"—and so I
> pursue a chimera, till it leads me to the edge of a precipice
> before which I shudder . . .
> —Goethe, *Werther* (Emphasis mine)[4]

> It is true, I have experienced the most rapturous emotions—
> short-lived delight!—*ethereal beam*, which only serves to
> shew my present misery—yet *lie still, my throbbing heart, or
> burst; and my brain—why dost thou whirl about at such a
> terrifying rate? why do thoughts so rapidly rush into my
> mind, and yet when they disappear leave such deep traces?* I
> could almost wish for the madman's happiness, and in a
> strong imagination lose a sense of woe. . . . I am now the
> *prey of apathy*. . . . Too well have I loved my fellow
> creatures! I have been *wounded by ingratitude*; from every
> one it has something of the *serpent's tooth*.
> —Mary (*Works*, 1.23.57) (Emphasis mine)

As illustrated by the italicized passages above, Wollstonecraft's language of sensibility relies heavily on certain forms of indirection to approximate its meaning: especially simile, metaphor, metonymy, and allegory. The referent teases, yet eludes the mind's eye. It is not an external object but a fluctuating state of mind, an ineffable capacity not easily located with any certainty or exactitude within—surely one reason why both speakers have a sense that they are suspended in dreams, in nonreality. Even the word "sensibility" itself, like the word "emotion,"[5] is a metaphor. Applied to the body, as it is in some of the earliest examples supplied in the *Oxford English Dictionary* from Chaucer, Lydgate, and Elyot, it at first means "capability of being perceived by the senses" or "readiness of an organ or tissue to respond to sensory stimuli." Its meaning is then extended metaphorically in the mid-eighteenth century to indicate certain qualities of mind: "emotional consciousness"; "quickness and acuteness of apprehension or feeling"; "capacity for refined emotion"; "delicate sensitiveness of taste"; also "readiness to feel compassion for suffering, and to be moved by the pathetic in literature or art."

Since, like other qualities of mind, sensibility itself cannot be directly observed, Wollstonecraft's contemporaries rely on external signs of its presence and find them in certain words, names, and behaviors; to name just a few of the most popular: feeling, heart, pity, affection, tenderness, sentiment, genius, particular poets, titles, characters, tears, sighs, faints, changes of color, speechlessness, charity, irascibility, melancholy. Not only do these external signs have the power to imply the presence of sensibility, they gradually gain the metonymic power to stand for the thing itself, so that a melancholy artist, a blushing woman, a *Hamlet* or *Werther* enthusiast, or a tender but irascible guardian are all assumed to have sensibility of mind. This, then, is the general nature of the language system of sensibility: metaphors flanked by metonyms, including a number of highly ambiguous nonverbal metonyms like sighs, tears, and silence.

To anyone disconcerted by the thought that the language of sensibility seems to have no anchors in reality, two points can be made. First, it does not differ in kind from other languages used to describe the mind, all of which are necessarily metaphorical because, as Kearns notes, "except for facts about the structure and function of the nervous system and sensory apparatus, nothing having to do with the mind can be described literally."[6] The language of mind is clearly as metaphorical as ever—superego, id, ego; parent, child, adult; homo sapiens, mammalian, and reptilian brains are still the rough equivalents of metaphors common in the eighteenth century derived from faculty psychology: the intellect, the senses, the will; reason, the passions. Second, the language of sensibility is, in any event, at least grounded in the observation of the physical, a grounding which frequently makes its words perfectly ambiguous, invoking at one and the same time both the spirit and the flesh. "Sensibility" suggests at once acuteness of the physical senses and emotional susceptibility, as do the closely allied terms "feeling," "delicacy," and "tenderness." "Sympathy" usually implies a capacity for fellow-feeling, but eighteenth-century physicians also employ it to describe connections between various parts of the human body. A "warm heart" may suggest a kind, sympathetic heart— or a heart consumed by anger. The venerable term "passion" itself also demonstrates the same doubleness with its connotations of physical and emotional agony.

The language of sensibility also impacts on that physical reality. Much more than "mere language," a metaphoric system like the language of sensibility, according to Lakoff and Johnson, structures "our thoughts, attitudes, actions." Beyond the general functions of orienting and structuring everyday thought and action, Lakoff and Johnson believe that extended metaphors like "sensibility" serve in broader ranging cognitive activities as well: they reinforce or negate existing theories ("theory-constitutive metaphors") or generate new ones ("theory-generative metaphors"); they highlight and hide features of experience; and they set boundaries.

Countering objectivists' reductive views of metaphor-as-mere-language, Lakoff and Johnson develop a new way of discussing metaphor that pays attention to both "inherent properties" and "interactional properties" involving "how human beings get a handle on a concept— how they understand it and function in terms of it." Viewing the metaphor "love is a physical force" interactively, they suggest, reveals an implicit assumption that lovers are its passive, and perhaps helpless, victims— a negative, limiting assumption that is clearly not implicit in the "love is a journey" metaphor.[7] Similarly, viewing the metaphors of Werther's claim about Albert interactively points up the drastically limited notion of communication shared by professors of sensibility: "He lacks a certain sensibility . . . their hearts do not beat in unison." They encourage others to believe that they are having a more complete, quite unique, communicative experience, yet the only level of communication they seek to cultivate or attenuate is affective communication. They are overwhelmingly interested in seeking out spaces and times where they can escape the necessity of thinking and doing to attend to their emotional maintenance. Characteristically, moreover, speakers of sensibility rely on the prefabricated language of others to aid them in their self-expression; particularly well-known examples are Pamela's use of scripture and Werther's extensive use of Homer and Ossian.

The Consequences of Indirection

> You should see how foolish I look in company when her
> name is mentioned, and particularly when I am asked how I
> like her. How I like her!—I detest the phrase. What sort of
> creature must he be who merely likes Charlotte, whose
> whole heart and senses are not entirely absorbed by her?
> Like her! Someone asked me the other day how I liked
> Ossian.   —Goethe, *Werther*[8]

> Sensibility is indeed the foundation of all our happiness.
> . . . But it is only to be felt; it escapes discussion.
>   —Mary (*Works*, 1.24.59–60)

Two other common characteristics of Wollstonecraft's language of sensibility may ultimately derive from its metaphoric nature: language skepticism and the reliance on non-empirical forms of verification, especially authority and analogy. How otherwise can auditors be certain that the person talking of a feeling heart is really experiencing heartfelt emotions, sufferers that the lamenting spectator is actually experiencing compassion, or speakers that the indirect terms they choose to express their own emotions will in any way approximate their state of heart to someone else? Modern philosophy tells us that they cannot (the notorious problem of "other minds"),[9] but their response is frequently to blame the language. They lament its limitations, or they lapse into silence and dumb show.

They also frequently take refuge in the twin myths of spontaneity and imperfection, two of Wollstonecraft's favorites. They measure signs not by their exactitude or appropriateness but by their "quickness," their presumed velocity from heart to face, to hands, to tongue; and they come to prefer unguarded, even awkward, gestures and loose unfinished sentences to the decorous balance in manner and word admired by the preceding generation (it is now shunned as "affectation"). As fascinating as this skepticism may be to contemporary observers, its practical consequence is to render sensibility's advocates speechless or incoherent, hardly the best strategies for advocacy.

Deprived of the reassurance of proving the authenticity of sensibility by observation, inference, and argument, followers of sensibility, in need of some form of corroboration, fall back repeatedly on older, and frequently less satisfying, forms of verification: authority and analogy. Their lives become quests for literary and human analogues: authors, characters, fellow-sufferers, or friends whose states resemble—even duplicate—their own, and consequently to some degree authenticate their own. They are happiest when they can find a common literary text that captures both their and their companions' feelings. Lotte's mention below of Klopstock, the German Milton, provides Werther and herself with double legitimation: with a means both to verify the rightness of their own emotional responses to life and, at the same time, to enjoy chaste emotional communion with a sympathetic, if not identical, other.

Literature Dependency

We went to the window. It was still thundering in the distance; a soft rain was pouring down over the country, and filled the air around us with delicious fragrance. Charlotte leaned on her elbow; her eyes wandered over the scene; she looked up to the sky, and then turned to me; her eyes were filled with tears; she put her hand on mine and said, "Klopstock!" I remembered at once that magnificent ode of his which was in her thoughts, and felt overcome by

the flood of emotions which the mention of his name called
forth. It was more than I could bear. I bent over her hand,
kissed it in a stream of ecstatic tears, and again looked into
her eyes. Divine Klopstock! If only you could have seen
your apotheosis in those eyes! And your name, so often
profaned, would that I never heard it repeated!
—Goethe, *Werther*[10]

One of the sailors, happening to say to another, "that he
believed the world was going to be at an end"; this
observation led her into a new train of thoughts: some of
Handel's sublime compositions occurred to her, and she
sung them to the grand accompaniment. The Lord God
Omnipotent reigned, and would reign for ever, and ever!—
Why then did she fear the sorrows that were passing away,
when she knew that He came out of great tribulation. She
retired to her cabin; and wrote in the little book that was
now her only confident [*sic*]. It was after midnight.
—*Mary* (*Works*, 1.20.51)

The close ties of Wollstonecraft's language of sensibility to both reading and writing—both potential sources of indirect verification—are
made abundantly clear in these two passages. First inspired by literature, it returns constantly to literature for reinforcement, thereby
repeatedly betraying traces of its origins in textual rather than actual
experience. In both scenes cited above, two such literary traces are visible: the static observer stance of the protagonists before a storm-swept
landscape, as if they were reading land, sky, themselves, their words;
and the use of literature—in the first instance, secular literature, in the
second, sacred—as a frame of reference for (even a substitute for any
other language to describe) what they have just witnessed. In Werther's
case, an author's name serves as a code word, rendering all other words
unnecessary; in Mary's, a similar function is served by phrases from
Scripture mediated by Handel's music.

Surely this is the behavior among devotees of sensibility that gave
them the reputation of a manic cult. They maintain exclusive loyalty
to others who use the same abitrary, secret sign system they do, which
is based on documents they alone have determined to be authoritative;
and their emotional responses to events, and the individual signs, are
often incomprehensible outside that system, a naïve reading response
that theorist Hans-Robert Jauss aptly terms "cultic participation."[11]
The exclusivity bound up with this highly literary language of sensibility causes conflict not only, as might be expected, between professors and nonprofessors of sensibility, but, as will soon be apparent,
within the code itself and, most regrettably, even among the people who
prefer that code to any other.

The Language of Feeling and Mind-As-Entity Metaphor

> The senses at first let in *particular* ideas, and furnish the
> yet empty cabinet, and the mind by degrees growing
> familiar with some of them, they are lodged in the memory,
> and names got to them. (Emphasis Locke's)
> —John Locke, *Essay on Human Understanding* [12]

> It is this quickness, this delicacy of feeling, which enables
> us to relish the sublime touches of the poet, and the painter;
> it is this, which expands the soul, gives an enthusiastic
> greatness, mixed with tenderness, when we view the
> magnificent objects of nature; or hear of a good action.
> . . . Softened by tenderness; the soul is disposed to be
> virtuous.
> —*Mary* (*Works*, 1.24.59)

The metaphor "sensibility" sometimes serves a theory-generative
function for thinkers of Wollstonecraft's day, suggesting alternative
ways of viewing the self, the other, and their relationship, but more
often it serves a theory-constitutive function for them in relation to the
dominant metaphor of mind of the eighteenth century, the mind-as-
entity metaphor as refashioned by Locke. Wollstonecraft is no exception; no other philosopher figures so prominently, or so persistently,
in her works. Chief inherent properties of Locke's mind-as-entity are
blankness, narrowness, and duskiness. For Locke the mind is, on one
occasion, a "dark Closet" with little openings representing the senses,
on another, "white paper, void of all characters." Ideas, impressions,
and emotions become, in this model, discrete entities within a larger
entity, "coupled together but still separate." Chief interactive properties of Locke's mind-as-entity are tangibility, initial passivity, and
impressibility yet brittleness:

> In this part the understanding is merely passive; and whether or no it will
> have these beginnings, and as it were materials of knowledge, is not in its
> own power. For the objects of our senses do, many of them, obtrude their
> particular ideas upon our minds whether we will or not; and the operations
> of our minds will not let us be without, at least, some obscure notions of
> them. No man can be wholly ignorant of what he does when he thinks.
> These simple ideas, when offered to the mind, the understanding can no
> more refuse to have, nor alter when they are imprinted, nor blot them out
> and make new ones itself, than a mirror can refuse, alter, or obliterate the
> images or ideas which the objects set before it do therein produce. As the
> bodies that surround us do diversely affect our organs, the mind is forced
> to receive the impressions; and cannot avoid the perception of those ideas
> that are annexed to them. [13]

The envisioned raw material of Locke's mind-as-entity is, variously, paper, slate, clay or wax, each of these having its own set of features and implications. All have in common a certain brittle fragility: once hardened by cold or heat, wax or clay can break or crumble as easily as slate; paper is subject to destruction by all the elements—air, water, or fire—and can also simply age, effacing any writing on its surface. However, wax, unlike any other of these materials, can be rewarmed and made soft. It is malleable, newly impressible, and effaceable; it offers, one might say, a slightly more optimistic metaphoric image of mind than the others.

The mind-as-entity metaphor itself sets up certain psychological boundaries, and it masks some features of mind while it highlights others. It assumes a considerable barrier, for example, between the higher and lower faculties; and although Locke does argue to dismantle barriers imagined between the "understanding" and the "will" in one part of his *Essay*, he nonetheless urges that the dike be reinforced between reason and the passions, for that alone enables the mind to operate freely and without bias by shutting out unpredictable waves of irrationality:

> But if any extreme disturbance . . . possesses our whole mind, as when the pain of the rack, an impetuous uneasiness, as of love, anger, or any other violent passion, running away with us, allows us not the liberty of thought, and we are not masters enough of our own minds to consider thoroughly and examine fairly . . . But the forbearance of a too hasty compliance with our desires, the moderation and restraint of our passions, so that our understandings may be free to examine, and reason unbiassed give its judgment, being that whereon a right direction of our conduct to true happiness depends; it is in this we should employ our chief care and endeavours.[14]

In addition, the Lockean model, by choosing to highlight the mind's openness to experience and the simplicity and transparency of its operations, hides both the mind's complexities and its potentially dynamic nature:

> These, if they are not all, are at least (as I think) the most considerable of those simple ideas which the mind has, and out of which is made all its other knowledge; all which it receives only by the two forementioned ways of sensation and reflection.
>
> Nor let any one think these too narrow bounds for the capacious mind of man to expatiate in, which takes its flight further than the stars, and cannot be confined by the limits of the world; that extends its thoughts often even beyond the utmost expansion of Matter, and makes excursions into that incomprehensible Inane . . . Nor will it be so strange to think these few

simple ideas sufficient to employ the quickest thought, or largest capacity; and to furnish the materials of all that various knowledge, and more various fancies and opinions of all mankind, if we consider how many words may be made out of the various composition of twenty-four letters.[15]

Whatever its limitations, Locke's model proves enormously popular, its influence, as the editor of a modern facsimile of the *Essay* notes, phenomenal in education, political thought, theology, and philosophy.[16] It maps hitherto uncharted domains, thereby allowing people a means of thinking about the nature and acquisition of knowledge, the operations of the mind. It proves especially useful for making distinctions, many of which become the public domain property of writers of the eighteenth century: simple and complex ideas, sensation and reflection, primary and secondary qualities, reason and passions, wit and judgment. Men differ from men, notes Locke, primarily in terms of the extent of their knowledge and their thoughtfulness: "Men then come to be furnished with fewer or more simple ideas from without, according as the objects they converse with afford greater or less variety; and from the operations of their minds within, according as they more or less reflect on them."[17] Women differ from men, according to Lockean moralists of the age, in their abilities both to acquire significant knowledge and to reflect dispassionately on that knowledge, once acquired. They are regularly described as being more open to "casual impressions," to "things external"; more driven by passions; and less able to "engage in fruitful reflections."[18]

Sensibility as metaphor has its own limitations, but at the same time, it eases many limitations present in the Lockean mind-as-entity model. To the image of a mind blank and half-lit, for example, it offers a counterimage of a mind flooded with the light of sensations and impressions that result from extraordinary sensitivities. To the image of mind as a narrow "presence chamber" or "Closet," it offers one "enlarged" or "extended" by the sublime experiences it is especially vulnerable to. To counter the mechanistic picture of discrete entities within another entity, it offers the metaphorical notion of "sympathy," frequently envisioned as a mysterious substance traveling the gaps between body and mind, heart and head, self and other.[19] And to other implications of the Lockean metaphor—the brittleness (hence breakability), passivity, simplicity or transparency of the human mind—it offers countersuggestions. The mind of sensibility frequently vibrates as a result of experiences, rather than breaks; it not only succumbs to experience, it grows as a result of it; and its structural simplicity does not stretch to the uncharted realm of the passions. The language of sensibility, visibly preoccupied by inexplicable attractions and aversions, whims, and mood swings, insists on their mystery—insists, in the words of Sterne's Yorick, that "there is no regular reasoning upon the ebbs and flows of our humours," [20] thereby indirectly reasserting the unpredictability of humans that distinguishes them from machines.

Finally, the consciousness of the Lockean mind becomes the heightened awareness[21] of the mind of sensibility, an awareness that not only includes equal cognizance of internal and external events but percipience on several levels: sensory and affective as well as intellectual. Both Yorick and Werther exemplify the heightened awareness, sympathy, dynamism, and mystery of the mind-as-sensitive-entity metaphor. They vibrate in the presence of books, nature, art, and people; they continually find themselves arrested by compassion or passion: Yorick admits to "having been in love with one princess or another almost all of [his] life";[22] Werther wonders "What is the world to our hearts without love?" Werther provides the quintessential example of this heightened awareness as he drinks in the sights, sounds, and other sensations of a fine spring day:

> When the lovely valley teems with mist around me, and the high sun strikes the impenetrable foliage of my trees, and but a few rays steal into the inner sanctuary, I lie in the tall grass by the trickling stream and notice a thousand familiar things: when I hear the humming of the little world among the stalks, and am near the countless indescribable forms of the worms and insects, then I feel the presence of the Almighty who created us in His own image, and the breath of that universal love which sustains us, as we float in an eternity of bliss; and then . . . I often think with longing, Oh, would I could express it, could impress upon paper all that is living so full and warm within me, that it might become the mirror of my soul, as my soul is the mirror of the infinite God! O my friend—but it will kill me—I shall perish under the splendor of these visions.[23]

The two metaphors, Locke's mind-as-entity and sensibility's mind-as-percipient entity, along with their host of subservient metaphors, work well enough together to allow authors to take journeys into the interior—something they do, of course, with increasing frequency. Two assumptions operative in the mind-as-entity metaphor collide with sensibility's model, however, causing authors, especially late-century authors like Wollstonecraft, consternation: the certainty of boundaries and rational supremacy.

The Lockean model assumes the existence, and the desirability, of discernible boundaries between external and internal experience, passions and ideas; the sensibility metaphor, in contrast, alters the nature of those boundaries radically, rendering them much more permeable and less certain. The much-praised character of "exquisite sensibility" in novels of the age is, by definition, a character extraordinarily open to experience, both external and internal. This special vulnerability raises troubling questions about the wisdom of cultivating sensibility in the minds of the disciples of reason; this same vulnerability, however, is the badge of honor of professors of sensibility and one that they would not trade for all the tranquility in the world.

Reason reigns as the preferred faculty in most eighteenth-century models of the mind, even in the satiric inversions of the Scriblerians, whose exceptionally mad or dull anti-heroes frequently have topsy-turvy brains in which the lower faculties are pictured sitting astride the higher ones. Going against that grain, members of the antisociety of sensibility argue in earnest for the supremacy of sensory and emotional experience, and often in absolute terms. "I am proud of my heart alone," says Werther. "It is the sole source of everything—all our strength, happiness, and misery. All the knowledge I possess everyone else can acquire, but my heart is all my own."[24] They challenge the rationalist model of faculties in one of two ways: either by suggesting the heart as their own countermonarch, or by positing instead the possibility of a joint rule within, head and heart meeting in the realm of "sentiments"—that mode of expression the eighteenth-century perfected which, by definition, synthesizes affective and intellectual responses.[25]

To the person of sensibility, the sentiment is more to be trusted and valued than the purely reasoned argument; the presence of emotion guarantees spontaneity and purity, and the participation of reason ensures reliability and cultural legitimacy. At the same time, the language of sentiments, by all accounts, frequently proves dissatisfying, deferring the pleasure and clarity its auditors or readers wish for. Mid-to late-century literary reviewers frequently complain that sentimental literature filters emotions until they lose their power, and refracts ideas until they lose their clarity. This may help to account for two verbal habits so common among speakers of sensibility: the reiteration and increasing exaggeration of their messages.

Wollstonecraft's Language of Feeling as Myth

> Sensibility is the most exquisite feeling of which the human
> soul is susceptible: when it pervades us, we feel happy;
> and could it last unmixed, we might form some conjecture
> of the bliss of those paradisiacal days, when the . . .
> impulses of the heart did not need correction.
>   —*Mary* (*Works*, 1.24.59)

I feel like the ghost that has returned to the burnt-out castle
which it had built in more splendid times, adorned with
costly magnificence, and left lavishly furnished, on its
death bed to a beloved son.   —Goethe, *Werther*[26]

If Wollstonecraft were dealing simply with a specialized language of
mind, her struggles might not consume so much of her creative energy
for so long. However, she is dealing instead with a particularly powerful language system functioning as myth—myth not so much in the
sense of "stories about legendary heroes" as in the sense of "stories to
live by." The premier English mythmaker of sensibility is Richardson;
the germinal mythic text is his *Pamela*. Although Wollstonecraft
shows no extraordinary interest in *Pamela*, she and her contemporaries
continue to spin stories of sensibility that are variations on Richardson's myth. The age finds it spellbinding.

Richardson, London printer and avid reader, gathers elements
(Barthes would say "signs") for his story from a wide variety of sources
both sacred and secular rich with cultural associations at the time—the
Old and New Testaments, Bunyan's *Pilgrim's Progress*, Milton's *Paradise Lost*, classical legend, Renaissance romance, Restoration drama,
and fairy tale—then reassembles them into the tale of attempted seduction and ultimate conversion that constitutes *Pamela*. Some of these
signs carry with them a message familiar to readers in the Judaeo-
Christian tradition of the talismanic power of faith, others the no-less-
familiar message to readers of romance or fairy tale of the talismanic
power of a young woman's chastity to neutralize the most brutal antagonist. In his version of the story of persecuted virtue, Richardson trans-
fers these talismanic powers to sensibility, lending it an aura of the
supernatural: the magic power to save the beauty and to tame the
beasts (in this case, to convert both Lord B— and his haughty sister
Lady Davers to the gentle gospel of the tender heart).

Responses of twentieth-century students to this novel often suggest
that they can no longer accept the premises of Richardson's myth.
Despite his best efforts to rationalize it, they no longer see Pamela's
acute passivity and Mr. B—'s persistent aggressivity as self-evident,
natural, or even plausible. Richardson's contemporaries and immediate heirs, on the other hand, most certainly do, for they make the myth
thrive, once launched, far beyond the confines of Richardson's novels.
Whether later authors take an earnest, scoffing, or ironical view of sensibility, sooner or later they all indulge, Richardsonian fashion, in some
magical thinking about sensibility itself, attributing to it an inherent
power to *significantly alter* persons who come in contact with it. Sometimes that refinement is merely physiological, sometimes aesthetic, or

moral, or both; whatever form it takes, catalysts of such refinement abound in the century; characters of "quickness" or "acuteness of apprehension or feeling," like Henry Fielding's Amelia, Tobias Smollett's Humphry Clinker, or Ann Radcliffe's Ellena Rosalba, work psychological magic on the feelings of others.

From the beginning, however, the myth has a potential dark side, for Richardson writes not simply of virtuous sensibility, but of persecuted sensibility. Readers infer from his *Pamela*, then even more from his *Clarissa*, that to be endowed with sensibility is to be subject to both greater joys and greater sorrows: it is to inhabit the realm of "exquisite" pain as well as pleasure. Richardson, Sterne, and Henry Mackenzie all point to this lesson from time to time, but their concomitant insistence on the gentle joys of sensibility tends to diminish its impact. It takes someone acting out the myth of sensibility in actuality, Jean-Jacques Rousseau, with his egotisms and pathologies, to first raise serious questions about the wisdom of habitually indulging in such ecstasy and agony. The ecstasy, Rousseau's life suggests, may become self-congratulatory narcissism, the agony, a persecution complex, a chronic state of mind that often leads to profound, sometimes irreversible, mental instability. Responding to that realization, and specifically to Rousseau's *Nouvelle Héloïse*, Goethe's *Werther* offers Wollstonecraft a devastating remythologization of sensibility, exposing its latent dark side: whether as antilanguage, antisociety, or individual propensity, it is a power to tap into cautiously; unfortunately, it can, Goethe suggests, shatter the elect as well as convert the damned. Although Wollstonecraft cannot know it, her contemporary Austen's *Sense and Sensibility* and *Mansfield Park* will reiterate this darker prophecy.

Other Dialects and Idiolects of Sensibility

> Nature is the nurse of sentiment,—the *true source of taste*;—yet what misery, and well as rapture, is produced by a *quick perception* of the *beautiful and sublime*, when it is exercised in observing animated nature, when every beauteous feeling and emotion excites responsive *sympathy*, and the *harmonized soul* sinks into melancholy, or rises to extasy [sic], just as the chords are touched, *like the aeolian harp* agitated by the changing wind. But *how dangerous* is it to foster these sentiments in such an imperfect state of existence. (Emphasis mine)
> —Letter VI, *Letters in Sweden* (*Works*, 6.271)

Myths proliferate, as mythographers well know; they generate new stories and new versions of stories, they inspire new beliefs, they add to the numbers of their converts, or they die. The myths of sensibility are no exception. Richardsonians tirelessly continue to produce books through two centuries and into the twentieth.[27] But three other eighteenth-century discourse communities besides the fiction writers also become especially interested in the myth-generative language of sensibility: philosophers, aestheticians, and scientists. These are communities with widely divergent beliefs about the nature and value of sensibility, and each creates its own dialect of sensibility, its own space within the larger lexicon, resulting in a code increasingly freighted with ambiguities, redundancies, and contradictions. Whether she moves outside or inside the frame of reference of this language, Wollstonecraft, so it seems, is destined to encounter paradox.

Philosophers are largely responsible for creating the ethics of feeling,[28] less so for the psychology of feeling. As a group, they tend to view sensibility as a virtue, or a propensity to virtue, and to assume that it is innate (sometimes God-given), a "self-fulfilling joy," and the essential tie that binds people together into societies. They multiply the various terms in the lexicon designating acts of fellow-feeling: charity, sympathy, benevolence, compassion, pity, tenderness, affection, love, sociability. Since they view sensibility as innate, they have no need to speculate on its origins; they concentrate on its benefits to society. Nowhere in the century does sensibility play a more central role in a philosopher's model than in Adam Smith's *Theory of Moral Sentiments*; it deserves mention as the representative of this discourse. He champions the "mild," "amiable," "gentle" human qualities over the "awful and respectable qualities of mind" preferred by the ancients. And at the heart of his ethical system stands sympathy, a wellspring of virtue, a cement of society, and a source of other definitions ("What is called affection, is in reality nothing but habitual sympathy").

> How selfish soever man may be supposed, there are evidently some principles in his nature, which interest him in the fortune of others, and render their happiness necessary to him, though he derives nothing from it except the pleasure of seeing it. Of this kind is pity or compassion. . . .[29]

The aesthetics of sensibility, inspired by Locke's sensationalism, then firmly wedded to the discourse of the sublime, beautiful and picturesque by Burke, and to Shakespeare mania by Edward Young's "Conjectures on Original Composition," presents sensibility as a propensity to genius or taste.[30] This allows aestheticians, if they wish, to finesse the question of origins: sensibility is either an inborn quality, an acquired one, or an amalgam of the two, a natural talent for making or viewing aesthetic objects that can be developed by the proper education. Their kind of sensibility does not readily yield answers to ethical, and particularly to utilitarian, inquiries about rightness, goodness, or usefulness. They tend to assume instead that sensibility, whatever its origins, is a self-justifying or self-explanatory virtue, perhaps because of the fruits it bears for all to see. Their essays, especially Young's and those of the continental Shakespeare enthusiasts, frequently let Shakespeare stand as sufficient proof of the cultural enrichment sensibility can provide. "We now gaze with amazement and delight," exclaims Young, and then adds:

> Perhaps he was as learned as his dramatic province required; for whatever other learning he wanted, he was master of two books, unknown to many of the profoundly read, though books which the last conflagration alone can destroy: the book of nature, and that of man. These he had by heart, and has transcribed many admirable pages of them into his immortal works. These are the fountainhead whence the Castalian streams of original composition flow.

If sensibility produces this caliber of openness to books of nature and man, art, so it follows, can also seek to elicit such feeling from its spectators; a new affective aesthetic theory is emerging: "The silent lapse of a single tear does the writer more honor than the rattling thunder of a thousand hands."[31] Terms abducted for this dialect of sensibility center around the creative individual in relationship to nature rather than society: nature and natural figure high on the list, as do prospect, profundity, beauty, sublimity, awe, charm, delicacy, imagination, fancy, spontaneity, and originality.

The scientists and medical men contribute to the psychology and the physiology of sensibility, and depending on their professions, they view sensibility as physiological fact or as medical symptom; in any event, for them it is primarily an extraordinary susceptibility to stimuli both internal and external, fostered by keen senses and enhanced by responsive nerves. For some of the medical men, this susceptibility too often leads to the illnesses of hypochondria (for men) and hysteria (for women). Physiological bias, of course, dominates their contributions to the lexicon: they speak of nerves and fibers, sensory organs, and the sensorium (a kind of nerve center), sensibility and irritability, and, in psychological applications, irascibility, misanthropy, indolence, melancholy, and madness. Their speculations can sometimes be cross-referenced to Burton's *Anatomy of Melancholy* or Descartes on the passions, but Michel Foucault's researches into the history of sexuality suggest that the origins of a central assumption of theirs can be traced to the ancient world: that the care of the self—and especially of the passions of the self—is first and foremost the responsibility of medical men.[32]

All of these dialects, in their turn, contribute to the gradual gendering of sensibility. The philosopher Adam Smith distinguishes stoical "manly" virtues from the "feminine" tender virtues; as an aesthetician, Burke associates rugged sublimity with masculinity and tender beauty with femininity; medical men like George Cheyne assume that women are more sensitive and susceptible to diseases of the nerves. In short, by midcentury, according to historian of sensibility G. J. Barker-Benfield, the notion that "women's nerves were normatively distinct from men's, normatively making them creatures of greater sensibility" becomes "a central convention of . . . literature." Following in the footsteps of Lockeans, writers of advice books to women stress their vulnerability to fleeting sensory impressions and the passions, hence to irrationality, distraction, immorality, and disease. Taking the opposite view of feminized sensibility as a potential gift rather than a weakness of character, both men and women novelists of the day work to reform men's manners "on women's terms," to make them, as Pamela does Lord B—, gentler, more affectionate, and more compassionate. They posit, with some frequency, a fictional world in which men and women converse with one another on—and in—the same terms.[33]

The genders do, to some extent, resist this gendering of sensibility, though in gender-specific ways, and for quite different reasons. Some men writing at the time (such as Fielding and Smollett) offer readers alternative masculine versions of sensibility in their benevolent misanthropes; others (such as Sterne and Rousseau) give sensibility a slightly exaggerated erotic edge; and still others (Cleland, M. G. Lewis, and de Sade) celebrate physical, phallic versions of sensibility. Barker-Benfield believes that many men writers of the day register uneasiness about the possibility of seeming effeminate if they cultivate, or recommend, sensibility. "Paradoxically," he writes, "the gendering of sensibility sexualized it."[34] Some women writers (chief among them, Radcliffe and Austen) also resist the feminization of sensibility, not, however, because it seems too feminine but rather because in some of its masculine transformations it seems too sexualized, too erotically charged. They prefer to stress its imputed cognitive benefits over its more visible physical effects. At the beginning of her writing career, Wollstonecraft is demonstrably among them. In her fiction and nonfiction, sensibility appears almost exclusively as a state of mind. As apt to be found in men as in women, it is also equally apt to bring to either sex its advantages or its disadvantages. Her women characters of sensibility may have genius, her men characters tenderness; at the same time, either her men or women characters may show such negative signs of sensibility as unhealthy self-absorption or enervation.

Resistance or not, eighteenth-century speakers of sensibility have an unparalleled variety and range of terms and attitudes about the passions and the body to choose from as they shape their own idiolects of

sensibility. Novelists move freely from one to the other, as Wollstonecraft clearly does in the epigraph given above, although they tend
to settle down in one. The ethics of sensibility dominates the fictions
of Richardson and his followers, especially Goldsmith, Sarah Fielding,
Sterne, Fanny Burney, Radcliffe, and Austen; the aesthetics of sensibility dominates the work of Gothic novelists like Radcliffe, Lewis, and
the Brontës; and the physiology of sensibility dominates that of the
medical man Smollett and, sometimes at least, Sterne. These three discourse communities are, however, discrete; each adapts the language
of sensibility to its own purposes and their definitions and assumptions
are frequently at odds with one another. Add to this the fact that English, French and (to a lesser extent) German vocabularies of sensibility are merging by the latter part of the century and the certainty that
the language of rational discourse dominating the century is at odds
with all of them, and the true labyrinthine complexity of the situation
begins to emerge.

   "What *is* sensibility?" Wollstonecraft asks irritably at one juncture
in her *Rights of Woman* (*Works*, 5.4.132). It is a question, by all accounts,
more than justified by 1792. Is sensibility something physical or mental? gender conscious or gender neutral? self-justifying or in need of
justification? a sign of health or sickness? benevolence or misanthropy? a cause for joy or gloom or both? something to develop or
something static, ineradicable, prohibiting development? Especially
troublesome to Wollstonecraft are these questions: Does it demand
social action or passive resignation or endurance? Does it lead to happiness, wisdom or genius, and virtue, or to vice, melancholy, or madness? Is it part of an ethic that men specifically designed to subordinate women or can it be a sexless virtue? Labeling this uncertainty on
her part simply indecisiveness or ambivalence is shortsighted to this
extent: the apparent inner turmoil of many professors of sensibility is
not completely of their own making, but language-generated. Not only
is the language of sensibility by late in the century replete with warnings, ambiguities, and omissions, it is brittle with incompatible absolutes
that make life for its followers, as Wollstonecraft herself complains, an
"intricate path." Many of the literary characters of the century are artificial constructs aiming to resolve—or paper over—these contradictions: the benevolent misanthrope, the irascible, shy, or clinically
depressed (wo)man of feeling, the sickly genius, the dying lover. And
all of these, as well as the beliefs implicit in the three distinct dialects
of sensibility, are potentially among the myths of sensibility.

   Among the contradictions with the most negative consequences for
Wollstonecraft's self–image as well as her fictional characters are two
lucidly presented by Stephen Cox in his study of the concept of the self

in eighteenth-century fiction: the high valuation of the self coupled with a very uncertain sense of that self's identity, and the simultaneous endorsement of self-awareness and selflessness.[35] On the one hand, valorization of the individual is at an all-time high; on the other, delimiting that self, by definition open, permeable, susceptible to stimuli, is difficult indeed. On the one hand, the literature of sensibility encourages both consciousness and self-consciousness "much like that," according to Williams, "of modern awareness"[36]; people of sensibility are expected to be keenly observant and introspective, on the model of Hamlet (one of Werther's role models). On the other hand, that same literature also praises selfless attentiveness to the needs and the feelings of others. This selflessness is valued by some as the moral justification for sensibility: sensibility is to be cultivated, apologists claim, not simply for its own sake, but because it produces a better kind of caring person and, as a result, a more cohesive and a happier human society.

The self's value, the self's identity, self-awareness, and selfless devotion to others are all, at this point in history, uneasy bedfellows. The secular self as yet has no clearly mapped terrain nor any clearly marked boundaries; neither self-awareness nor selflessness has set limits and each frequently expresses itself in oceanic feelings or a merging of subject and object that leaves the individual—especially the individual of sensibility—paralyzed and disoriented. When alone, Werther hears his every heartbeat, he marks the rise and fall of his spirits, he records the slightest alteration in his reactions to people, places, and books. He is the complete conscious man, in the eighteenth-century sense of the term: both open to feelings and a conscious consumer of feelings.[37] In nature, however, and around people, outside presences tend to inundate his own feelings; he feels compelled to respond emotionally to each situation, sometimes pitying or identifying with—even merging with—very unlikely and unfortunate objects: trees chopped down, for example, or a peasant murderer. He is dashed from Self to Other, and, in either case, finds himself overwhelmed by his emotional responses. What Goethe's novel demonstrates so well to its age is that, in encouraging affective experience, people make themselves prey to a number of problems they are not yet prepared to adequately handle.

Charting a course through this sea of complex contradictory claims and metaphors is, by midcentury, a far from easy task, something nowhere more memorably illustrated than in Sterne's *Tristram Shandy*. This story of the sensitive yet sadly limited Shandy family teases out many of the ambiguities in the language of sensibility; but while the narrator revels in the slipperiness of his language,[38] his life and his uncle Toby's life are "put in jeopardy" by it. So, too, it can be claimed, is Wollstonecraft's, yet she manages nevertheless to extend it, to apply it to "remote things"[39] in ways that are generative of new ideas, techniques, and forms. Her angry, highly critical response to the rich, yet troublesome, antilanguage of sensibility is most familiar; this study focuses on her creative responses to it.

Wollstonecraft's Acquaintance with the Literature of Sensibility

> One way home was through the cavity of a rock covered with a thin layer of earth, just sufficient to afford nourishment to a few stunted shrubs and wild plants, which grew on its sides, and nodded over the summit. A clear stream broke out of it, and ran amongst the pieces of rocks fallen into it. Here twilight always reigned—it seemed the Temple of Solitude; yet, paradoxical as the assertion may appear, when the foot sounded on the rock, it terrified the intruder, and inspired a strange feeling, as if the rightful sovereign was dislodged. In this retreat she read Thomson's *Seasons*, Young's *Night-Thoughts*, and *Paradise Lost*.
> —*Mary* (*Works*, 1.4.15)

Anyone wondering about the nature and extent of Wollstonecraft's early reading need only consult her anthology for women, the *Female Reader* (1789). Quite obviously an omnivorous reader, even at the dawn of her literary career she already seems at home with early modern classics of British literature by Shakespeare, Milton, Addison and Steele, Lord Chesterfield, Pope, Swift, and Johnson. She reveals as well the penchants of an eighteenth-century autodidact for history, the Bible, sermons, pedagogy, and periodical essays. Most important for present purposes, she is intimately acquainted with the languages, myths, and literature of sensibility. Her first novel *Mary* pays special tribute to Richardson, Rousseau, Young, and Thomson; later works reveal her knowledge of Locke's epistemology (so crucial to the cult of sensibility), Burke's treatise on the sublime, Goethe's *Werther*, Mackenzie's fiction and periodicals, Adam Smith's *Theory of Moral Sentiments*, Sterne's *Sentimental Journey*, and the novels and sonnets of Charlotte Smith. Nor is she only conversant with the high literature of sensibility. In her tenure as one of Joseph Johnson's reviewers, she reads stacks of women's sentimental novels, along with some more aesthetic treatises, poems, and sentimental travel books. She knows not only *Werther* and Rousseau, but their fervent English admirers.

In the *Analytical Review* and elsewhere, she is often a resistant reader—announcing her intention to create a counter-Richardsonian heroine in *Mary*, chiding Rousseau for his reductive view of women in *Rights of Woman*, laughing at the maudlin imitations of *Werther* in the *Analytical Review*, unleashing fury in her *Rights of Men* at Burke for his misappropriation of the sentimental. She is nevertheless an attentive reader, with the keenest possible ear for nuance. She hears implicit sensuality in the effusions of Rousseau, discerns insincerity in the sermons of Dr. Fordyce, and detects monarchist madness in the laments of Burke over the French Revolution. And she frequently displays a keen sense of reader decorum to match her keen ear. She guards herself equally against "blind homage" on the one hand and "cold reading" on the other.[40]

That, however, has to do with her public reading habits. Her private reading habits—though this is necessarily speculative—are probably less reasonable. There is evidence in her correspondence that she reads at least Goethe's *Werther* and Rousseau's *Émile* ritualistically, primarily for emotional exercise. Chances are very good that she also reads Milton, Young, Thomson, and Sterne in the same way. This kind of iterative, admirative reading is, of course, a cultic reading practice quite popular among professors of sensibility, and the possibility that Wollstonecraft engages in it should, at the least, prevent generalizations about her abjuration of the creed and practices of sensibility after about 1790. In fact, many of the attitudes she holds until her death find their origins in the literature of sensibility: a firm belief in an alliance between sensibility, virtue, and genius; a fascination with solitude, melancholy, and mental derangement; a heavy reliance on reading and writing; a love affair with nature; an admiration for sympathy and charity; a discontent with quotidian pursuits; and a morbid interest in death as solution and resolution.

Although her basic position on the literature of sensibility seems to shift, at no time does she give the impression that she has stopped reading it. At the outset of her literary career, she allows sensibility to work considerable magic in the mind of the beholder: mental health, poetic genius, taste, and virtue are all nurtured by its presence. Her midcareer polemics anatomize it text by text, and her later fictions and letters remythologize it, ultimately reshaping it into a virtue, born of woman, worth dying for, and capable of refining—even saving—the savage world. Sensibility as metaphor and myth, then, plays a steady role in Wollstonecraft's life and works. It is the wellspring of her creativity and a key to her character. If it sometimes alters her attitudes or actions, at other times she transforms it and gives it new forms of life.[41]

Mary Wollstonecraft
and the Language
of Sensibility

Part One
First Fictions of Sensibility

1
Epistolary Revelations

Perfect confidence, and sincerity of action is, I am
persuaded, incompatible with the present state of reason.
. . . There is certainly an original defect in my mind—for
the cruelest experience will not eradicate the foolish
tendency I have to cherish, and expect to meet with,
romantic tenderness.
>   —Wollstonecraft to Godwin, 21 May 1797,
>   *Godwin and Mary*, pp. 76 –77

Wollstonecraft's public documents reveal only half-truths about the story of her romance with the language of sensibility. They rightly suggest that it was tempestuous; they wrongly suggest that it was an on-again, off-again affair,[1] an impression given by her flamboyant renunciation of sensibility in the *Rights of Woman*. Midpoint in her career, with her feminism more radical, she feels herself constrained by the language of feeling of her youth and tries to banish it from her vocabulary. Only near the end of her career does she lift her own self-imposed public interdict, make peace with sensibility again, and turn myth-maker herself in order to refashion sensibility and its language for her own ends. At the same time, in private correspondence Wollstonecraft never strays too far from her lexicon of sensibility, presumably because she finds no other attractive alternative way to describe herself and others.[2] For twenty years her private vocabulary of self-assessment remains steadily affective, curiously repetitive, even oracular.[3] This is not a discourse of analysis but of cultic participation; even when she does find fault with sensibility (which is very seldom) it is from inside the belief system, and generally directed at an abuser of that system. She declares its recommended behaviors self-defeating, yet she continues to cultivate them; she realizes she is wandering in its conceptual blind alleys, yet continues to think in its terms. Her discontents remain criticisms rather than a more ambitious critique of underlying assumptions, framework, or conclusions. As a result, her letters to friends and family, spanning the period from her adolescence to her untimely death, offer modern readers an invaluable baseline against which to measure her public vacillations on the subject of sensibility.

•   •   •

Wollstonecraft's early letters to a friend, Jane Arden, reveal a fifteen-year-old girl who is already acquainted with the language, literature, and gestures of sensibility. Her initial letter announces her desire to cultivate an intimate friendship of the sentimental kind. "According to my promise I sit down to write to you," it begins, then shifts immediately to verse:

> "My promise and my faith shall be so sure
> "As neither age can change, nor art can cure
> "Perform thy promise, keep within faith's bounds
> "Who breaks his word, his reputation wounds."
>   (c. 1–20 May 1773, *Collected Letters*, p. 51)

The result, in editor Ralph Wardle's words, is "six quotations that Mary wove into [a] letter (or around which she wove it)".[4] Wollstonecraft ties each poetic fragment carefully to a word in her preceding paragraph, and each of these words would be quite at home in a lexicon of sensibility: "promise," a reminder of the importance of intimacy and fealty in sentimental friendships; "writing," of the dependence of the movement on literature; "indulgence," of the many characters of sensibility who luxuriate in joy, or more often perhaps in sorrow; "wrong," of the preoccupation of the movement with scenes of sorrow; and "friendship," of one of sensibility's preeminent values. None of the excerpts is mawkish; one is from Pope, two others clearly modeled on Pope, and the complete song transcribed and enclosed, "Sweet Beverley," is a rollicking mock-pastoral to a rural English retreat. Nevertheless the young Wollstonecraft uses the passages the way sentimental characters or readers frequently use the literature they read: to express feelings that might otherwise remain unexpressed, and to lend certain of those feelings an authority they might not otherwise have. As she issues a challenge, compliments herself, and justifies her criticism of another friend, she reveals herself, in the process, to be a speaker of sensibility keenly susceptible to the slights of others yet hungry for intimacy and, consequently perhaps, somewhat imperious in her demands on friends:

When you write to Miss G—— pray present my compliments to her, and tell her I should be obliged to her if she would write to me, and inclose it in her letter to you, and I flatter myself you will excuse my asking you to inclose it in your answer to this. —I thought Miss R—— behaved rather oddly on Saturday but I believe I was in the wrong—

> "I see the right, and I approve it too—
> "I blame the wrong and yet the wrong pursue."
> —"To you good gods I make my last appeal
> "Or clear my virtues or my crimes reveal
> "If in the maze of fate I blindly run
> "And backward tread those paths I ought to shun
> "Impute my errors to your own decree,
> "My hands are guilty, but my heart is free."
>   (*Collected Letters*, pp. 51–52)

When she takes offense at Miss Arden's (now "Dear Jenny") behavior in a subsequent letter, it is no surprise to find her reacting with the impulsiveness characteristic of a heroine of sensibility. She requests the instant return of all her letters and spills much ink in defense of her feelings. She has a heart, she claims, "too susceptible for my own peace. . . . I spent part of the night in tears; (I would not meanly make a merit of it.)— . . . If I did not love you so well ["so well" is written, then crossed out], I should not be angry.—I cannot bear a slight from those I love" (c. 4 June 1773–16 November 1774, *Collected Letters*, pp. 61–62). Besides having an oversensitive heart, she adds, she has exalted, "romantic notions of" love and friendship: "I must have the first place or none.— I own your behaviour is more according to the opinion of the world, but I would break such narrow bounds." She tries not to take pride in her overly sensitive nature ("I would not meanly make a merit of it"), yet betrays the conviction that her sensitivity, which fosters romantic notions of friendship, raises her above commonplace friends. In a second such self-congratulatory double move, she apologizes self-consciously for the "freedom" of her style, then justifies it in the next breath as a natural consequence of her faith in sincerity (a tenet central, of course, to the creed of sensibility): "If I did not love you I should not write so;—I have a heart that scorns disguise, and a countenance which will not dissemble" (*Collected Letters*, p. 60). Some might term Wollstonecraft's behavior here hypocrisy; certainly other characters of sensibility have been accused of hypocrisy, that catchall charge against any and all forms of human inconsistency.[5] In Wollstonecraft's words, however, can be heard just as easily a dialectic between the values of the antisociety of sensibility and rationalist society. Heard this way, Wollstonecraft is revealed clearly siding with the antisociety, yet keenly cognizant of the behavioral and stylistic rules of the society; she can be seen already very able to measure the gulf between the antilanguage of feeling and the discourse of propriety.

As a young woman Wollstonecraft is well on her way to developing what Godwin identifies after her death as her "female-Werther" complex: a persistent longing to find breathing space for her nonrational needs, especially needs for aesthetic stimulation and emotional intimacy; a conviction that the presence of such a longing is the best available inward sign of superior virtue and genius; and a mind almost too sensitive to endure either life's joys or woes (*Memoirs*, p. 73). Werther's sad story created quite a critical stir in England in the 1770s and 1780s, just as Wollstonecraft was growing up, and her reviews for the *Analytical Review* reveal that she was sympathetically inclined to the book's hero and well aware of the stir. Like Werther, whose name can be read as a play on the German word for "value" *(wert,* "value"; *werten,* "rate" or "evaluate"; hence *Werther* might be "one who values, rates, or evaluates," "a valuable man," or "a man who values himself," all of which are appropriate for Goethe's hero), Wollstonecraft values in herself and others the recently discovered and acclaimed heightened self-consciousness. Also like Werther, in her letters the young Wollstonecraft asks her friends to listen patiently while she traces minute fluctuations in her feelings.

Wollstonecraft's biographer Wardle doubts whether he should consider the language and gestures in these early letters an integral part of the emergent adult personality; to him they are rather signs of adolescent affectation. He argues instead that Wollstonecraft strips away the immature mask of sensibility once she joins Joseph Johnson's London literary circle and becomes a self-acknowledged disciple of reason.[6] Surely the distinction is academic; adolescent affectation can become adult habit, and in the case of Wollstonecraft, it does. Most of the sentimental attitudes she cultivates as a fifteen-year-old remain with her throughout her literary career, in some cases becoming generalized into dominant character traits.

Her already noted preference for a free style is one of the most striking examples of this process. Wollstonecraft's disregard for polished periods is a major hallmark of her prose; it serves her well in her personal and in her polemical writings, but less well in her fiction. In the young girl's letters, it is one of a complex of attitudes loosely allied to her ethics of feeling, but it is also, very specifically, limited in scope to her language attitudes and practices. As a self-declared writer of feeling, she distrusts sentences that become too calculated, too balanced, too ornamental, and trusts most a syntax that seems to spring, in emotionally laden fragments, from momentary feelings. Wollstonecraft apologizes for her rhapsodic style but persists in its use, and gradually her aversion to ornament begins to broaden to include dress and manners. She advertises *Mary* as "an artless tale," for example, and prefaces her *Education of Daughters* by protesting that she could not alter the naturally "grave" tone of her treatise without "writing affectedly" (*Works*, 4.5). In her preface to *Original Stories* she grows more adamant, not only defending her own stylistic aim, "perspicuity and simplicity," but attacking those who would write otherwise. She allies, for the first time, language, manners, and ornament of dress (jewels):

> In writing the following work, I aim at perspicuity and simplicity of style; and try to avoid those unmeaning compliments, which slip from the tongue, but have not the least connection with the affections that should warm the heart, and animate the conduct. By this false politeness, sincerity is sacrificed, and truth violated; and thus artificial manners are necessarily taught. For true politeness is a polish, not a varnish; and should rather be acquired by observation than admonition. And we may remark, by way of illustration, that men do not attempt to polish precious stones, till age and air have given them that degree of solidity, which will enable them to bear the necessary friction, without destroying the ɾ ɪain substance. (*Works*, 4.359)

By the time she pens her introduction to the *Rights of Woman*, her dissatisfaction with ornament has come to include all habits of body, mind, and tongue that women cultivate to please men: "elegance," "soft phrases, susceptibility of heart, delicacy of sentiment, refinement of taste." Not surprisingly, her usual stylistic apology sounds quite militant:

> Animated by this important object, I shall disdain to cull my phrases or polish my style; — I aim at being useful, and sincerity will render me unaffected; for, wishing rather to persuade by the force of my arguments, than dazzle by the elegance of my language, I shall not waste my time in rounding periods, or in fabricating the turgid bombast of artificial feelings, which, coming from the head, never reach the heart. — I shall be employed about things, not words! — and, anxious to render my sex more respectable members of society, I shall try to avoid that flowery diction whicʰ has slided from essays into novels, and from novels into familiar letteɪ ɜ and conversation.
>
> These pretty superlatives, dropping glibly from the tongue, vitiate the taste, and create a kind of sickly delicacy that turns away from simple unadorned truth; and a deluge of false sentiments and overstretched feelings, stifling the natural emotions of the heart, render the domestic pleasures insipid, that ought to sweeten the exercise of those severe duties, which educate a rational and immortal being for a nobler field of action. (*Works*, 5.75–76)

In the text of both her vindications, she shatters the icon of the silent, ornamental woman, openly criticizing many prominent seventeenth- and eighteenth-century men of letters (Milton, Chesterfield, Burke,

Rousseau) for their preference for such a woman. One available portrait of Wollstonecraft from this period suggests her casual attitude towards her own appearance: her hair is anchored carelessly under a headband; her dark, shapeless clothing is cast in shadow, while the light in the picture directs all eyes to her face and the book in her hands; she is unsmiling, and gazes steadily, even arrestingly, at the viewer.[7]

In the end, Wollstonecraft utterly disregards rules of public conduct as well as dress in her extramarital attachments to Henry Fuseli, Gilbert Imlay, and William Godwin. A dramatic demonstration that the slippery slope argument is not always a fallacy, Wollstonecraft's preference for the spontaneous style moves inexorably from written style to lifestyle, from manners to morals.

•   •   •

At her first job away from home, as companion to Mrs. Dawson of Bath, Wollstonecraft gives Jane Arden the following psychological assessment of herself at twenty-one:

> I have not been able to write so soon as I intended. . . . I fear I have a kind of *indolence growing upon me*, that I must endeavour to shake off. . . . To say the truth, I am very indifferent to the opinion of the world in general;— *I wish to retire* as much from it as possible— I am particularly *sick of genteel life*, as it is called;—the *unmeaning civilities* that I see every day practiced don't agree with my temper;—I long for a *little sincerity*, and *look forward with pleasure to the time when I shall lay aside all restraint.*—

> This is the gayest of all gay places;—nothing but dress and amusements are going forward;—*I am only a spectator*—I have lost all relish for them;— early in life, before misfortune had broken my spirits, I had not the power of partaking of them, and now I am both from habit and inclination averse to them.— My wishes and expectations are very moderate.— I don't know which is the worst—to think too little or too much.— 'tis a difficult matter to draw the line, and keep clear of *melancholy and thoughtlessness*:—I really think it is best sometimes to be deceived—and to expect what we are never likely to meet with;—deluded by false hopes, the time would seem shorter, while we are hastening to a better world, where the follies and weaknesses that disturb us in this, will be no more:—In that abode of peace I hope to meet you, and there our *early friendship will be perfected.* (Emphasis mine, c. April-June 1780, *Collected Letters*, pp. 71–72)[8]

Absent in this later letter is the studious transcription of the words of poets she might have used as a younger correspondent as a substitute for expressions of personal feeling. Even so, the letter still unmistakably speaks the language of sensibility, if somewhat less self-consciously. The speaker may have abandoned particular texts but nevertheless relies in a quiet, unresisting manner on the literary code, circumscribing her feelings primarily in terms of the familiar metaphors and metonyms of the meditative graveyard literature of sensibility. Her "spirits" are "broken," she has lost all "relish" for life, she is "only" life's "spectator," she suffers from "indolence," "melancholy," and she "longs for death" as an "abode of peace" where her "friendship" with Jane can achieve its "perfected" state. Sensibility in this passage is presented as an illness of spirit, a list of symptoms, but one caused, Wollstonecraft is careful to suggest, not by some inherent weakness in the self but by the spiritual starvation of that self. The speaker has chafed and sickened under the incessant triviality of the demands of "genteel life": its serious pursuit of "unmeaning civilities," "dress and amusement," and gaiety. Code flirts with preestablished myth as she indulges in magical thinking at two points—in her explanation of both the cause of her illness ("unmeaning civilities") and its cure (death). Like Werther, she assumes that a life without emotional involvement is tantamount to living death; also like Werther, ironically, she pursues death as the only possible cure for the discontents of civilization.

The letter offers other proofs, too, that Wollstonecraft has internalized the language of sensibility, has adopted it as a part of her own subjective reality. It casts its spell over her past ("early in life, before misfortune had broken my spirits") as well as her present; it defines her self ("indolence"; "I am only a spectator"), delimits her discontent ("I am very indifferent to the opinion of the world"; "I have lost all relish for . . . amusements"), and designates her wishes ("I wish to retire"; "I long for a little sincerity"; "and look forward with pleasure to the time when I shall lay aside all restraint"; "keep clear of melancholy and thoughtlessness"; "in that abode of peace I hope to meet you"). She also allows it, just like a character of sensibility, to structure her external world, to divide it into the "sensitive hearts" and the "insensible ones"—and to act and write accordingly. The language of sensibility, then, liberates her to air certain feelings, at the same time that it holds her perceptual powers captive, enabling her to see some things but blinding her to many others.

It frees her, for certain, from the quiet tyranny of decorum, allowing her to articulate alternative forms of social interaction: sincerity, absence of restraint, friendship. These terms are hardly synonymous, but they do have in common the implication (indeed, in this case, the expectation) of intimacy, of the breaking down of the boundaries of propriety in favor of that ideal state for the advocate of sensibility, freer communication of one self with another—in short, sympathy. While it articulates values that the "world in general" seems not to comprehend, however, that language—precisely like Werther's—creates new barriers between the self and that world, rendering that self isolated. The world in general becomes an unattractive realm where amusement takes the place of thought, where life is a round of "unmeaning civilities," where friendship is only possible in an imperfect form. Faced with such a world, yet still longing for a nonexistent sanctuary for introspection and intimacy, the self transforms its longing into a wish to "hasten to a better world." Wollstonecraft's early language of sensibility, then, liberates her self and its secret longings, but only to alienate and isolate—to imprison that self again within itself, with death the only imaginable escape.[9]

•   •   •

Nearly all other meditations on herself or others in the *Collected Letters* are variations on this early letter; all draw upon the lexicon of sensibility. Such meditations occur at crucial junctures in her life, moments of transition when she is taking stock of herself and her situation. When her sister Eliza develops a post-partum revulsion to her husband Meredith Bishop, for example, Wollstonecraft couches her analysis in terms of a distinction to become of increasing importance to her—sensibility versus sensuality:

> Her ideas are all disjointed and a number of wild whims float on her imagination and unconnected fall from her—something like strange dreams when judgement sleeps and fancy sports at a fine rate— Don't smile at my language—for I am so constantly forced to observe her . . . that my thought continual turn [sic] on the unaccountable wanderings of her mind—She seems to think she has been very ill used. . . . My spirits are hurried with listening to pros and cons and my head is so confused that I sometimes say no when I ought to say yes— My heart is almost broken with listening to B. while he *reasons* the case. . . . May my habitation never be fixed among the tribe that can't look beyond the present gratification—that draw fixed conclutions [sic] from general rules—that attend to the literal meaning only . . .
> (c. 7 January 1784, *Collected Letters*, pp. 80, 83)

Considering that the sufferer in this obviously hurriedly written passage is Wollstonecraft's sister, her sympathy hardly needs justification. Yet that sympathy may gain some of its strength as well from certain attitudes adopted by disciples of sensibility: sympathy for nonrational states of mind and a marked aversion to rationalism, especially when in the service of selfishness. Wollstonecraft witnesses her sister's delirium with pained fascination ("my thought continual turn on the unaccountable wanderings of her mind"), ranging for nonjudgmental terms to describe it: "ideas are all disjointed"; "something like strange dreams when judgment sleeps." Her sympathy becomes empathic response when she is forced to listen to the husband reason his case: "My spirits are hurried"; "my head is so confused"; "my heart is almost broken."

Deductive reason clearly seems to her an alien invader, a faculty least able to grapple humanely with Eliza's problems because fettered by its willful literal-mindedness, its blindness to extenuating circumstances ("can't look beyond the present gratification—that draw fixed conclusions from general rules—that attend to the literal meaning only"), and, at least in this case, its close alliance with sensuality. What Bishop is reading "literally" cannot be known with certainty, although likely candidates for texts are the marriage vows or contract. Nor can it be known what particular case Bishop is "reasoning"; but it seems to be a case for some kind of "present gratification" argued deductively, drawing "fixed conclusions" from "general rules" without any consideration for Eliza's state of body or mind. And here Wollstonecraft certainly prefers Eliza's sensitive, "wandering" mind to Bishop's sensual, reasoning one.

Just beneath the surface of this letter floats the image of a dishonored and distracted Clarissa, and several of the assumptions of that novel operate here and elsewhere for Wollstonecraft as mythic premises: that women tend towards physical and emotional sensitivity or sensibility, men towards sensuality and brutality; that the two are, as a result, very frequently incompatible; that women can easily grow too refined for the world they must inhabit and become sick to death. Wollstonecraft sees her friend Fanny Blood's father, brother, and eventual husband Hugh Skeys as variations on the same type that Bishop represents to her. As she struggles to make sense of a second major crisis in her adult life, Fanny's death in Lisbon, Clarissa again seems to haunt her thoughts:

> How Hugh could let Fanny languish in England while he was throwing money away at Lisbon, is to me inexplicable . . . I much fear he loves her not for the qualities that render her dear to my heart— Her tenderness and delicacy is not even conceived by a man who would be satisfied with the *fondness* of . . . women— . . . He has formed to himself a picture of a perfect creature— The principal features may be just—but the little minute things sensibility can only feel and teach—refinement of sentiment and the general notion of goodness is very different—according to the vulgar phrase the one may assist them to escape Hell but the other is wanted to give a relish for those pure joys that we cannot form a conception of in our present imperfect state. (25 July 1785, *Collected Letters*, pp. 95–96)

Here Wollstonecraft identifies feminine sensibility, particularly "tenderness" and "delicacy," as an amiable infirmity, a sign of moral and spiritual superiority, and masculine insensitivity as a sensual blindness that endangers women's safety as well as their happiness. She does not pretend that the distinction between sensibility and sensuality is always a clear-cut one; on the contrary, she becomes increasingly certain that even sensibility can easily slip into sensuality and blindness, that even people of delicacy must be ever on their guard against such an occurrence.

She laments to Eliza shortly before her return to England from Ireland in 1787, for example, that she is sad to see a "man of sensibility and cleverness . . . sink into sensuality" and says, "Such will ever I fear be the case with the inconsistent human heart when there are no *principles* to restrain and direct the wayward impulses of it" (27 June 1787, *Collected Letters*, p. 155). There is a tone of resignation in these lines often to be detected in Wollstonecraft's letters, a tone which may be the consequence of giving too much credence to the myths of sensibility and the Lockean mind-as-entity metaphor they rest upon. These myths—as Wollstonecraft complains herself in *Rights of Woman*—tend to essentialize the differences between men and women, and to exaggerate the irresistible power of the lower faculties, passion, senses, and the imagination. Women of sensibility, who are defined as more susceptible to impulses from without and within than men, can presumably be much more easily swept away by such impulses. The chances of blocking such emotional transports by an act of will or rational exertion apparently seem quite remote to Wollstonecraft at this point in her life.

After the death of Fanny Blood and the failure of the school at Newington Green, Wollstonecraft writes Fanny's brother George in 1786 from her new position with the Kingsboroughs in Ireland, inscribing her unhappiness in the medical dialect of sensibility. It is very well suited to describe melancholy, but not to suggest cures for it:

> I am indeed very unwell, a kind of melancholy langour consumes me— all my active spirits are fled— every thing is tasteless—and uninteresting— I am grown beyond measure indolent, and neglect the few comforts, which are within my reach— I find exercise fatiguing and irksome— Inshort my nerves have been so much injured I am afraid I shall never be tolerably well— These disorders are particularly distressing as they seem intirely to arise from the mind—and that an exertion of the reasoning faculties would banish them and bring it to a proper tone—but slackened nerves are not to be braced by arguments physical as well as mental causes have contributed to reduce me to my present weak state.

Then she drifts to the past—"About this time last year I closed my poor Fanny's eyes"—and then to the future and self-analysis:

This warfare will in time be over—and my soul will not vainly pant after happiness—or doubt in what it consists—I have fostered too great a refinement of mind, and given a keener edge to the sensibility nature gave me—so that I do not relish the pleasures most people pursue—nor am I disturbed by their trifling cares—yet it would be well if I had any hope to gild my prospect—any thing to animate me in my race besides the desire of reaching the goal. (4 December "12 O'clock Night" 1786, *Collected Letters*, p. 128)

Wollstonecraft's profound dejection after Fanny's death has a corrosive psychological effect on her. Not only does she regret Fanny's loss, she voices loss of faith in the refinements of sensibility Fanny represents. Still another woman of sensibility has sickened, then died, and her death seems to close a chapter in Wollstonecraft's life while it confirms the medical myth about sensibility: that it is death-inducing, a physical and mental condition too fragile to survive in an insensitive world. Wollstonecraft is now bereft of her ideals as well as her friend. She nevertheless clings to the language and literature of sensibility to articulate her desire and pain in her own "night thoughts" (the letter is identified as a midnight epistle): "I may sometimes long for the bosom of a friend"; "nerves . . . injured," "slackened nerves," "melancholy langour," "keener edge to the sensibility nature gave me." While this language makes possible a diagnosis of her pathological condition—sensibility, again, fosters illness—at the same time it erects many barriers to any cure, barriers that Wollstonecraft does not seem to see.

First, it assumes a mind divided against itself into faculties or entities—both reason and nerves—and consequently powerless to resist any "physical as well as mental causes." Second, it suggests a mind without self-recuperative powers, one subject to the breakdown of internal communication and to irreversible damage ("slackened nerves . . . not to be braced by arguments"; cf. "broken spirit" above). Third, this passage, like the previous one, underlines the utopian nature of sensibility's desires. Although the speaker seems dissatisfied with her "slackened" state, the exit from that state that she finds attractive is inaccessible and ultimately self-defeating—continued friendship in death: "This warfare will in time be over—and my soul will not vainly pant after happiness—or doubt in what it consists." Fourth, it represents sensibility as a superior state of mind despite its proclivity to illness. Sensibility is vastly preferable to the state of mind of the world in general, with which the sensitive self imagines itself at "war": "I have fostered too great a *refinement* of mind, and given a *keener edge* to the sensibility *nature gave* me—so that I do not relish the pleasures *most people pursue*—nor am I disturbed by *their trifling cares*." The language of sensibility drives Wollstonecraft swiftly—and repeatedly, as it turns out—to the very edge of inescapable sorrow and unfulfillable desire; at the same time, it flatters her into fatalistic resignation with its delusions of exceptionality.

Wollstonecraft shows the first signs of a self-conscious struggle with illogic in the jumbled belief system of sensibility in a letter to the Reverend Henry Gabell in the spring of 1787, when she is about to return to London to join the group of writers working for publisher Joseph Johnson. As she reviews her own unhappy life thus far as daughter, companion, friend, schoolmistress, sister, and governess, she comes to question the value of both intellectual and emotional endowments. Yet intellect, she quickly decides, can be easily defended. Surely God, she ventures, "created nothing in vain"; and surely the exercise of curiosity makes people happier, wiser, and better. At sensibility, however, she balks and, unable to justify its existence so effortlessly, she shifts from a declarative to an interrogative mood:

> The main hinge on which my argument turns is this, refinement genius— and those charming talents which my soul instinctively loves, produce misery in this world—abundantly more pain than pleasure. Why then do they at all unfold themselves *here*? If useless, would not the Searcher of hearts, the tender Father, have shut them up 'till they could bloom in a more favorable climate; where no keen blasts could blight the opening flower.

The terms of her question reveal no eagerness to abandon the "charming talents" of sensibility; so completely has sensibility colored Wollstonecraft's views that, like both Werther and Yorick, she must even imagine God to be a man of feeling, a "tender Father," a "Searcher of hearts." Her doubts do not have to do with sensibility's rightness but rather with its usefulness in a world hostile to it. Its usual consequences, because of this "unfavorable climate," are negative. It produces pain more often than pleasure; it renders life more complex, more "severe," more "wretched":

> Besides sensibility renders the path of duty more intricate—and the warfare *much* more severe— Surely *peculiar* wretchedness has something to balance it! I . . . beg you to continue to write to me. . . . My reason has been too far stretched, and tottered almost on the brink of madness—no wonder then, if I humbly hope, that the ordeal trial answered some end, and that I have not suffered in vain. (16 April 1787, *Collected Letters*, p. 150)

Just what actual ordeal or trial Wollstonecraft is referring to is not clear. It could be her father's cruelty, her sister's flirtation with madness, or her friend's death, or it might be some experience more immediate—perhaps working for the unsympathetic Lady Kingsborough.[10] Whatever it is, it seems serious enough to her to inspire the metaphor "warfare." Two things are clear, however: the nature of her complaint, and the extent of her continuing investment in sensibility. She questions the value of a propensity for which the world seems to have no use, and which causes much more suffering than pleasure. Despite these doubts, she uses the language of sensibility to structure her self and her world. She presents herself as a heroine of sensibility whose "soul instinctively loves" refinement and genius, but who has suffered "*peculiar* wretchedness" for that love; and she presents God as tender, as a searcher of hearts, as the gentle gardener protecting fragile plants of sensibility from the "blasts" of an unfriendly climate. The latter image of God as gardener will ultimately help Wollstonecraft to represent the mind as dynamic, and capable of growth.

But at this juncture the language of sensibility proves more troublesome than helpful to Wollstonecraft as she struggles to see sensibility's part in the divine plan. The references to a maze ("intricate path") and a brink ("tottering reason") suggest all too well her sense of frustration in the face of what seem to be unanswerable questions. She cannot understand the existence of mental powers that only render people miserable. She clearly cannot see any definite place for sensibility, either inside the mind or outside in the world. The main metaphors in the passage are mind-as-entity metaphors: talents as delicate young plants, reason as stretched and tottering. Yet sensibility is assigned neither shape nor place. Is it a delusive guard or substance? Either could, presumably, render a "path" more "intricate" or life's "warfare" more "severe." Is it twin, parent, sibling, or child of "refinement and genius"? Again, Wollstonecraft's passage takes no stand.

In addition to uncertainty about the psychological role—indeed, the ontological nature—of sensibility, the passage also intimates Wollstonecraft's questions about its social-ethical role as well. It does not fit very well at all into a larger scheme of things, and there are signs, here and elsewhere, that she is working to construct a larger, coherent view of things. During the same spring she reports to her sister Eliza that she is reading William Paley's *Principles of Moral and Political Philosophy*,[11] a book that defines duty as whatever best promotes the general welfare. Does his particular brand of theological utilitarianism prompt her to this questioning of the usual rationale for sensibility's usefulness? Does it cause her to question whether sensibility actually renders people happier, wiser, and more virtuous? Her experience, she admits, suggests the contrary: that it makes people miserable and renders them useless. Why, then, she questions Gabell, has God given us these gifts?

This will not be the last time Wollstonecraft questions sensibility's utility, nature, or role in the psychic well-being of the individual. A theory of personality based on Locke's seventeenth-century static model of mind, it is clearly showing signs of age by the late 1780s. The chief social use of the classic man of sensibility (and his primary moral justification for being) is his exercise of compassion or benevolence, and Wollstonecraft's early preference for the moral discourse of sensibility (with the medical the second most favored) suggests that at the time she still finds this moral justification of sensibility persuasive. However, by the 1780s new views are emerging: that the individual and society in general are capable of moral and intellectual development, even perfectible—that the mind and its constructs, in other words, are dynamic. To a great extent, Wollstonecraft grows to embrace those views, at least intellectually, and with them the conviction that the truly virtuous people are obliged to do more than simply sympathize or distribute occasional alms. They also should work to improve life for the greatest number of people, which might mean to educate them, to invent labor-saving machines for them, or perhaps, to become their political advocates—concrete interventionist tactics of which the retiring, resigned, conservative, and sensitive midcentury man of feeling would never have dreamt. Wollstonecraft questions the classic credo of sensibility without wishing to relinquish the notion itself, a gesture important because it epitomizes the struggle she will have for the rest of her adult life: the struggle to reshape the notion of sensibility in order to integrate it into the reformist and feminist philosophy of life she embraces as an adult.

•   •   •

The other most significant passages employing the language of sensibility are in Wollstonecraft's letters to Gilbert Imlay beginning in 1793, and, somewhat later, to William Godwin. Her tone is frequently less ambivalent, less speculative, and more urgent than that in her early letters, as if, in addition to enjoying less leisure, she is now convinced that she can no longer afford to question the value of a code she is trying to persuade nonbelievers to respect. And nonbelievers they both certainly are. When they meet Wollstonecraft assumes Imlay to be a man of sensibility and a heroic revolutionary; his abandonment of her and their child eventually reveal him to be an untrustworthy womanizer. Godwin is free of these faults but, at least at the outset of their relationship, is no great friend of sensibility. He imagines properly trained reason capable of getting people out of trouble, and excess sensibility getting them into it.

Despite her preference, in these love letters, for imperative and declarative sentences (compare the interrogatives that punctuate the letter to Gabell) and an accompanying commanding tone, she is nevertheless more frequently imposed upon by the language of sensibility than in command of it. If it helps her to image her self and her world, it also makes her relationships with others markedly more difficult. In an early letter to Imlay, with their three-month romance still flourishing, Wollstonecraft distinguishes herself from him in the following terms:

> —Cherish me with that dignified tenderness, which I have only found in you; and your own dear girl will try to keep under a quickness of feeling, that has sometimes given you pain— Yes, I will be *good*, that I may deserve to be happy; and whilst you love me, I cannot again fall into the miserable state, which rendered life a burden almost too heavy to be borne.
>
> But good-night!— God bless you! Sterne says, that is equal to a kiss— yet I would rather give you the kiss into the bargain, glowing with gratitude to Heaven, and affection to you. I like the word affection, because it signifies something habitual; and we are soon to meet, to try whether we have mind enough to keep our hearts warm. (Past Twelve o'Clock Monday night [c. August 1793, *Collected Letters,* p. 233])

The predominant tone of this letter is certainly loving, but it contains, as well, many signs of sentimental discontent. She is hypersensitive and self-critical, exacting difficult demands on herself ("Yes, I will be *good*, that I may deserve to be happy") and Imlay ("we are soon to meet, to try whether we have mind enough to keep our hearts warm"); she is also irritable ("your own dear girl will try to keep under a quickness of feeling"). Even a favorite author cannot quite please her; she corrects Sterne's insistence that the language of tenderness may substitute for the action itself: "God bless you!— Sterne says, that is equal to a kiss— yet I would rather give you the kiss into the bargain." And while her words endorse familiar virtues of sensibility that few believers would challenge—"dignified tenderness," "quickness of feeling," "affection," "hearts warm"—they also unwittingly betray Wollstonecraft's vulnerability. Forced to acknowledge that her valued "quickness of feeling" has caused her lover "pain," she vows to be "*good*," then fears the return, if she is not, of suicidal melancholy: "I cannot again fall into the miserable state, which rendered life a burden almost too heavy to be borne." Wollstonecraft quite clearly suffers throughout her life from what today would be termed chronic depression. In her case, a childhood inclination to be unhappy because of home life becomes the dominant mood of a young person acutely conscious of herself as a woman of sensibility, and from that habitual mood comes, at last, as Ryle suggests can happen,[12] a permanent, and highly dangerous, feature of her character.

A few weeks later, in another love letter to Imlay, Wollstonecraft begins by touching on the subject of sensibility playfully: "One rea-

son, in short, why I wish my whole sex to become wiser, is, that the foolish ones may not, by their pretty folly, rob those whose sensibility keeps
down their vanity." Then, as she wonders whether "continual separations" are necessary to fuel Imlay's affection, she grows suddenly
melancholy:

> —Of late, we are always separating.—Crack!—crack!—and away you
> go.— This joke wears the sallow cast of thought; for, though I began to
> write cheerfully, some melancholy tears have found their way into my eyes,
> that linger there, whilst a glow of tenderness at my heart whispers that you
> are one of the best creatures in the world.— Pardon then the vagaries of a
> mind, that has been almost "crazed by care," as well as "crossed in hapless
> love," and bear with me a *little* longer!— When we are settled in the coun-
> try together, more duties will open before me, and my heart, which now,
> trembling into peace, is agitated by every emotion that awakens the remem-
> brance of old griefs, will learn to rest on yours, with that dignity your char-
> acter, not to talk of my own, demands.
>
> Take care of yourself—and write soon to your own girl (you may add
> dear, if you please) who sincerely loves you, and will try to convince you
> of it, by becoming happier. Mary (Friday Morning [c. September 1793, *Col-
> lected Letters*, pp. 236–37])

Imlay's absence haunts this letter, as it does Wollstonecraft's thoughts.
He is still in or near Paris, but is no longer visiting Mary in Neuilly,
where she has settled to avoid the summer Terror, with as much regu-
larity as before. She does not mention it outright, but his faithfulness
has clearly become a worry in her mind; her fear of being jilted, in fact,
is what unifies the letter, which lacks coherence or sustained thought
on the surface. Paragraph one mentions his absence, two follows him
"along the road," three jokes of foolish women luring men away from
wise ones, and four speculates on these "continual separations."

The letter makes every attempt to end on a cheerful note, with visions
of their idyllic mutual future and a wish for his health, surely an attempt,
along with the passim "my heart whispers that you are one of the best
creatures in the world," to convince herself that *she* cannot be betrayed.
As her biographer Claire Tomalin remarks most perceptively, "If you
believe, as she did, that love derives first of all from a mental and spiritual sympathy, it becomes very difficult to acknowledge to yourself that
you have been wrong in your estimate of your partner."[13] Doubts rise to
the surface about Imlay's capacity for sustained sympathy—"The way
to my senses is through my heart; but, forgive me! I think there is sometimes a shorter cut to yours"—but she explodes them, deferring to sensibility's mythic paradigm, before they can become convictions.

By September of 1793 Wollstonecraft is essentially alone in a Paris
in the beginning throes of the Reign of Terror, without any regular
income, an *Englishwoman* writing a *book about the Revolution*—two

facts that make her potentially suspect to the French authorities. Her letter, however, makes no mention of these things; she instead absorbs herself completely in her love for Imlay, and she doubly shields herself from reality by periodic reversion to literary analogues. While her situation rather than her self-talk is her main problem at this time, her language—and the myths it generates in her own mind—creates an identity for her that complicates that situation. Allusions to *Hamlet* and Gray's "Elegy," and to Laurence Sterne in the letter cited, suggest a self woven in part from materials firmly allied with the literary vogue of sensibility (Goethe's Werther also compared himself to Hamlet, and Sterne's Yorick to Hamlet's "poor Yorick"). The self assessing itself here as "crazed by care" and "crossed in hapless love" accepts the plots of certain stories (Ophelia's, for example, or Maria's from Sterne's *Sentimental Journey*) as mythic imperatives—accepts, in other words, that separation from loved ones must necessarily have tragic consequences, madness or death. Wollstonecraft's two suicide attempts in 1795, precipitated by Imlay's abandonment, show all too poignantly the degree to which she believes in this particular myth.

The discussion of the heart reinforces this myth by making her self seem even more fragile. Her heart seems out of touch with reason, seems instead to have its own independent existence in this extended metaphor as a sentient being: yet, like a lyre in the wind, it "whispers," is "agitated," can be "at rest," at the mercy of—and extremely vulnerable to— external stimuli. The use of the word "girl" in both letters to Imlay also reinforces the unfortunate emerging self-portrait of vulnerability. "Girl" is not a term she chooses for herself; it is, she mentions in the previous letter, Imlay's term of endearment for her. ("You have often called me, dear girl," August 1793, *Collected Letters*, p. 235.) It rests awkwardly on the shoulders of the vindicator of the rights of woman, something she seems to sense. Each time she employs it, she does so in a sentence that strives to substitute "good" or "happy" for "dear":

> Cherish me . . . and your own dear girl . . . will be *good*, that I may deserve to be happy; and . . . cannot again fall into the miserable state. . . . (c. August 1793, *Collected Letters*, p. 233)
>
> You have often called me, dear girl, but you would now say good. (Wednesday morning, c. August 1793, *Collected Letters*, p. 235)

She insists on mentioning it, however, perhaps revels in it as an affectionate diminutive, but it diminishes her even as it guarantees her Imlay's affection, strips her linguistically of adulthood and autonomy, hardly a good label for someone in her situation feeling as helpless, as vulnerable, as gloomy as she does. An instance of Robin Lakoff's double bind,[14] the label "dear Girl" exposes her, if she rejects it, to Imlay's possible rejection, condemns her, if she embraces it, to immaturity, and their relationship to the lopsided one of parent and child. The letter offers some evidence, moreover, that she assumes, whether consciously or not, the infantile role the label bestows on her. A small child bereft of its parental support would certainly experience terror, hysteria, and, very probably, fears of death. And so does she: she complains of "trembling," "agitation," disorientation, near madness, and fears of the return of suicidal depression. That she hopes by expressing her "vagaries of mind" to recall her caretaker is clear.

In this case, Wollstonecraft's inherited language of sensibility clearly precipitates as well as expresses her personal crisis. It hints to her the artificiality and the fragility of her sense of self, it wishes for a utopian union with Imlay, it insists upon the irrevocable dire consequences of separation from Imlay, and it cuts her off from cognitive assessment of her difficulties; it feeds her fears and fans her desires. She becomes increasingly agitated as her life-sustaining intimacy with him begins to crumble, and that despite her most valiant epistolary efforts.

By December of 1793, she is urging Imlay, now in Le Havre, to "have some . . . sensibility," and by September of the next year, she is lecturing him, now on his way to London, on the benefits of cultivating imagination and the dangers of cultivating trade:

> To honour J. J. Rousseau, I intend to give her [their daughter Fanny] a sash, the first she has ever had round her—and why not?—for I have always been half in love with him.
>
> Well, this you will say is trifling—shall I talk about alum or soap? . . . Believe me, sage sir, you have not sufficient respect for the imagination— I could prove to you in a trice that it is the mother of sentiment, the great distinction of our nature, the only purifier of the passions— animals have a portion of reason, and equal, if not more exquisite, senses; but no trace of imagination, or her offspring taste, appears in any of their actions. The impulse of the senses, passions, if you will, and the conclusions of reason, draw men together; but the imagination is the true fire, stolen from heaven, to animate this cold creature of clay, producing all those fine sympathies that lead to rapture, rendering men social by expanding their hearts, instead of leaving them leisure to calculate how many comforts society affords.
>
> If you call these observations romantic, a phrase in this place which would be tantamount to nonsensical, I shall be apt to retort, that you are embruted by trade and the vulgar enjoyments of life— Bring me then back your barrier-face, or you shall have nothing to say to my barrier-girl; and I shall fly from you, to cherish the remembrances that will ever be dear to me; for I am yours truly
>
> Mary
> (22 September 1794, Collected Letters, p. 263)

This letter is most often cited for its homage to Rousseau, which is taken to be a sign of Wollstonecraft's continuing ambivalence about both sensibility and the father of French *sensibilité*. Although no reason exists to dispute this claim, in this context the mention of the father of the French Revolution is certainly rhetorical as well as self-referential: it is the first in a chain of comments in the letter designed to goad Imlay into coming back to her: "this you will say is trifling," "sage sir, you have not sufficient respect for the imagination," "I could prove to you in a trice," "if you call these observations romantic, a phrase in this place . . . tantamount to nonsensical," "I shall be apt to retort, that you are embruted by trade and the vulgar enjoyments of life," "Bring me then back your barrier-face."

The dominant tone of the letter is defiant; the new mother is clearly angered, yet may fear the backlash of an all-too-direct attack on men as self–indulgent sensualists (she accuses Rousseau of such an attitude in the *Rights of Woman*), so shifts her target metonymically to the commercial trade that Imlay represents in her mind. She moves the blame for sensuality from men to the world of having and getting; trade becomes the purveyor of self-indulgent sensualism. At the same time she intensifies her defense of sensibility, changing the terms of her discourse from medical or moral to aesthetic, and turning from simple praise of sensibility to a self-conscious mythologization of its virtues. It is no longer characterized as a fosterer of amiable illness, but of geniuses and benefactors, people who could save, or at least improve, the world: "sentiment, the great distinction of our nature, the only purifier of the passions." Its siblings are sympathy and sociability, its parent imagination, a virtue with a proven mythic genealogy of its own as Prometheus's "true fire, stolen from heaven, to animate this cold creature of clay."

In contrast to earlier pronouncements on the subject of sensibility—in the letter to Reverend Gabell, for example—here Wollstonecraft seems to find a place for it, and a new, happier myth for it, both in the mind and in society. Even so, the metaphors of sensibility continue to define her relationship with Imlay in self-defeating ways, tempting her to abandon reason to the beasts, and encouraging her to make idealistic demands, to assume antisocial postures, and to place herself in either-or situations that make her brittle, hence fragile. Here, just two-and-a-half years after the polemic against sensibility in the *Rights of Woman*, Wollstonecraft has never sounded more like Goethe's apostle of sensibility, young Werther, who insists that having to do work of any kind stifles one's capacity to love and create. He disdains the hard-working bourgeois, calls him a Philistine:

Along comes some Philistine, a man of position and respectability, and says to him [a "warmhearted youth"]: "My good young friend, to love is human; but you must love within human bounds. Divide your time: devote a portion to business, and give the hours of recreation to your sweetheart. Calculate your fortune; and of what you have left over, you may make her a present, only not too often—on her birthday, and such occasions, etc. etc." If he were to follow this advice, he might become a useful member of society, and I should advise every prince to give him a post; but it is all up with his love, and, if he be an artist, with his genius. O my friend! why is it that the torrent of genius so seldom bursts forth, so seldom rolls in full-flowing stream, overwhelming your astounded soul? Because, on either side of this stream sedate and respectable fellows have settled down; their arbors and tulip beds and cabbage fields would be destroyed; therefore in good time they have the sense to dig trenches and raise embankments in order to avert the impending danger.

In response to his mother's wish, some time later, that he cease his idle existence and find some work to engage in, Werther laughs: "Am I not sufficiently employed? And is it not in the end the same, whether I count peas or lentils? The world runs on from one folly to another; and the man who, purely for the sake of others, and without any passion or inner compulsion of his own, toils after wealth or dignity, or any other phantom, is simply a fool."[15] Faced with the option of continued leisure or work to attain wealth, power, or prestige, Werther opts to remain at leisure and use fewer resources, to simply withdraw into himself, where he can, he insists, be perfectly content.

Wollstonecraft might be acting out Werther's attitudes, so closely does she adhere to his script in this instance. She, too, expresses contempt for the world of trade and commerce; she, too, prefers withdrawal, in this case flight through her imagination into a more congenial romantic past, the brief period when she and Imlay secretly meet outside a Paris tollgate (the "barrier" mentioned). Her expressed longing for the return of Imlay's "barrier-face" is ambiguous: is it the face of temporary sensibility that Imlay reveals as a new lover,[16] or is it the impassive, "embruted" face of Imlay the tradesman? The reference to his own "barrier-girl" is even more ambiguous: does she refer to herself or to their daughter? The combination "barrier/girl" is revealing in any event. At first, it seems to suggest something vaguely revolutionary, something independent and courageous: a woman of keen sensibility who both longs for barriers and for their demolition, who wishes to remain at the periphery of a society perceived as mundane and unfeeling, ready to flee all but the most refined and intimate of relationships. The associations cannot hold for long, however; for, in context, the phrase also suggests a self barricaded in the solitude of remembrance of the past rather than one facing a less-than-perfect present, an immature and defensive self: "Bring me then back your barrier-face, or you shall have nothing to say to my barrier-girl; and I shall fly from you, to cherish the remembrances."

In December 1794 and January 1795, after four months of solitude with her infant daughter, Wollstonecraft sends a flurry of letters to Imlay in a futile attempt to persuade him either to return to her in Paris or to end the relationship once for all. As her circumstances grow grimmer—few friends remaining out of jail, insufficient funds to heat her rooms—she becomes entangled in "the same perpetually recurring cycle of emotion,"[17] a cycle that also functions, unfortunately, like a downward spiral, one always ending in melancholic despair. Any happy emotion she feels, and at this point in time there appear to be mainly two, her desire for Imlay and her love for her daughter Fanny, evokes a powerful chain of unhappy emotions—hurt, loneliness, anger, anxiety, self-recrimination, despair—and she cannot seem to free herself from the chain. Letters may begin or end anywhere in the cycle, but they document her increasing despair without fail:

> Come to me, my dearest friend, husband, father of my child!— All these fond ties glow at my heart at this moment, and dim my eyes.— With you an independence is desirable; and it is always within our reach, if affluence escapes us—without you the world again appears empty to me. But I am recurring to some of the melancholy thoughts that have flitted across my mind for some days past, and haunted my dreams.
>
> My little darling is indeed a sweet child; and I am sorry that you are not here, to see her little mind unfold itself. You talk of "dalliance," but certainly no lover was ever more attached to his mistresses, than she is to me. Her eyes follow me every where, and by affection I have the most despotic power over her. She is all vivacity or softness—yes; I love her more than I thought I should. When I have been hurt at your stay, I have embraced her as my only comfort—when pleased with you, for looking and laughing like you; nay, I cannot, I find, long be angry with you, whilst I am kissing her for resembling you. But there would be no end to these details. Fold us both to your heart; for I am truly and affectionately
>
> Yours
> Mary
> (26 December 1794, *Collected Letters*, p. 269)

> I will not importune you.— I will only tell you, that I long to see you, and, being at peace with you, I shall be hurt, rather than made angry, by delays.— Having suffered so much in life, do not be surprised if I sometimes, when left to myself, grow gloomy, and suppose that it was all a dream, and that my happiness is not to last. I say happiness, because remembrance retrenches all the dark shades of the picture.
>
> (28 December 1794, *Collected Letters*, pp. 270–71)

How I hate this crooked business! This intercourse with the world, which obliges one to see the worst side of human nature! Why cannot you be content with the object you had first in view, when you entered into this wearisome labyrinth?— I know very well that you have imperceptibly been drawn on; yet why does one project, successful or abortive, only give place to two others? Is it not sufficient to avoid poverty? . . . I will own to you that, feeling extreme tenderness for my little girl, I grow sad very often when I am playing with her, that you are not here, to observe with me how her mind unfolds, and her little heart becomes attached!— These appear to me to be true pleasures—and still you suffer them to escape you, in search of what we may never enjoy.— It is your own maxim to "live in the present moment." *If you do*—stay, for God's sake; but tell me the truth—if not, tell me when I may expect to see you, and let me not be always vainly looking for you, till I grow sick at heart.

Adieu! I am a little hurt.— I must take my darling to my bosom to comfort me.

Mary
(29 December 1794, *Collected Letters*, pp. 271–72)

I have gotten into a melancholy mood, you perceive. You know my opinion of men in general; you know that I think them systematic tyrants, and that it is the rarest thing in the world, to meet with a man with sufficient delicacy of feeling to govern desire. When I am thus sad, I lament that my little darling, fondly as I doat on her, is a girl.— I am sorry to have a tie to a world that for me is ever sown with thorns.

(30 December 1794, *Collected Letters*, p. 273)

Fatigued during my youth by the most arduous struggles, not only to obtain independence, but to render myself useful, not merely pleasure, for which I had the most lively taste, I mean the simple pleasures that flow from passion and affection, escaped me, but the most melancholy views of life were impressed by a disappointed heart on my mind. Since I knew you, I have been endeavouring to go back to my former nature, and have allowed some time to glide away, winged with the delight which only spontaneous enjoyment can give.— Why have you so soon dissolved the charm? . . . Still as you talk of your return, even in February, doubtingly, I have determined, the moment the weather changes, to wean my child.— It is too soon for her to begin to divide sorrow!— And as one has well said, "despair is a freeman," we will go and seek our fortune together.

This is not a caprice of the moment—for your absence has given new weight to some conclusions, that I was very reluctantly forming before you left me.— I do not chuse to be a secondary object.— If your feelings were in unison with mine, you would not sacrifice so much to visionary prospects of future advantage.

Mary
(9 January 1795, *Collected Letters*, pp. 274 –75)

Werther criticizes Lotte's husband Albert for failing to synchronize his heartbeat with hers; Wollstonecraft sees the same fault in Imlay. In both cases, the ideal affective harmony of lovers of sensibility has yet to be achieved. By the next summer, she has fallen into a melancholy very much like (indeed, linguistically almost identical to) Werther's before his suicide, speaking wildly of her "sickness of heart." However, even as she sinks into a suicidal despair that her language of sensibility condones, even helps to create, she nevertheless clings loyally to that language. In June 1795, about to depart England again as Imlay's business agent to Scandinavia after a first attempt to take her life, she writes him rapturously of the "ineffable," but actually quite self-defeating, "joys" of sensibility:

> I shall always consider it as one of the most serious misfortunes of my life, that I did not meet you, before satiety had rendered your senses so fastidious, as almost to close up every tender avenue of sentiment and affection that leads to your sympathetic heart. You have a heart, my friend, yet, hurried away by the impetuosity of inferior feelings, you have sought in vulgar excesses, for that gratification which only the heart can bestow. . . .
>
> Ah! my friend, you know not the ineffable delight, the exquisite pleasure, which arises from a unison of affection and desire, when the whole soul and senses are abandoned to a lively imagination, that renders every emotion delicate and rapturous. Yes; these are emotions, over which satiety has no power, and the recollection of which, even disappointment cannot disenchant; but they do not exist without self-denial. These emotions, more or less strong, appear to me to be the distinctive characteristic of genius, the foundation of taste, and of that exquisite relish for the beauties of nature, of which the common herd of eaters and drinkers and *child-begeters*, certainly have no idea. (Friday, 12 June 1795, *Collected Letters*, p. 291)

This passage offers the nearest thing to an analysis of psychological functions of sensibility that Wollstonecraft's letters yield. It places the virtues of sensibility and the vices of sensuality on a physiological map, connecting them causally with one another, with bodily organs, and with the faculties into which Enlightenment philosophers tended to divide the mind. It insists that feeding the senses sets up roadblocks to the heart along the usual "avenues" of access—sentiment and affection—but that denying the senses will remove those roadblocks, allowing the free flow of sympathy (presumably in either direction, either *to* or *from* the heart) and also allowing affection and desire to unite. This, in its turn, will stimulate imagination, which in its turn will transform all emotions into "delicate," "rapturous" internal events, and foster genius, taste, and a love of nature. It all sounds blissful, if vaguely so.

At the same time, the letter sets up stark, mutually exclusive choices between a life of devotion to senses or sentiment: "satiety" or "self-denial"; "the common herd" or "genius"; eating, drinking, and child-begetting, or taste, genius, and love of nature. Certainly Wollstonecraft makes her rhetorical point: after reading this letter, who would be tempted to praise the life of sensual excess? More than any other passage to this point, however, this one reveals clearly the drastic limits of the language of sensibility. The internal process it describes is hazy (indeed fantastical) and circular, and the mental map is unnervingly incomplete. The only faculties mentioned are lower faculties: will and reason are left out of the picture entirely. Besides, the person of sentiment is promised a series of unverifiable gifts: ineffable delight, exquisite pleasure, genius, taste, relish for nature. Invulnerable these emotions may be, as she boasts, to "satiety" and "disappointment"; but perhaps because they represent ineffable and unfulfillable desires, they do not save her from profound dejection. In the same letter, she admits, "I have looked at the sea, and at my child, hardly daring to own to myself the secret wish, that it might become our tomb; and that the heart, still so alive to anguish, might there be quieted by death. At this moment ten thousand complicated sentiments press for utterance, weigh on my heart, and obscure my sight" (*Collected Letters*, p. 291). Listing the joys of sensibility does not make her happy, but, as she notes in concluding her letter, detailing its sorrows makes her unhappier: "The train of thoughts which the writing of this epistle awoke, makes me so wretched, that I must take a walk, to rouse and calm my mind" (p. 292).

From Norway later that same summer, having received almost no correspondence from Imlay though she commands him, at her departure, to write frequently, a much more subdued Wollstonecraft records the grief she feels in the certainty of having lost all but her infant daughter:

> I have just received two of your letters . . . and you must have received several from me, informing you of my detention, and how much I was hurt by your silence. . . .
>
> Write to me then, my friend, and write explicitly. I have suffered, God knows, since I left you. Ah! you have never felt this kind of sickness of heart!— My mind . . . I feel almost rises to agony. But this is not a subject of complaint, it has afforded me pleasure,—and reflected pleasure is all I have to hope for—if a spark of hope be yet alive in my forlorn bosom.
>
> I will try to write with a degree of composure. I wish for us to live together, because I want you to acquire an habitual tenderness for my poor girl. I cannot bear to think of leaving her alone in the world, or that she should only be protected by your sense of duty. Next to preserving her, my most earnest wish is not to disturb your peace. (30 July 1795, *Collected Letters*, pp. 306 –7)

Dramatized here is the last, worst double bind of anyone whose life has been defined and circumscribed, at every turn, by sensibility. Alienat-

ed from the "common herd," yet born to "sympathy," her only gratification lies in the successful communication of that sympathy to a few
like-minded, sympathetic others. At this point, however, only one of
her friends remains—her daughter. Her other chosen friend has rejected her, leaving her a prey to her own, apparently almost overwhelmingly intense, solitary feelings. The terms of sensibility highly value
intimate friendship, hence the terms of sensibility encouraged her to
mingle her joys, her sorrows, her interests, even her identity, with his;
yet despite the utter futility of hoping for the continuance of that intimacy, that same language of sensibility offers her no way to extricate
herself from it. She sees her self as wedded to his by the repeated ceremony of compassion; and since that self, by her own description—"I
am born to sympathy"—has no clear-cut borders but is rather defined
in terms of openness to others, she cannot retreat from that compassion. She translates it, in this case, from a hope for love into a wish to
be dutiful: "my most earnest wish is not to disturb your peace."

Letters from Imlay in the month that follow make Wollstonecraft
certain that their relationship is over, and that she has nothing to hope
from him, not for herself or for her daughter. She promises on 26 August
1795 not to disturb him anymore, and writing down that promise
induces in her a remarkable involuntary physiological response:

> You tell me that my letters torture you; I will not describe the effect yours
> have on me. . . . I mean not to give vent to the emotions they produced.—
> Certainly you are right; our minds are not congenial. I have lived in an
> ideal world, and fostered sentiments that you do not comprehend—or you
> would not treat me thus. I am not, I will not be, merely an object of com-
> passion—a clog, however light, to teize you. Forget that I exist: I will never
> remind you. Something emphatical whispers to me to put an end to these
> struggles. Be free—I will not torment, when I cannot please. I can take
> care of my child; you need not continually tell me that our fortune is insep-
> arable, *that you will try to cherish tenderness* for me. . . .
>
> Adieu! I am agitated—my whole frame is convulsed—my lips tremble,
> as if shook by cold, though fire seems to be circulating in my veins.
>
> God bless you.
> Mary
> (26 August 1795, *Collected Letters*, p. 310)

While the last paragraph here might seem, to some, to be melodramat-
ic posturing, the physical state it aims to describe, however literary the
language, follows quite plausibly from the paragraphs before. In these,
Wollstonecraft quite consciously closes the lexicon of sensibility,
denies Imlay access to it, and denies herself the use of it, for, as she
notes, "Our minds are not congenial. I have lived in an ideal world, and

fostered sentiments that you do not comprehend." This refusal to speak the language of the heart may be motivated by the desire to withdraw a valuable medium from a person who cannot appreciate it, or by a recognition of the inadequacy of that medium to either express her pain or move her reader to change his mind; in either case, she finally realizes that that language does not gain her access to Imlay's heart. The passage is clogged with negatives that signal the exertion of will required: "I will not describe," "I mean not to give vent," "I am not, I will not be, merely an object," "I will never remind you." Robbed of her language of the heart, she struggles in vain to express the pain of deprivation with other words; only her body is left to register it: "My whole frame is convulsed—my lips tremble, as if shook by cold, though fire seems to be circulating in my veins."

Despite their obvious estrangement, Imlay promises to meet her in Dover upon her return from Scandinavia. When she arrives, however, he is not there. Just a little over a week later her dalliance with melancholy bears its final, bitter fruit: she tries to take her own life in the Thames, her suicide note to Imlay laced with bitter accusations and a keen desire to effect his remorse:

> I write you now on my knees; imploring you to send my child and the maid with——, to Paris, to be consigned to the care of Madame ——, rue ——, section de ——. Should they be removed, —— can give their direction.
>
> Let the maid have all my clothes, without distinction.
>
> Pray pay the cook her wages, and do not mention the confession which I forced from her—a little sooner or later is of no consequence. Nothing but my extreme stupidity could have rendered me blind so long. Yet, whilst you assured me that you had no attachment, I thought we might still have lived together.
>
> I shall make no comments on your conduct; or any appeal to the world. Let my wrongs sleep with me! Soon, very soon, shall I be at peace. When you receive this, my burning head will be cold.
>
> I would encounter a thousand deaths, rather than a night like the last. Your treatment has thrown my mind into a state of chaos; yet I am serene. I go to find comfort, and my only fear is, that my poor body will be insulted by an endeavour to recal [sic] my hated existence. But I shall plunge into the Thames where there is the least chance of my being snatched from the death I seek.
>
> God bless you! May you never know by experience what you have made me endure. Should your sensibility ever awake, remorse will find its way to your heart; and, in the midst of business and sensual pleasure, I shall appear before you, the victim of your deviation from rectitude.
>
> Mary
>
> (c. 10 October 1795, *Collected Letters*, pp. 316-17)

The language of sensibility, needless to say, does not push Wollstonecraft off Putney Bridge. It is, however, an accomplice in this crime. Its overlexicalization of words for emotion, especially negative emotion; its labyrinthine metaphors of mind; and its myths about the human psyche in love—all increase Wollstonecraft's susceptibility to a death wish. Throughout her affair with Imlay, Wollstonecraft writes, according to Tomalin, like "a creature almost entirely at the mercy of emotional impulse," and at the moment of self-annihilation, she acts out a sentimental hero(ine)'s death: "She had arrived at full romantic status: prepared to die for lack of love."[18] More than once in the final months before this, she compares her lot in her letters to that of tragic or pathetic literary figures: Shakespeare's Hamlet (p. 300), Sterne's Maria (p. 305), Shakespeare's Lear (p. 305). Can she have failed to remember, at this juncture, that Werther, in his own impassioned defense of suicide as "natural," as physical infirmity, uses as his primary example the story of an unfortunate abandoned woman who "plunges into the deep, to end her sufferings in the broad embrace of death"?[19]

Her letters to Godwin, however, which already begin a few months after her last letter to Imlay, take up the language again. Take, for example, this attempt dating from early in their relationship to help him to understand and value her sensitive nature:

I have not lately passed so painful a night as the last. I feel that I cannot speak clearly on the subject to you, let me then briefly explain myself now I am alone. Yet, struggling as I have been a long time to attain peace of mind (or apathy) I am afraid to trace emotions to their source, which border on agony.

Is it not sufficient to tell you that I am thoroughly out of humour with myself ? Mortified and humbled, I scarcely know why—still, despising false delicacy I almost fear that I have lost sight of the true. Could a wish have transported me to France or Italy, last night, I should have caught up my Fanny and been off in a twinkle, though convinced that it is my mind, not the place, which requires changing. My imagination is for ever betraying me into fresh misery, and I perceive that I shall be a child to the end of the chapter. You talk of the roses which grow profusely in every path of life— I catch at them; but only encounter the thorns. . . . Consider what has passed as a fever of your imagination; one of the slight mortal shakes to which you are liable—and I—will become again a *Solitary Walker*. Adieu! I was going to add God bless you! (17 August 1796, *Godwin and Mary*, pp. 14 –15)

Her tone in this letter and in others to Godwin is rarely as desperate or angry as it was with Imlay, in part, no doubt, because Godwin reciprocates her affection more successfully than Imlay. He also launches a campaign to subdue her passions, while she engages in a counter-campaign to fire his imagination and inspire his sensibility; both, to a degree, succeed, as the following interchange between the two illustrates:

> (Godwin to Wollstonecraft)
> I know the acuteness of your feelings, & there is perhaps nothing upon earth that would give me so pungent a remorse, as to add to your unhappiness. . . . Upon consideration I find in you one fault, & but one. You have the feelings of nature, & you have the honesty to avow them. In all this you do well. I am sure you do. But do not let them tyrannise over you. . . . Be happy. Resolve to be happy. You deserve to be so. Every thing that interferes with it, is weakness & wandering; & a woman, like you, can, must, shall, shake it off. Afford, for instance, no food for the morbid madness, & no triumph to the misanthropical gloom. . . . Call up, with firmness, the energies, which, I am sure, you so eminently possess. (17 August 1796, *Godwin and Mary*, pp. 16–17)

Wollstonecraft responds, calmed but not entirely subdued, determined to banish fears of another rejection yet eager to rationalize, rather than alter, her sensitivities:

> I like your last—may I call it *love* letter? better than the first—and can I give you a higher proof of my esteem than to tell you, the style of my letter will whether I will or no, that it has calmed my mind—a mind that had been painfully active all the morning, haunted by old sorrows that seemed to come forward with new force to sharpen the present anguish—Well! well—it is almost gone—I mean all my unreasonable fears—and a whole train of tormentors, which you have routed—I can scarcely describe to you their ugly shapes so quickly do they vanish—and let them go, we will not bring them back by talking of them. . . . My affections have been more exercised than yours, I believe, and my senses are quick, without the aid of fancy—yet tenderness always prevails. (17 August 1796, *Godwin and Mary*, pp. 18–19)

Wollstonecraft shows no willingness to abandon the language of self-definition she has used since her youth, even though she at least half-recognizes in this letter that the language of sensibility, too long indulged, may breed or increase the very sorrows it seeks to articulate and exorcise. In letter after letter, her attitudes spring from this metaphoric language that has become second nature to her, determining her reactions, shaping her self-concept and her expectations, structuring her thoughts and her perceptions of the world. Even now, writing to reason itself, in the person of the rational philosopher Godwin, it rarely occurs to her to react to persons, places, or things any other way but emotionally; and she still divides the world, as she always has, into the have-hearts and the have-no-hearts. Just three months before she dies she makes this remark about a mutual acquaintance: "I am not much surprised at Miss Parr's conduct. You may remember that I did not give her credit for as much sensibility (at least the sensibility which is the mother of sentiment, and delicacy of mind) as you did, and her present conduct confirms my opinion. Could a woman of delicacy seduce and marry a fool?" (10 June 1797, *Godwin and Mary*, p. 93).

At every turn, moreover, in this quiet but not quite tranquil time following her two attempted suicides, Wollstonecraft seems in danger of slipping back into a mythic role, one of the archetypical protagonists of sensibility whose lives are inscribed, then reinscribed, throughout the century by a series of novelists. When she fears abandonment, she vows to "become again" a "*Solitary Walker*" (p. 15); like Werther, she is convinced that she has a "sick heart" (pp. 43, 112); and, faced with the prospect of a grammar lesson from Godwin, she hopes it will proceed like Adam's affectionate lessons to Eve in Milton's mythic paradise.[20] Godwin, whether consciously or not, tries to intervene directly at such moments, and counter or rewrite the mythic script before it overwhelms her. "Do not become again a *solitary walker*," he pleads (p. 17); later he reminds her, "I found a wounded heart, &, as that heart cast itself upon me, it was my ambition to heal it" (p. 75).

Yet the slightest sign of disapproval from him can upset the delicate balance she has achieved, something nowhere clearer than in her overreaction to his (probable) suggestion that she improve her grammar. She sinks into melancholy, indolence, anger; she tells him her life history to point up the absolute importance of writing to her wellbeing; she reviews what she has accomplished; and she outlines what *she* values most in her writing. Throughout the letter, the tone remains one of near desperation:

What is to be done, I must either disregard your opinion, think it unjust, or throw down my pen in despair; and that would be tantamount to resigning existence; for at fifteen I resolved never . . . to endure a life of dependence. . . . In short, I must reckon on doing some good, and getting the money I want, by my writings, or go to sleep for ever. . . . I am compelled to think that there is some thing in my writings more valuable, than in the productions of some people on whom you bestow warm elogiums [sic]—I mean more mind—denominate it as you will—more of the observations of my own senses, more of the combining of my own imagination—the effusions of my own feelings and passions than the cold workings of the brain on the materials procured by the senses and imagination of other writers.

I am more out of patience with myself than you can form any idea of, when I tell you that I have scarcely written a line to please myself (and very little with respect to quantity) since you saw my M.S. (4 September 1796, *Godwin and Mary*, pp. 28–29)

The defensiveness, the veiled threats to end it all, the either-or constructions, the sudden writer's block—all suggest that Godwin has touched a nerve here, much, no doubt, to his surprise; what he may not know is that he has threatened to undercut her own philosophy of writing, one quite dependent on certain assumptions in the credo of sensibility. Wollstonecraft has consistently valued content over style, spontaneity over perfection; indeed, on various occasions, she expresses a suspicion, or even a contempt, for stylistic perfection. Her threat to write her own way—recording the spontaneous overflow of her perceptions, her imagination, and her feelings—or die must stand as a measure of the degree to which she remains wedded, both as writer and as woman, to the frame of reference provided to her by the language of sensibility.

From first to last, then, Mary Wollstonecraft is, in her private life, a disciple of sensibility, always (to paraphrase her confession about Rousseau) at least "half in love" with it.[21] Its language helps her to structure, and necessarily to circumscribe, herself, others, her values, the world. This is what her letters reveal. The houses of fiction and persuasion she builds on this foundation are sometimes rather surprising ones, but are definitely less surprising if one keeps the foundation in view, and postulates, even when it is fully submerged during Wollstonecraft's most polemic period, that it exists.

2
Mary, A Fiction

L'exercise des plus sublimes vertues élève et nourrit le
génie.   —Selected for the title page of *Mary*

While the metaphors and myths of sensibility tend to become truths for
Wollstonecraft to live by, her novels allow her sufficient critical distance to sometimes celebrate, sometimes challenge, those same
metaphors and myths. The epigraph for *Mary* (1788) from Rousseau's
Pensées[1] hints at a story about the power of sensibility (a collection of
"sublime virtues") to produce genius; and a letter to Reverend Gabell
on 13 September 1787 corroborates that intention, describing *Mary* as
"a tale, to illustrate an opinion of mine, that a genius will educate itself"
(*Collected Letters*, p. 162).[2] The Advertisement promises to weave that
myth around a new kind of heroine, not just an "echo," or "reflection"
of one of Richardson's or Rousseau's women, but an original creation,
drawn from nature: "the mind of a woman, who has thinking powers"
(*Works*, 1.5). Despite all this, however, the story frequently demythol-
ogizes sensibility even as the heroine and, occasionally, the narrator
laud it.[3] The story revisits the claim that benevolence is its own reward;
presents sensibility sometimes as a form of illness or madness, sometimes as a form of self-deception; and contradicts its heroine's assumption that sensibility is the fountainhead of human happiness, virtue, and
wisdom. These contradictions, and more, illustrate the radical linguistic instability of the notion of sensibility by the 1780s, while *Mary*
documents the beginning of Wollstonecraft's lifelong struggle to cut
through the complex tangle of ideas associated with the term, to shape
it to her own steady purpose: the creation of a new, less reductive and
restrictive, feminine ideal.

   The first contradiction greets readers in the very first chapters, for
although the Advertisement promises a new thinking heroine, the
heroine unveiled in the exposition is an all-too-familiar woman of feel-

ing. Sometimes she seems to act out tableaus from the poems of William Collins, James Thomson, or Edward Young: an ardent friend of nature and literature, she rambles through mountains near her father's home reading Thomson, Young, or Milton (*Works*, 1.4.15); an enthusiastic believer in a personal, immanent God, she sits up nights "*conversing* with the Author of Nature, making verses, and singing hymns of her own composing" (1.4.16). Tending her invalid mother as a child has exercised "her compassion so continually, that it became more than a match for self-love, and was the governing propensity of her heart through life" (1.2.11); she habitually forgets herself in her zeal to attend to the needs of others, denying herself, for example, "every childish gratification, in order to relieve the necessities" of poor families in the vicinity (1.4.15). Such benevolence endears her to the local "servants and the poor," who "adore her," just as the servants of two other classic protagonists of sensibility, Pamela and Werther, adored them.

Self-denial comes naturally to Mary; she has the marked asceticism of Clarissa coupled with her passion for cerebral experience of any kind: "When her understanding or affections had an object, she almost forgot she had a body which required nourishment" (1.4.17). She is also, by turns, quiet, reflective, sensitive, affectionate, empathetic, enthusiastic, and constitutionally melancholy: her understanding is "strong and clear, when not clouded by her feelings"; but she is "too much the creature of impulse, and the slave of compassion" (1.2.12). Throughout her story, her feelings hurry her between two poles: an all-consuming love for two dear friends, Ann and Henry, and an ever-growing aversion to the stranger her parents foist on her as husband: "The sound of his name made her turn sick; but she forgot all, listening to Ann's cough, and supporting her languid frame" (1.6.22).

Modern readers are apt to think that Wollstonecraft's first novel suffers from lack of clear focus. Is she, they may ask, writing about feeling, education, intellect, or all three? If all three, just what is their connection? The three as advertised—sensibility, self-education, and genius—are not quite synonymous in *Mary*, but they are intimately allied, as they are in the aesthetics of sensibility. They stand in reversible metonymic relationship to one another: sensibility is a sure sign of the presence of (or at least the potential for) intellect or genius; genius, in turn, is a sign of the presence of sensibility. The presence of either ensures the proximity of self-education: the presence of sensibility holds the promise of educability; the presence of genius suggests the fulfillment of that promise. At all times the wild card in this triad is sensibility. Expressible in a wide variety of metonymic behaviors, its presence does not always guarantee an increase in wisdom or knowledge.[4]

Sometimes sensibility seems to halt growth, other times to foster it. As an inclination to moodiness, introversion, agitation, or oceanic longings, it can become an obstacle to self-development—even, as some recent critical essays have suggested, an inducement to static or regressive behavior.[5] As an inclination to reflection, openness to stimuli, consciousness, impressibility, or compassion, however, it can become the fertile ground of self-education. Wollstonecraft generally sees sensibility as a necessary precondition for education. People who have it may still go astray; but people without it are only barely educable, if at all. Sensibility's special feature for Wollstonecraft is its capacity to soften the waxen mind, make it, as it is in childhood, newly impressible or malleable, hence open to change: "Softened by tenderness," as Mary puts it in her meditation on sensibility, "the soul is disposed to be virtuous" (1.24.59). In Wollstonecraft's eyes, endowing Mary with extraordinary sensibility identifies her as a possible genius, and certainly as a highly educable young woman.

It takes a whole cluster of ideas to make possible the metonymic triad sensibility-education-genius. Many of those ideas originated in Locke's *Essay Concerning Human Understanding* as mediated by Rousseau's *Émile*.[6] Wollstonecraft, at the time a governess well read on the subject of education and an education writer herself, embraces these ideas and the new, revolutionary epistemological and pedagogical paradigms that come along with them: the image of the individual not as a thinking machine but as a sentient organism; the possibility of extraordinarily sensitive individuals; the presence of sensibility to stimuli as a precondition for growth in organisms; the centrality of the senses in conveying impressions to the mind; the importance of experience and reflection as the sole sources of knowledge; the uniqueness of each individual's experiences; the educability of the individual. As revolutionary as the implications of the triad are its effects: a series of political, cultural, and literary revolutions, one of which is the creation of an important new novelistic subgenre, the *Bildungsroman*. A late eighteenth-century refinement of other novels of education, both Christian (*Pilgrim's Progress*) and neoclassical (Wieland's *Agathon* and Fielding's *Tom Jones*), the *Bildungsroman* presents individual experience as teacher, and self-actualization as education's goal. Education is no longer seen as the product of a series of lessons to mold the shapeless clay or tame the wild child, but as an organic process, involving the dynamic interaction of an individual's unique potentialities with his or her environment.[7] To some writers at the time (Goethe, Radcliffe, and Austen, to name a few), the protagonist of sensibility seems the best candidate for such an educational process; and Wollstonecraft is certainly among them. *Mary* is her experiment in this new subgenre.

In opting for a feeling heroine of intellect, it should be said, Wollstonecraft creates a challenge for herself in her first novel; for only a few of the many protagonists of sensibility can be said to achieve successful self-development. Earlier novels of sensibility, on the contrary, stress the exemplary, static qualities of sensibility;[8] they are not interested in demonstrating to their readers how to grow but rather how to cope: how to handle a variety of difficult situations as fully formed people of sensibility. Pamela, chastity itself, teaches her readers how to handle sex harassment; the Vicar of Wakefield, soul of fortitude, demonstrates how to endure poverty and disgrace without losing self-respect; Tristram's Uncle Toby, the essence of benevolence, shows his readers how to adapt to an embarrassing injury without becoming morose, self-centered, or bitter; and Mackenzie's "man of feeling," Harley, demonstrates ways of dealing with a heartless world. This exemplary pattern is visible in *Mary* as well.

The hero Henry and others in *Mary* exemplify the sensitivity of the prototypical character of sensibility (Pamela, Clarissa, Harley, Werther, and Yorick included): an exceptionally acute self-consciousness. Sometimes the exceptional awareness translates itself into unusually keen perceptive powers, at other times into an extraordinary capacity for empathy or sympathy, but it can also become all-consuming and self-consuming: overwhelmed by the emotion or sensation of the moment, these characters frequently lose their sense of time, place, or self, becoming passive prisoners of that moment. Mary's mother Eliza studies the role of the sentimental heroine so successfully that her "voice" becomes "but the shadow of a sound": "She had, to complete her delicacy, so relaxed her nerves, that she became a mere nothing" (*Works*, 1.1.7). Mary's friend Ann, like Clarissa, has a mind so in tune with her body that the cares of the one translate into consumption in the other: "A number of uneasy thoughts obtruded themselves; and apprehensions about Mary, whom she loved as well as her exhausted heart could love, harassed her mind. After a sleepless, feverish night she had a violent fit of coughing, and burst a blood-vessel" (1.7.23). Henry is so susceptible to suffering that he, like Ann, contracts consumption; and so keenly aware is he of the moral ambiguity of his relationship with the married Mary that he cannot bring himself to express his affection for her until he lies on his deathbed. In this context, of course, it becomes a subjunctive declaration of love, and a perfectly sentimental one as well, since it must content itself with thoughts and feelings rather than acts. To the end, Henry remains a static, exemplary man of sensibility:

— I loved thee ever since I have been acquainted with thine: thou art the being my fancy has delighted to form; but which I imagined existed only

there! In a little while the shades of death will encompass me — ill-fated
love perhaps added strength to my disease, and smoothed the rugged path.
. . . I could have wished, for thy sake, that we could have died together —
or that I could live to shield thee from the assaults of an unfeeling world!
Could I but offer thee an asylum in these arms — a faithful bosom, in which
thou couldst repose all thy griefs — (*Works*, 1.27.67)

In an attempt to allow her heroine an escape from this static, exemplary mode, Wollstonecraft creates an alternative response to the
moment that allows for learning rather than affective stasis or disinte-
gration. Far from being a passive receptor or reactor like her mother,
her friend, or her lover, Mary transmutes her ordinary, often painful,
daily experiences, just as Wollstonecraft promises she will at the
novel's outset, into the gold of intellectual growth[9] signaled by courageous decisions and actions. The alchemical metaphor seems appropriate, for there is perceptible magical thinking about the talismanic
powers of sensibility in Mary's emergence from a dismal childhood
unscathed by any corrosive emotions. Instead, Wollstonecraft charts
Mary's development as a series of acts of creative resistance to her
environment. As a result, *Mary* is more a female *Bildungsroman* than
a romance, its heroine more an evolving organism than a model character, and sensibility more a gift with a price than a badge of excellence.

Just as sensibility and genius are linked organically in the novel's epigraph, feeling and thought are united in the person of the heroine: Mary
is neither a thinker *despite* her feeling nor sensitive *despite* her thinking.
Her intellect makes her more sensitive to emotional experience, and her
emotional experience enables her to grow intellectually; and that is the
first of three highlighted features of Mary's *Bildung* in this story. Examples of this positive reversible relationship between thought and feeling
abound in *Mary*, but it is nowhere more succinctly captured than in a
passage recounting her early reaction to Ann's consumption:

> Her anxiety led her to study physic, and for some time she only read
> books of that cast; and this knowledge, literally speaking, ended in vanity
> and vexation of spirit, as it enabled her to foresee what she could not pre-
> vent.
> As her mind expanded, her marriage appeared a dreadful misfortune.
> (*Works*, 1.6.22)

Here emotions spur Mary to the conscious cultivation of new knowledge, then her "expanded" intellect, in its turn, fosters new, intenser
emotions. Mary's responses to other challenges are comparable: in
Portugal, with Henry, Ann's mother, and, at last, her husband, thoughts
and feelings work, if not altogether in harmony, nevertheless in con-

cert, to expand her mind. Hardly any major occurrence, in fact, fails
to inspire a combination of thoughts and feelings, and, in addition,
those thought-feelings the eighteenth century termed "sentiments."
The most quoted passage from the book collects a bundle of such
thought-feelings, her "rhapsody on sensibility," which begins:

> Sensibility is the most exquisite feeling of which the human soul is suscep-
> tible: when it pervades us, we feel happy; and could it last unmixed, we
> might form some conjecture of the bliss of those paradisiacal days, when
> the obedient passions were under the dominion of reason, and the impuls-
> es of the heart did not need correction. (*Works*, 1.24.59)

Wollstonecraft, in such moments, reconstitutes the reflective mode of
the eighteenth-century's uniquely holistic language of the sentiments
in order to suggest in Mary a comparable holistic psychological
development.

A second noteworthy feature of Mary's *Bildung* is its presentation as
natural and spontaneous. Without the advantages of either tutor or public school, Mary nevertheless becomes a literary enthusiast, teaches
herself to write, teaches herself the catechism, grows quite expert in
acts of kindness and charity, and even displays, to sympathetic observers,
signs of genius. Surely a comfort to Wollstonecraft, largely an autodidact, and to many of her women readers who were self-educated, the
novel presents self-education as inevitable, lifelong, and often preferable to formal education, since it is more apt to foster individuality and
genius. An organic metaphor signals this kind of education in Wollstonecraft's texts; her preferred verb to describe it is "unfold."

Genius or not, Mary might have profited from some formal guidance; this is a point Wollstonecraft seems willing to make as well in
her story. Wollstonecraft offers a completer picture of the natural,
spontaneous self-educative process of unfolding in chapter 5 of *Rights
of Woman*, which points up missing elements in Mary's development:

> The business of education in this case, is only to conduct the shooting ten-
> drils to a proper pole. . . . the tree, and even the human body, does not
> strengthen its fibres till it has reached its full growth.
> There appears to be something analogous in the mind. The senses and
> the imagination give a form to the character, during a childhood and youth;
> and the understanding, as life advances, gives firmness to the first fair pur-
> poses of sensibility — till virtue, arising rather from the clear conviction
> of reason than the impulse of the heart, morality is made to rest on a rock
> against which the storms of passion vainly beat. (*Works*, 5.5.183)

There comes a point in any child's development when the senses and
the imagination (together constituting, in the next paragraph, "sensi-

bility") must yield to understanding; educators can offer help at this point, restraining sensibility, encouraging the understanding, guiding various talents in the proper direction. Mary has no such guidance. In her the "first fair purposes of sensibility" continue unchallenged: she dissolves her worries in the beauties of the hills; she basks in the sentiments of Thomson or Milton; she learns self-denial for charity's sake; she cultivates religious enthusiasm. "These various movements of her mind were not commented on," the narrator must admit ruefully, "nor were the luxuriant shoots restrained by culture" (*Works*, 1.4.17). Neglected except for servants, the "luxuriant" productions of Mary's youthful imagination grow unchecked, until her best features also become her flaws: compassion to a fault, bookishness to the exclusion of society, and otherworldliness to the point of apathy. This context clarifies the narrator's assessment of Mary's youthful character considerably: "In this manner was she left to reflect on her own feelings; and so strengthened were they by being meditated on, that her character early became singular and permanent. Her understanding was strong and clear, when not clouded by her feelings; but she was too much the creature of impulse, and the slave of compassion" (*Works*, 1.2.12). Mary's sensibility dominates her adult life; the narrator notes this but does not condemn her for it.

A third significant feature of Mary's *Bildung* is its gradual, experiential quality: it involves a subtle and constant dialogue not only with herself but also with her environment, an environment that sometimes deflects her from certain avenues or encourages her along others but is never exclusively responsible for her development. Her own intelligence and sensibility also bear some of the burden of that responsibility. Three phases mark the *Bildung* of Mary. In each phase she changes opinions and experiments with new activities in response to the demands of new surroundings, but she also develops and maintains a core identity, one related primarily to the virtues of sensibility that first command her heart. First impressions, in Wollstonecraft's understanding of Locke, are least effaceable. Each phase reveals new insights into sensibility, especially about its effects on the individual personality, some of which are salutary, some limiting, even debilitating. In its outline this short novel, although it may seem thin on plot (Wollstonecraft herself advertises it as a novel "without episodes"), is well thought out and subtly executed.

• • •

Mary grows up amidst the criminal neglect and abuse of her parents. Her mother, a self-centered, ailing woman of "delicacy" or false sensibility, loves her dogs more than her children, and her son more than her daughter. When Mary comes to her from the nursery she sends "the awkward thing away"; later, when Mary tries to confide secrets to her, she laughs at her, so that Mary "determined never to do it again." Her father, tyrannized by his own vices, also tyrannizes his family, especially "when inebriated." Mary, the narrator confides, lives "continually in dread lest he should frighten her mother to death," a fear augmented after "her father had a dog hung in a passion" (*Works*, 1.2.10, 12, 10–11). Left almost entirely to herself, Mary takes long walks, listens to the housekeeper's stories, and learns to read and think. These latter activities spring spontaneously from Mary's fertile mind, but receive a particular stamp from her environment.

The narrator records that Mary "perused with avidity every book that came in her way," and says that "neglected in every respect, and left to the operations of her own mind, she considered every thing that came under her inspection, and learned to think" (*Works*, 1.2.10). "This habit of thinking, this kind of absorption," the narrator adds, paradoxically "gave strength to the passions (*Works*, 1.4.17)." Her environment especially encourages the "luxuriant" growth of religious enthusiasm and compassion: "Could she have loved her father or mother, had they returned her affection," for example, "she would not so soon, perhaps, have sought out a new world." As it was, however, "sublime ideas filled her young mind—always connected with devotional sentiments." Deep in the woods, she talks and sings to angels and the spirits she imagines "inhabited every part of nature" (*Works*, 1.2.11); and the lack of anyone to love on earth inspires her to turn her thoughts towards the "Great First Cause" and her ultimate home in heaven:

> She was now fifteen, and she wished to receive the holy sacrament; and perusing the scriptures, and discussing some points of doctrine which puzzled her, she would sit up half the night, her favourite time for employing her mind; she too plainly perceived that she saw through a glass darkly; and that the bounds set to stop our intellectual researches, is one of the trials of a probationary state. (*Works*, 1.4.16)

This loveless world also sets the "governing propensity of her heart through life"; her mother's perpetual illness habituates Mary to the role of caretaker, calling forth and exercising her compassion on a daily basis. The passage that sums up the progress of Mary's young mind reiterates both the importance of environment and native genius. It also reveals, however, an unmistakable awareness of the potentially crippling effects of an all-too-great sensibility:

> She had once, or twice, told her little secrets to her mother; they were laughed at, and she determined never to do it again. In this manner was she

left to reflect on her own feelings; and so strengthened were they by being meditated on, that her character early became singular and permanent. Her understanding was strong and clear, when not clouded by her feelings; but she was too much the creature of impulse, and the slave of compassion. (*Works*, 1.2.12)

•   •   •

The child Mary in this book certainly mothers the woman, who is also "the creature of impulse, and the slave of compassion." This second phase of her development begins with her decision to cultivate the friendship of a local young woman, Ann, several years older than herself, who, like Mary's mother, calls forth "all her tenderness . . . like a torrent" (*Works*, 1.3.14). Ann, impoverished, disappointed in love, and sickly, provides Mary with a distraction from her own family cares. While their friendship grows, Mary's brother dies, making her, quite suddenly, an heiress; then her mother dies, a loss that proves doubly catastrophic to Mary because it precipitates her into an arranged marriage, a business deal struck by her father to save his estate: "The clergyman came in to read the service for the sick, and afterwards the marriage ceremony was performed. Mary stood like a statue of Despair, and pronounced the awful vow without thinking of it; and then ran to support her mother, who expired the same night in her arms. Her husband set off for the continent the same day, with a tutor, to finish his studies at one of the foreign universities" (*Works*, 1.5.20). The one consolation in these developments for Mary is Ann's arrival to live with her as a female companion for the duration of her new husband's absence on a grand tour.

Their friendship benefits Mary; it refines her character and moderates her urges more than her parents ever could. With Ann's encouragement, Mary improves her writing skills; softens her manners (for, as the narrator volunteers, Ann's manners had such a "bewitching softness . . ., a delicacy so truly feminine, that a man of any feeling could not behold her without wishing to chase her sorrows away" *Works*, 1.5.18); strengthens her "taste and her judgment" by "contracting" the "habit of observation" of an artist "and permitting the simple beauties of Nature to occupy her thoughts" (*Works*, 1.6.21); and, finally, expands her mind (she studies medicine, a study that Wollstonecraft recommends to young women, both in *Education of Daughters* and in the *Rights of Woman*). Ann's friendship alone, however, cannot reverse Mary's development, cannot eradicate, for example, the propensity to melancholy that gives "the colour" to her "unsettled mind."

If friendship finally causes Mary more pain than pleasure, then much of the fault lies with her sensibility-dominated psyche. It causes her to wish for perfect emotional union with Ann, whom she loves "better than any one in the world. . . . To have this friend constantly with her . . . would it not be superlative bliss?" (*Works*, 1.5.20). When it does not occur, when Ann seems indifferent, shrinking back from Mary's "warm greeting," Mary retreats into intense despondency and an equally intense, if unfocused, longing: "Before she enjoyed Ann's society, she imagined it would have made her completely happy: she was disappointed, and yet knew not what to complain of" (*Works*, 1.6.21). She succumbs to wide, self-consuming mood swings: "She would then imagine that she [Ann] looked sickly or unhappy, and then all her tenderness would return like a torrent, and bear away all reflection" (*Works*, 1.3.14). As her friend's physical condition deteriorates, Mary's unhappiness increases. Even the knowledge of medicine Mary gains contributes to her discontent—first of all, because "it enabled her to foresee what she could not prevent"; second, because as "her mind expanded, her marriage appeared a dreadful misfortune; she was sometimes reminded of the heavy yoke, and bitter was the recollection!" (*Works*, 1.6.22).

So pronounced is the aversion to her husband that when she writes him to tell him of her plan to accompany her ailing friend to the Mediterranean, her "heart revolt[s]" at the thought of asking his permission. She successfully avoids it: "Irresolutely she wrote something about wishing him happy. — 'Do I not wish all the world well?' she cried, as she subscribed her name — It was blotted, the letter sealed in a hurry, and sent out of her sight; and she began to prepare for her journey" (*Works*, 1.8.25). Both these decisions—to leave England and not to ask permission—must be read, in part, as signs of a new independence of judgment and hence as personal triumphs for Mary, and triumphs directly inspired by her sensibility. It has enabled her to take control of her own destiny in a world that grants women very little autonomy, yet to do so without rushing visibly into rebellion. As much as her sensibility has been a private enabler for Mary, however, it also increasingly becomes a public crippler, alienating her from those around her, and gradually transforming her, in the eyes of her society, into a misfit and a zany.

Shortly after arriving in Lisbon, Mary encounters three "fashionable women" whose minds, according to the narrator, are "shackled with a set of notions concerning propriety, the fitness of things for the world's eye, trammels which always hamper weak people," and whose comments dramatize vividly just how far Mary's natural development has taken her beyond the boundaries of the accepted norm. These women approve of her wealth—"Riches, and the consequent state, are the sublime of weak minds" (*Works*, 1.11.30 –31)—but not of her manner of dress, her bookishness, or her all-consuming devotion to Ann:

" 'She is a foolish creature,'" pronounces one, " 'this friend that she pays as much attention to as if she was a lady of quality, is a beggar.' 'Well, how strange!' cried the girls" (*Works*, 1.11.31). They cannot understand Mary's desperation over her friend's worsening condition, which finds expression, in this case, in her silence and in her emotional outbursts:

> The ladies wondered that a person of her sense should be so little mistress of herself; and began to administer some . . . trite consolations, which Mary did not answer; but waving her hand, with an air of impatience, she exclaimed, "I cannot live without her! — I have no other friend; if I lose her, what a desart will the world be to me." "No other friend," re-echoed they, "have you not a husband?"
> Mary shrunk back, and was alternately pale and red. A delicate sense of propriety prevented her replying; and recalled her bewildered reason. — Assuming, in consequence of her recollection, a more composed manner, she made the intended enquiry, and left the room. Henry's eyes followed her while the females very freely animadverted on her strange behaviour. (*Works*, 1.11.32)

Mary does what her sensibility has trained her to do best—practice charity and piety. She spends her nights calming Ann's bedside fears of "terrifying dreams" and supporting her "to avoid suffocation" (*Works*, 1.9.28); and her days are spent touring Roman Catholic Lisbon, reading theological treatises, and questioning the value of cathedrals, choirs, ceremonies, and convents. People around Mary, however, find her antisocial and imagine her to be a bizarre, or unacceptably irreverent, wife.

Unfortunately, the taciturn Mary does little to correct their false impressions. Although her failure to speak is attributed to her sense of propriety, her "delicacy" or sensibility is also implicated. Her solitary, melancholy childhood increases her tendency to silence: "Mary had not said much, for she was diffident; she seldom joined in general conversations. . . . mirth did not interest her" (*Works*, 1.9.27). Her ethic of feeling encourages her to value doing over speaking: "They who imagine they can be religious without governing their tempers, or exercising benevolence in its most extensive sense," she reflects on the Roman Catholics around her in Portugal, "must certainly allow, that their religious duties are only practised [*sic*] from selfish principles; how then can they be called good? The pattern of all goodness went about *doing* good" (*Works*, 1.13.34). Finally, her unquestioning acceptance of the inexpressibility topos found in much of the literature of sensibility completes her alienation from speaking, her retreat into silence: as she insists in her meditation on sensibility, "It is only to be felt; it escapes discussion" (*Works*, 1.24.60).

To say that Mary is linguistically handicapped by her sensibility
would hardly be an exaggeration. At critical moments in her life, words
fail her; and she is forced to rely on body language or borrowed language. Told she is to marry immediately at her dying mother's bedside,
both Mary's tongue and her brain are struck dumb:

> Overwhelmed by this intelligence, Mary rolled her eyes about, then, with a
> vacant stare, fixed them on her father's face; but they were no longer a
> sense; they conveyed no ideas to the brain. . . . "My child," said the languid
> mother. . . . "God forgive me! do you?" — Mary's tears strayed in a disre-
> garded stream; on her bosom the big drops fell, but did not relieve the flut-
> tering tenant. "I forgive you!" said she, in a tone of astonishment. The
> clergyman came. . . . Mary stood like a statue of Despair. (*Works*, 1.5.19–20)

Both Ann's and Henry's deaths also strike her dumb. Ann's " 'slow,
sudden-death' [a citation from Young's *Night Thoughts*] disturbed her
reasoning faculties; she seemed stunned by it; unable to reflect, or
even to feel her misery" (*Works*, 1.15.38). Henry's death drives her to
dumb show, prayer, and finally unconsciousness.

Nor is Mary only speechless in times of great sorrow; fear, joy, love,
any powerful emotion that wells up, as Locke predicts, ties her tongue
and clouds and distorts her perceptions. Attending a church concert in
Lisbon, she is mute with awe and devotion at the beauty of the moment:
"Tears of gratitude and tenderness flowed from her eyes. My Father,
I thank thee! burst from her — words were inadequate to express her
feelings" (*Works*, 1.9.26). At these moments she characteristically loses
her grasp of the subject and the thread of her logic in her pursuit of self-
expression. There are several striking instances in her story: her well-
known reflections on sensibility in chapter 24, and her long and very
indirect declaration of love to Henry in chapter 18; but an excerpt from
her briefer meditation on a storm at sea in chapter 20 will illustrate her
style just as well:

> I have not words to express the sublime images which the bare contempla-
> tion of this awful day raises in my mind. Then, indeed, the Lord Omnipo-
> tent will reign, and He will wipe the tearful eye, and support the trembling
> heart — yet a little while He hideth his face, and the dun shades of sorrow,
> and the thick clouds of folly separate us from our God; but when the glad
> dawn of an eternal day breaks, we shall know even as we are known. Here
> we walk by faith, and not by sight; and we have this alternative, either to
> enjoy the pleasures of life, which are but for a season, or look forward to
> the prize of our high calling, and with fortitude, and that wisdom which is
> from above, endeavour to bear the warfare of life. We know that many run
> the race; but he that striveth obtaineth the crown of victory. Our race is an

arduous one! How many are betrayed by traitors lodged in their own breasts, who wear the garb of Virtue, and are so near akin. . . . Surely any thing like happiness is madness! Shall probationers of an hour presume to pluck the fruit of immortality, before they have conquered death? it is guarded, when the great day, to which I allude, arrives, the way will again be opened. Ye dear delusions, gay deceits farewel! [*sic*] . . . Eternity, immateriality, and happiness, — what are ye? How shall I grasp the mighty and fleeting conceptions ye create?

After writing, serenely she delivered her soul into the hands of the Father of Spirits; and slept in peace. (*Works*, 1.20.51–52)

Here is sentimental discourse at its weakest, the kind its detractors must always have in mind: strained, hyperbolic, diffuse and digressive or associative, emotionally saturated, and heavily derivative. Granted, its function is not communication but meditation, self-talk designed to achieve and sustain emotional tranquility in the face of fear; and, to that extent, it serves its purpose, putting Mary to sleep. Yet it is hardly the kind of language she could use in conversation to much advantage, except, perhaps, to yield her the universal reputation of a "dear enthusiastic creature" (Henry's designation for her, *Works*, 1.19.46). In such moments, Mary's sensibility arrests the development of her mind and she becomes a prisoner of its language.

•   •   •

Acquaintance with Henry in Lisbon marks the beginning of Mary's third phase of development: he offers her a friendship beneficial both to mind and heart. Identified as a "man of learning," he also shares many of Mary's sentimental propensities. He is melancholy, having been disappointed in love; a "thrilling" musician; and well versed in literature and "the intricacies of the human heart" (*Works*, 1.12.33). A gentle purveyor of sympathy, his prime mover, like hers, seems to be compassion, as it is in this scene just after the death of Mary's friend Ann: "She [Mary] ran eagerly up to him — saw the tear trembling in his eye, and his countenance softened by the tenderest compassion; the hand which pressed hers seemed that of a fellow-creature. She burst into tears . . . " (*Works*, 1.16.40).

She reads "strong lines of genius" (*Works*, 1.9.28) in his face on their first meeting; and she soon realizes that her own intellect will thrive around him. He increases her "stock of ideas," improves her taste, and stimulates her genius:

When she conversed with him, all the faculties of her soul unfolded themselves; genius animated her expressive countenance; and the most graceful, unaffected gestures gave energy to her discourse. . . . Mary could not help thinking that in his company her mind expanded, as he always went below the surface. (*Works*, 1.12.33)

Just as valuable to Mary as this intellectual stimulation is the emotional outlet Henry provides. Like Ann, he is ill and consequently gives Mary a second object for her compassion. She reads to him and converses with him, when she is not attending Ann, "with a degree of tenderness that she was not conscious of" (*Works*, 1.14.36). As a result of their increasing attachment, after Ann's death, Henry is able to intercept Mary before she plummets into a "black wave" of "sullen sorrow":

> She called herself "a poor disconsolate creature!" — "Mine is a selfish grief," she exclaimed — "Yet, Heaven is my witness, I do not wish her back now she has reached those peaceful mansions, where the weary rest. Her pure spirit is happy; but what a wretch am I!"
> Henry forgot his cautious reserve. "Would you allow me to call you friend?" said he in a hesitating voice. "I feel, dear girl, the tenderest interest in whatever concerns thee." His eyes spoke the rest. (*Works*, 1.16.39–40)

Henry's offer of friendship, unlike offers from the hero of Wollstonecraft's later novel, *Maria*, cannot be construed as a trope for the sexual exploitation of an inferior. Rather it signals, within its context, a desire for a radically new kind of male-female relationship: a bonding of like to like rather than a joining of opposites, a love between equals rather than a contract between master and servant. Henry's words suggest equivalencies between his gesture to Mary and Mary's gesture to Ann, and beyond these gestures, between his character and hers. Henry shares many traits with Mary, speaks her antilanguage of sensibility, and, given the right circumstances, will duplicate her actions: selfless empathy, charity, affection. Henry's posited likenesses to Mary cannot be stressed too much, for they reveal some of Wollstonecraft's earliest attitudes towards sensibility: a prereflective and gender-neutral faith, coupled with an erotically charged enthusiasm. The paradox in these attitudes is a seeming one, insofar as Wollstonecraft makes no attempt to erase the attractiveness of sensibility, but only the gender-exclusivity her age begins to assign to it—frequently called its "feminization." In her fictions both men and women may have this human propensity; and when they do, they are more attractive to one another.

Primarily idyllic rather than satiric in their presentation of sensibility, her two earliest fictions, *Mary* and "Cave of Fancy," show little evidence of the dark feminist suspicions of sensibility as male conspiracy that mark her later writings. Nevertheless, seen in the context of the widening rift between men and women's spheres in her day so detrimental to women's liberty, her insistence on sensibility as a belief system with a common language and set of behaviors for men and women can be seen as progressive, utopian proto-feminism rather than reactionary conventionality. In this belief system, sensibility becomes a way to bridge the rift, a means to the revolutionary end of enduring affectionate relationships between equals. At this first stage of her career her attitude towards sensibility is very close to Radcliffe's, her Henry and Mary very close to Radcliffe's Valancourt and Emily St. Aubert, or Vivaldi and Ellena Rosalba. Both Wollstonecraft and Radcliffe "hoped much from the cult of sensibility, the effect of which was to induce some measure of approximation in the ethical ideals and emotional sensitiveness of the two sexes."[10]

Two obstacles frustrate Henry's proffered friendship no matter what he and Mary do: his illness and her married state. The acute distress these obstacles cause Mary nearly outweighs the intense joy she feels in Henry's company. These are both formidable barriers to the fulfillment of desire, problems without visible solutions; nevertheless Mary mulls them over repeatedly, plaguing herself with bouts of painful questioning and periods of gloom, her mind, as the narrator notes, on occasion quite "unhinged." If Henry has allowed Mary to achieve a new level of intellectual and emotional integration, he has also precipitated, however unwittingly, a new degree of dissatisfaction. Again sensibility is implicated: it is both bait and trap, both the primary cause of the mutual attraction and the reason for the lovers' scrupulous avoidance of any cruel, impious, or improper actions.

> Her mind was unhinged, and passion unperceived filled her whole soul. . . .
>
> By these kind of conflicts the day was lengthened; and when she went to bed, the night passed away in feverish slumbers; though they did not refresh her, she was spared the labour of thinking, of restraining her imagination; it sported uncontrouled. . . .
>
> What was she to do? where go? Could she set a seal to a hasty vow, and tell a deliberate lie; promise to love one man, when the image of another was ever present to her — her soul revolted. "I might gain the applause of the world by such mock heroism; but should I not forfeit my own? forfeit thine, my father!" (*Works*, 1.16.42)

The longer her stay in Lisbon, the more repugnant her stranger-husband Charles becomes to her, now "mentioned . . . with such disgust that he [Henry] trembled for her. 'I cannot see him; he is not the man formed for me to love!' Her delicacy did not restrain her, for her dislike to her husband had taken root in her mind long before she knew Henry" (*Works*, 1.18.45). While the recorded monologues of her conflicted feelings on this subject have a surface sameness about them, the tone in which she speaks gradually becomes firmer. In this instance, Mary's sensibility is her friend; her habitually affective self-expression—the forte of the language of sensibility—gradually leads her to increased understanding and decisiveness. Just before her return to England, she announces her resolve to continue to live apart from her lawful spouse:

> With these notions can I conform to the maxims of worldly wisdom? can I listen to the cold dictates of worldly prudence, and bid my tumultuous passions cease to vex me, be still, find content in grovelling pursuits, and the admiration of the misjudging crowd, when it is only one I wish to please — one who could be all the world to me.... My conscience does not smite me, and that Being who is greater than the internal monitor, may approve of what the world condemns; sensible that in Him I live, could I brave His presence, or hope in solitude to find peace, if I acted contrary to conviction, that the world might approve of my conduct — what could the world give to compensate for my own esteem? it is ever hostile and armed against the feeling heart! ... you may tell me I follow a fleeting good, an *ignis fatuus*; but this chase, these struggles prepare me for eternity — when I no longer see through a glass darkly I shall not reason about, but *feel* in what happiness consists. (*Works*, 1.18.46 – 47)

In this impassioned speech, Mary reveals her Werther-like convictions that the world views "the feeling heart" with hostility, but that God may approve of decisions in favor of the heart that the world condemns. She is quite certain that if she does not attend to her own "tumultuous passions," she will forfeit her own self-esteem, even though to attend to them will inevitably condemn her in the eyes of the "misjudging crowd." This notable decision not only to live apart from her husband but to live openly *for* Henry again signals a new degree of independence in Mary's attitude: even if she remains emotionally dependent on the approval of certain friends, she demonstrates a new ability to do without the approval of society at large. As a young woman of sensibility, she submerges her own wishes entirely in the wishes of her father and dying mother; in her sentimental friendship with Ann, she neglects all her own troubles to tend a dying friend. Here, at last, she comes of age as only the most daring among the heroes and heroines of sensibility do: she determines to follow the wishes of her own heart, and, if necessary, to flaunt the world.

Because Henry is "afraid to discover his passion," it should be added, Mary reenters England in a state of suspense, if not irresolution. She plunges into charity work to silence her reveries and to find some modicum of satisfaction. When a poor family she has just aided spurns her, however, she realizes that benevolence, far from being the self-rewarding experience it is reputed to be, can sometimes be an acutely

painful and lonely enterprise: "Too well have I loved my fellow creatures! I have been wounded by ingratitude; from every one it has something of the serpent's tooth" (*Works*, 1.23.57). At this point Henry's
return to England and a simultaneous letter from her absent husband
revive her attachment to the one and her revulsion to the other. For a
brief moment, a renewed sense of Henry's needs and his "disinterested
affection" (*Works*, 1.28.69), coupled with new proof of her husband's
folly, nearly move her to renounce permanently both husband and fortune. Henry obviates the necessity for this by going to live with his
mother in the country near Mary's house. She follows him, and for a
few halcyon weeks, they spend all their time together singing, reading,
and enjoying the "luxury of wretchedness" (*Works*, 1.26.65). Just
before he dies, he declares his love; and Mary finds the declaration,
under the circumstances, nearly as devastating as his death.

Mary's response to Henry's declaration is a sleepless night torn by
"tumultuous emotions" and a "wandering" mind, in which her new certainty of his love repeatedly encounters the equal certainty of his immi-
nent death:

> I could be happy listening to him, soothing his cares. — Would he not smile
> upon me — call me his own Mary? I am not his — said she with fierceness
> — I am a wretch! and she heaved a sigh that almost broke her heart, while
> the big tears rolled down her burning cheeks . . . the barrier of reason was
> almost carried away, and all the faculties not restrained by her, were run-
> ning into confusion. (*Works*, 1.27.68)

His death shortly thereafter—anticipated, yet hardly easier to accept
because anticipated—triggers a comparable near-death experience in
her that has all the marks of trauma, of catastrophic emotional dis-
ablement:

> She left the room, and retired to one very near it; and sitting down on the
> floor, fixed her eyes on the door of the apartment which contained the body.
> Every event of her life rushed across her mind with wonderful rapidity —
> yet all was still — fate had given the finishing stroke. She sat till midnight
> — (*Works*, 1.29.71)

She lives to return to her husband, but not to love him. She divides the
rest of her adult days between land reform and charity, but never recov-
ers any real interest in life. With shattered nerves and a "heart in which
there was a void, that even benevolence and religion could not fill," her
thoughts alternate between past and future: between the rehearsal of
"all her former woes" and the dream of reunion with Henry in death.
"Her delicate state of health did not promise long life. In moments of

solitary sadness, a gleam of joy would dart across her mind — She thought she was hastening to that world *where there is neither marrying*, nor giving in marriage" (*Works*, 1.31.73; italics hers).

As the other two do, the third phase of Mary's education expands her mind and spurs her to courageous decisions. In this process, however, sensibility reveals itself to be foe *and* friend, for, to recall one of her earlier observations in the letters, it "renders the path of duty more intricate—and the warfare *much* more severe" (*Collected Letters*, p. 150). First of all, it makes both lovers far too scrupulous, too driven and bound by the imagined impact of their words on each other. Their sensibility makes them more amiable and compassionate, on the one hand, but, on the other, their highly tuned sensors register the minutest reaction of pleasure or pain in others and their "internal monitors" censor even the slightest deviations from propriety and piety. This necessarily thwarts—and simultaneously fans—their passion.

A case in point is Henry's first very indirect verbal declaration of affection (he has, on earlier occasions, shown nonverbal signs of it, *Works*, 1.14.37):

> He . . . looked Mary full in the face; and, with the most insinuating accents, asked "if he might hope for her friendship? If she would rely on him as if he was her father; and that the tenderest father could not more anxiously interest himself in the fate of a darling child, than he did in her's [*sic*]." (*Works*, 1.16.41)

On the face of things, this looks like a step forward. Henry has, in veiled terms declared himself; and Mary, in the night that follows, is lost in a joyful "delirium" over it, "her mind . . . unhinged, and passion unperceived" filling "her whole soul" (1.16.42). Surely she has no trouble translating his measured words into the declaration of passion that they really are; but she is also particularly taken with the words themselves: "He had called her his dear girl; the words might have fallen from him by accident; but they did not fall to the ground. My child! His child, what an association of ideas! If I had had a father, such a father! — She could not dwell on the thoughts, the wishes which obtruded themselves" (*Works*, 1.16.42). However thrilling these words may seem to her, however, both she and Henry remain bound and imprisoned by this decorous language of sensibility, effectively separated by his parent-child metaphor of friendship. Such a language raises invisible, yet powerful, barriers to the sexual consummation of their love, encouraging Mary and Henry to interact instead with asexual, caretaking behaviors, and so they do: guiding, supporting, depending, and loving in a kind of sexless and absolute way that excludes other alternatives.

The language of sensibility makes their lives more complicated, then, by radically delimiting their choices. It encourages them to speak in terms of absolutes. It assumes in its devotees an infinitude of sensitivity, passion, and creativity, then cautions them to invest themselves very selectively, to absolutize a few relationships and activities to the exclusion of all others. When these relationships are, for whatever reason, severed, then the believers are inevitably devastated. All "nature," as Mary experiences after the death first of her mother, then Ann, then Henry, is a "blank" and her "heart" a "void." Moreover, the list of approved activities in Mary's language of sensibility is drastically short: charity and piety, two kinds of nonspecific and usually nonerotic love, and, just possibly, the cultivation of creativity or genius. When those activities fail to satisfy Mary, she is left to herself, cast adrift to ruminate on her own and others' feelings. The diseases that Ann, Henry, and finally Mary, all fall ill of—nervous disorders and consumption—are particularly appropriate, even metaphoric. Their hearts and imaginations are constantly overstimulated without enough "proper" outlets; and they are then plagued by self-consuming, oceanic, frequently unnamed longings.

A second and more disturbing way that sensibility renders Mary's life more complex is by sapping her of reason, will, sense of self and its value, and even the desire to go on living. Ann's "slow, sudden death" disturbs Mary's "reasoning faculties"; she seems "stunned by it; unable to reflect, or even to feel her misery" (*Works*, 1.15.38). The world has become the "desart" she predicted it would (*Works*, 1.11.32), and she is immobilized by "impenetrable gloom." Henry's death, discussed just above, elicits similar paralysis and death-longing, as does her encounter with ingratitude. Sinking into "apathy," she loses all sense of life's meaning: "Surely life is a dream, a frightful one! and after those rude, disjointed images are fled, will light ever break in? Shall I ever feel joy?" She also loses touch with, and control over, her self several times in the course of her story:

> Yet lie still, my throbbing heart, or burst; and my brain — why dost thou whirl about at such a terrifying rate? why do thoughts so rapidly rush into my mind, and yet when they disappear leave such deep traces? I could almost wish for the madman's happiness. . . .

> Oh! reason, thou boasted guide, why desert me, like the world, when I most need thy assistance! Canst thou not calm this internal tumult, and drive away the death-like sadness which presses so sorely on me, — a sadness surely very nearly allied to despair. I am now the prey of apathy — (*Works*, 1.23.57)

Such apathy is the natural response to catastrophic loss but is not, under normal circumstances, a permanent state of mind. Only if people image or talk to themselves continually of their grief, depression, or apathy can they sustain the state: "Feelings," says the narrator, are "strengthened . . . by being meditated on" (*Works*, 1.2.12). Mary's language of sensibility is, unfortunately, well suited to this task: it highlights the feelings and multiplies the shades of feelings, especially feelings of love, fear, and melancholy, at the expense of reason; it presents a mind consisting in separate faculties frequently at war with one another; and it just as frequently assumes helpless passivity in the subject, and a hopeless inadequacy on the part of words to express the most important experiences of all, feelings. Consider the phrases for the self cited already: governing propensity of heart, understanding clouded by feelings, slave of compassion, sensibility pervades us, a torrent of tenderness, constitutional black bile, lost in waking dreams, imagination sported uncontrolled, reason's barrier carried away, tumultuous passions, faculties running into confusion, unhinged mind, rushing thoughts leave deep traces, whirling brain, void heart. This is a language of psychic catastrophe, of potential mental illness, presenting a bleak interior landscape to all men and women of feeling.

Mary undoubtedly spends considerable time contemplating just such a bleak interior world; she publicly extols the pleasures of sensibility, but her private journal entries and conversations suggest that she pays a high psychological price in order to live her life according to the gospel of the heart. Gary Kelly, editor of the Oxford edition of *Mary*, concludes in his introduction that both heroine and novel are ultimately the "prisoners" of sensibility: "Mary is a prisoner of her sex's sensibility," he suggests, and likewise, "The novel itself becomes imprisoned by its author's feminine sensibility."[11] Yet the effects of sensibility on heroine, narrator, novel, are far from unequivocal: instead they all reveal the liberating as well as the constraining qualities of the language of sensibility.

It enables Mary to think, act, and express herself in ways that foster her own self-awareness and development, even if it channels all that activity in just a few directions—self-analysis, loving, reading, praying, giving alms, feeling compassion for the suffering of others. It offers to Mary and her friends ways to exempt themselves from many cultural expectations; they live outside the realm of conventionality, without children, employment, or other social obligations. All three of them retain a fair degree of personal autonomy, even if none of them has any power beyond a narrow domestic circle. Its invitation to cultivate interiority—whether in the form of sentiments, virtues, or pure emotions—is its most appealing feature to Mary, Ann, and Henry, living in an alien world devoted to trivial pursuits like riches and reputation. All this may constitute pleasant house arrest but not quite imprisonment.

• • •

Wollstonecraft's complicity in her subject may help to explain a paradox that lies at the very center of *Mary*: while the heroine praises sensibility, the story gradually demystifies it, unearthing the pain, paralysis, and confusion that often haunt its followers. And where does Wollstonecraft's narrator stand? Essentially, on the heroine's side, although that statement needs some qualification. Wollstonecraft's narrator controls focalization, tone, and narrator-protagonist proximity to counterbalance the doubts raised by the story. The narrator takes a very partial, limited third-person perspective, one that portrays Mary and Henry with quiet but steady respect, and presents satirically all the characters who are out of sympathy with Mary. Mary's parents, her husband, and occasional detractors are consistently handled with a dismissive tone that ranges from light irony to invective. Of the mother, for example, the narrator remarks, "She read all the sentimental novels . . . and, had she thought while she read, her mind would have been contaminated" (*Works*, 1.1.9); of the father, "Death is indeed a king of terrors when he attacks the vicious man!" (*Works*, 1.7.23); and of the "fashionable women" in Lisbon who criticize Mary, "their minds had received very little cultivation" (*Works*, 1.11.30). The arranged husband Charles receives different but comparably reductive treatment: he gains attention only as a young man interested in foreign frivolities or as an object of Mary's increasing revulsion: "The sound of his name made her turn sick" (*Works*, 1.6.22).[12] Otherwise he remains banished from the book until the last pages, where he enters in name only to become a part of Mary's final, grim reality. In a serious parodic reversal of the ending of Swift's *Gulliver's Travels*, now told from the wife's point of view, it is the returning husband who nauseates, not she who repels him:

> He came in person to answer the letter. Mary fainted when he approached her unexpectedly. Her disgust returned with additional force, in spite of previous reasonings, whenever he appeared; yet she was prevailed on to promise to live with him, if he would permit her to pass one year, travelling from place to place; he was not to accompany her.
> The time too quickly elapsed, and she gave him her hand — the struggle was almost more than she could endure. She tried to appear calm; time mellowed her grief, and mitigated her torments; but when her husband would take her hand, or mention any thing like love, she would instantly feel a sickness, a faintness at her heart, and wish, involuntarily, that the earth would open and swallow her. (*Works*, 1.30.72)

The narrative avoidance of the husband leaves the impression that the narrator feels the same aversion as the heroine.

This is not to suggest that the narrator's and the heroine's perspectives are consistently identical. The narrator's use of free indirect discourse,[13] a technique just emerging in the 1790s, allows her to trace the heroine's psychological actions and reactions minutely but, at the same time, provides the built-in distancing device of reported rather than dramatized actions, thoughts, and feelings. A steady and fairly quick pace also contributes to this distancing effect; the narrator does not linger over scenes of emotional intensity. Typical of such passages is one recounting Mary's early religious promptings, just precise enough to serve as a plausible transcript of her sentiments, yet cautiously worded enough to serve as an objective account, and distanced by the use of a narrator's "I," a heroine's "she," and a quick pace:

> Many nights she sat up, if I may be allowed the expression, *conversing* with the Author of Nature, making verses, and singing hymns of her own composing. She considered also, and tried to discern what end her various faculties were destined to pursue; and had a glimpse of a truth, which afterwards more fully unfolded itself.
>
> She thought that only an infinite being could fill the human soul, and that when other objects were followed as a means of happiness, the delusion led to misery, the consequence of disappointment. Under the influence of ardent affections, how often has she forgot this conviction, and as often returned to it again, when it struck her with redoubled force. Often did she taste unmixed delight; her joys, her ecstacies arose from genius. (*Works*, 1.4.16)

On two other occasions, the narrator tells the reader what Mary does not know or has forgotten—"She forgot that happiness was not to be found on earth" (*Works*, 1.16.42)—leaving the impression that she knows more than the heroine, is indeed somewhat wiser than the heroine, even if she chooses most of the time not to exploit that wisdom. Above all, however, the technique enforces a distance between the reader and the protagonist, something that readers of the first-person novels of sentiment of Richardson, Rousseau, and Goethe had, by all reports, considerable trouble finding.[14] The reader can know, but cannot easily participate in, the heroine's feelings. And Wollstonecraft maintains this distance for at least the first two-thirds of the book; in fact, the more emotional her heroine becomes, the more distanced, crisply analytical, even clinical, the narrator's treatment grows. Mary's state reaches its most distraught point after the death of Ann, when Henry offers disinterested friendship; and at this point the narrator actually deploys descriptors implying illness, descriptors that hover on the brink of negative judgment:

> She dwelt on Henry's misfortunes and ill health; and the interest he took in her fate was a balm to her sick mind. She did not reason on the subject; but she felt he was attached to her: lost in this delirium, she never asked

herself what kind of an affection she had for him, or what it tended to; nor
did she know that love and friendship are very distinct; she thought with
rapture, that there was one person in the world who had an affection for her,
and that person she admired — had a friendship for. (*Works*, 1.16.41–42)

In a mode of description that goes on for another long paragraph, terms
like "sick" and "delirium" are passed over too brusquely to invite much
pity from the readers; rather they are put on their guard.

In other instances, however, it must be added, the readers are thrown
off guard, even invited to experience Mary's sentiments without the benefit of a narrator's distancing mediation. In these instances, the divid-
ing line between Mary's thoughts and the narrator's dissolves, making
it impossible to be absolutely sure whether the narrative voice speaking
is recording its or Mary's sentiments. One long example, in this case,
serves best for many: the recording of the death of Mary's father.

Terrified at seeing him so near death, and yet so ill prepared for it, his
daughter sat by his bed, oppressed by the keenest anguish, which her piety
increased.

Her grief had nothing selfish in it; he was not a friend or protector; but
he was her father, an unhappy wretch, going into eternity, depraved and
thoughtless. Could a life of sensuality be a preparation for a peaceful death?
Thus meditating, she passed the still midnight hour by his bedside.

The nurse fell asleep, nor did a violent thunder storm interrupt her
repose, though it made the night appear still more terrific to Mary. Her
father's unequal breathing alarmed her, when she heard a long drawn
breath, she feared it was his last, and watching for another, a dreadful peal
of thunder struck her ears. Considering the separation of the soul and body,
this night seemed sadly solemn, and the hours long.

Death is indeed a king of terrors when he attacks the vicious man! The
compassionate heart finds not any comfort; but dreads an eternal separation. No transporting greetings are anticipated, when the survivors also
shall have finished their course; but all is black! — the grave may truly be
said to receive the departed — this is the sting of death! (*Works*, 1.7.23)

Where do Mary's thoughts end and the narrator's begin? At "Could a
life of sensuality . . . ?" The "thus meditating" seems to rule out that
possibility; besides, given the information the text provides about her
father's drunken brutality, that Mary should have such a thought is more
than plausible—it is probable. At "Death is indeed a king of terrors
. . . ?" More plausible perhaps, yet elsewhere Mary shows a predilection for preaching to herself in her journal in just such an elevated tone.
Recall, for example, the reflections she records after the storm at sea:
"At this solemn hour, the great day of judgment fills my thoughts; the
day of retribution, when the secrets of all hearts will be revealed; when
all worldly distinctions will fade away" (*Works*, 1.20.51).

The inescapable conclusion to be drawn from such an analysis is that Wollstonecraft sometimes does not take care to distinguish the voices of narrator and protagonist. So long as Mary's sentiments are not self-defeating or self-destructive, she does little to disentangle the two voices. In this category, obviously, are the remarks made about the "Romish religion" in the middle of the book: "The pattern of all goodness went about *doing* good. Wrapped up in themselves, the nuns only thought of inferior gratifications" (*Works*, 1.13.34). Wollstonecraft's narrator cultivates a guarded, general approval of the heroine, coupled, however, with a dogged refusal to make her perfect or to entirely condone her occasional hysteria. The narrator throughout retains the right to mention Mary's faults as well as her virtues—"The exercise of her various virtues gave vigor to her genius, and dignity to her mind; she was sometimes inconsiderate, and violent; but never mean or cunning" (*Works*, 1.13.35)—but never with any acrimony. Mary is, after all, advertised as a heroine drawn from nature. This tone of honest, yet sympathetic, analysis maintains a delicate balance between approval and disapproval, but a very delicate one ultimately tipped in favor of sympathy in the last third of the story by the increasing dominance of Mary's own voice, which is fervent, plaintive, melancholy.[15]

Gradually Mary herself is more frequently quoted directly, either from her writings or from conversation; when she speaks, the passages almost inevitably have more emotive appeal than the narrator's, since her two most characteristic modes of discourse are the complaint and the rhapsody. It is under the sun of Henry's kindly disposition in Lisbon that Mary first begins to express herself, distinguishing the nature of her affections, lamenting her failures to find happiness, articulating the conflict she feels between duty and desire. After separation from him, she turns increasingly to her journal, now "her only confident," recording her sorrows, fears, wishes, and reflections. After a storm at sea she records in fervent terms her increasing detachment from life's "dear delusions" and her revived faith in God's ability to "speak peace to her troubled spirit" (*Works*, 1.20.51–52). Back in London, engaged in charity work, she uses her journal as an outlet for her increasing frustration; writing in it enables her to go on, and also enables her to revive her faith in sensibility. Despite trouble, she continues to believe, echoing Sterne, that sensibility is the "source inexhaustible" of all virtue and joy (*Works*, 1.23.57–58).

The narrator-heroine relationship becomes perfectly complicated near the end of the book when Mary's voice begins to sound like the narrator's by taking up the narrator's habit of submitting sensibility to self-conscious, critical analysis. At the end of her "rhapsody" on sensibility, for example, she pauses to reflect on a dangerous counterfeiter of this exquisite sensitivity, the sensualist: "Sensibility is indeed the foundation of all our happiness; but these raptures are unknown to the depraved sensualist, who is only moved by what strikes his gross senses; the delicate embellishments of nature escape his notice; as do the gentle and interesting affections." Shortly after she writes her rhapsody, Mary meets such an intelligent man of the world, a good conversationalist who admires her "genius, and cultivation of mind" but who is, unfortunately, too much "the slave of beauty" and "the captive of sense." He troubles Mary, and her record of that unease forms a lengthy caveat to all followers of sensibility:

> Every individual has its own peculiar trials; and anguish, in one shape or other, visits every heart. Sensibility produces flights of virtue; and not curbed by reason, is on the brink of vice talking, and even thinking of virtue.
>
> Christianity can only afford just principles to govern the wayward feelings and impulses of the heart: every good disposition runs wild, if not transplanted into this soil; but how hard is it to keep the heart diligently, though convinced that the issues of life depend on it. (*Works*, 1.20.59–61)

Since Mary's cautious tone at this juncture is nearly impossible to distinguish from the narrator's, it is tempting to assume that Wollstonecraft approves of the attitudes of her older, more mature heroine. She certainly seems to invite the readers to share Mary's newly chastened and measured admiration of sensibility. Mary, in the words of narrative theorist Rimmon-Kenan, at last becomes the dominant focalizer,[16] and her perspective on sensibility becomes the dominant ideology. Difficult as it is to achieve and maintain, and much as it may tyrannize its best believers, true sensibility is, in the last analysis, clearly recommended as the best of all possible frames of mind for gentle, sensitive people like Mary and Henry who inhabit a "world in ruins" (*Works*, 1.22.54). Sensibility has not given Mary everything she wanted nor has it enabled her to change the world. It has, however, provided her with a list, even if a short one, of alternative attitudes and behaviors, alternatives she, as a thinking and feeling person, finds considerably more attractive than the subservience in marriage recommended by her family.

If all that emerged in *Mary* were this guarded endorsement of sensibility, however, it would hardly be the unique document that it is. More important than the book's final resolution is the degree of ambivalence towards sensibility that it manages to hold in suspension; for out of that ambivalence comes creative innovation. Wollstonecraft's uneasiness with the standard sentimental heroine—doubly registered in the book's advertisement and in its satiric portrayal of Mary's mother—spurs her to create a new kind of dynamic, intellectual heroine. And that, in turn, leads to the construction of a new kind of novel, one tracing the organic development of human character in its natural, social, and intellectual environment. Wollstonecraft's ambivalence also modifies the book's point of view, a point of view too unstable to be called entirely successful, perhaps, but nevertheless risk-taking and much more thought provoking than the fatherly comfort of a Fielding or the light ironic steadiness of an Austen.

Finally, that ambivalence crystallizes in Mary's well-known apostrophe to sensibility on her return to London:

> Sensibility is the most exquisite feeling of which the human soul is susceptible: when it pervades us, we feel happy; and could it last ummixed, we might form some conjecture of the bliss of those paradisiacal days, when the obedient passions were under the dominion of reason, and the impulses of the heart did not need correction.
>
> It is this quickness, this delicacy of feeling, which enables us to relish the sublime touches of the poet, and the painter; it is this, which expands the soul, gives an enthusiastic greatness, mixed with tenderness, when we view the magnificent objects of nature; or hear of a good action. . . . Softened by tenderness; the soul is disposed to be virtuous. Is any sensual gratification to be compared to that of feeling the eyes moistened after having comforted the unfortunate?
>
> Sensibility is indeed the foundation of all our happiness; but these raptures are unknown to the depraved sensualist, who is only moved by what strikes his gross senses; the delicate embellishments of nature escape his notice; as do the gentle and interesting affections. . . .
>
> Every individual has its own peculiar trials; and anguish, in one shape or other, visits every heart. Sensibility produces flights of virtue; and not curbed by reason, is on the brink of vice talking, and even thinking of virtue.
>
> Christianity can only afford just principles to govern the wayward feelings and impulses of the heart: every good disposition runs wild, if not transplanted into this soil. (*Works*, 1.24.59–61)

Doubts about sensibility surface even in this, Wollstonecraft's first and most credulous, fictional presentation of it. Reason must check it, and Christianity must guard it from sensualist usurpation. Wollstonecraft's faith in sensibility, however, both as a unique propensity and an agent for remarkable change, surfaces as well. She grants it mythic status by placing it in a prelapsarian paradise, a world before the fall into a divisive awareness of gender difference; and she allows it to work magical growth in the minds of the faithful. Doubts about feeling, for Wollstonecraft, are not an invitation to apathy but to action: her response to it is neither to reject it out of hand nor to succumb to it but to extricate herself from it in a lifelong series of acts of creative resistance. *Mary* is her first such act.

3
"Cave of Fancy"

Ye who listen with credulity to the whispers of fancy, and
pursue with eagerness the phantoms of hope; who expect
that age will perform the promises of youth, and that the
deficiencies of the present day will be supplied by the
morrow; attend to the history of Rasselas prince of
Abyssinia.[1]   —Samuel Johnson, 1759

A fictional fragment written about the same time as *Mary* (1788),
"Cave of Fancy" (1787), is unique among Wollstonecraft's works for its
dreamlike, antimimetic qualities. It shares with *Mary* a preoccupation
with the notion of sensibility—sensibility underlies the protagonist's
genius, serves as a touchstone of human identity and merit, and dominates the cautionary tale for a younger woman that forms the climax of
the fragment. Unlike *Mary*, however, much of "Cave of Fancy" takes
place in an unnamed fairy-tale realm where characters remain untouched
by everyday concerns about psychosocial, political, or economic survival, a realm where the myths of sensibility can be represented without an immediate challenge from actuality. According to Roland
Barthes, myths "abduct" much of their material, building powerfully
appealing stories by freely using culturally laden "signs" as "signifiers," stripped of their historical context and naturalized in a new setting.[2] Wollstonecraft's fictional fragment seems to be a particularly
pure example of such an experiment; it gathers together largely derived
materials on a utopian island to create a mosaic of legitimacy for sensibility.

It borrows its opening cadences, for example, from Samuel Johnson's
oriental tale, *Rasselas*, the story of a prince's education:

Ye who expect constancy where every thing is changing, and peace in the
midst of tumult, attend to the voice of experience, and mark in time the footsteps of disappointment, or life will be lost in desultory wishes, and death
arrive before the dawn of wisdom. (*Works*, 1.1.191)

Thereafter elements of the Gothic, the sublime, and the Oriental tale all jostle each other to become the story's legitimizing framework. Chapter 1 introduces a landscape remote, threatening, and enchanted in language fairly straining to evoke two of sensibility's favorite moods, awe and melancholy. The valley near the eponymous cave holds sandy wastelands scattered with "mangled limbs"; woods inhabited by "hissing" serpents, croaking ravens, screeching owls, and roaring lions and "tygers" and having "noxious vapors" and an "everlasting twilight"; and a mountainous coastline conducive to landslides and shipwrecks (*Works*, 1.1.191).

The hermit Sagestus, who presides over this dubious realm, is both sage and magician "to whom nature had unlocked her most hidden secrets"(*Works*, 1.1.191). His location and his powers make him faintly reminiscent of Shakespeare's Prospero: he can penetrate solid rocks, enter the mystic underworld of the Cave of Fancy, and commune with departed human spirits attempting to purify themselves in the earth's dark, subterranean waters. He is, so it seems, their confessor, judge, jury, and pardoner, in charge of their release when they achieve purification:

> Some, who were refined and almost cleared from vicious spots, he would allow to leave, for a limited time, their dark prison-house; and, flying on the winds across the bleak northern ocean, or rising in an exhalation till they reached a sun-beam, they thus re–visited the haunts of men. These were the guardian angels, who in soft whispers restrain the vicious, and animate the wavering wretch who stands suspended between virtue and vice. (*Works*, 1.1.192)

A seer extraordinaire, Sagestus's "hollow eyes, sunk in their orbits, retired from the view of vulgar objects, and turned inwards, overleaped the boundary prescribed to human knowledge" (*Works*, 1.1.191). His vision extends not so much to the future as to the past and the present. But Sagestus also has the additional visionary power, one that identifies him as a sage of sensibility as well as wisdom, to penetrate human appearances to their essences. Lavaterian physiognomist without equal,[3] he can discern temperament and character from the faces and bodies of both the living and the dead:

> He was perfectly acquainted with the construction of the human body, knew the traces that virtue or vice leaves on the whole frame; . . . nay more, he knew by the shape of the solid structure, how far the spirit could range, and saw the barrier beyond which it could not pass: the mazes of fancy he explored, measured the stretch of thought, and, weighing all in an even balance, could tell whom nature had stamped an hero, a poet, or philosopher. (*Works*, 1.2.194)

When a shipwreck leaves a beach littered with bodies, the hermit-magician discovers a small orphaned girl alive and adopts her as his "Sagesta." Finding the best method of accomplishing her general education thereafter becomes his professed goal. In the course of the remaining three extant chapters, Sagestus offers Sagesta an extended introduction to sensibility. He first reduces sensibility to its essence for his young charge and teaches her to search it out in those few places where it cannot be feigned: in the psyche, in gestures, and in the face and voice. He then teaches Sagesta the familiar catechism of sensibility: that it is the sister of wisdom and the mother of fancy, love, and virtue, but that it, like all human inclinations, must be indulged in moderation. At last he initiates her into the mysteries of the Cave of Fancy, allowing her to hear a cautionary tale—a testimonial—about the dangers of sensibility to women in love. Given the imputed wisdom of the "sage, to whom nature had unlocked her most hidden secrets," readers are certainly encouraged to assume that they see a priest, or even an oracle of sensibility, in Sagestus, and in the Cave of Fancy an oracle's cave. Setting and sage together suggest that the "Cave of Fancy" not only aims to tell what the Wollstonecraft of 1787 believes (or hopes) is the truth about sensibility, but also strives to persuade others— through the seduction of mythic presentation—to believe in that truth.

The shipwreck that yields Sagestus his orphan also gives him the opportunity to walk the beach and "scrutinize" the faces of the corpses washed ashore. In what may well be Wollstonecraft's most haunting fictional scene, he walks "leisurely among the dead," "narrowly" reading "their pallid features" for signs of vice and virtue, now "indelibly fixed by death" (*Works*, 1.2.194). He divides the bodies into two categories, those who had sensibility or benevolence when alive and those who lacked it.[4] He ties external structures to internal processes, and to describe those processes, he relies heavily on the metonyms of sensibility.

Sagestus reads benevolence, for example, in the face of a young man who apparently saved the infant's life before he died: "The head was square, though the features were not very prominent; but there was a great harmony in every part, and the turn of the nostrils and lips evinced, that the soul must have had taste. . . . benevolence indeed strung the nerves that naturally were not very firm; it was the great knot that tied together the scattered qualities, and gave the distinct stamp to the character" (*Works*, 1.2.196). And he infers a large sensorium—and a whole array of cognitive and emotive activities—from the countenance of another:

A spacious forehead met his view; warm fancy had revelled there, and her airy dance had left vestiges, scarcely visible to a mortal eye. Some perpen-

dicular lines pointed out that melancholy had predominated in his constitu-
tion; yet the straggling hairs of his eye-brows showed that anger had often
shook his frame; indeed, the four temperatures, like the four elements, had
resided in this little world, and produced harmony. The whole visage was
bony, and an energetic frown had knit the flexible skin of his brow; the king-
dom within had been extensive; and the wild creations of fancy had there
"a local habitation and a name." So exquisite was his sensibility, so quick
his comprehension, that he perceived various combinations in an instant . . .
and the flash of his eye spoke the quick senses which conveyed intelligence
to his mind; the sensorium indeed was capacious, and the sage imagined he
saw the lucid beam, sparkling with love or ambition, in characters of fire,
which a graceful curve of the upper eyelid shaded. (*Works*, 1.2.194)

Everywhere in these passages Sagestus's descriptive language
assumes things about mind and body that are essentially beyond observation and verification: that the mind is a collection of discrete entities, that the quiescent face and body are the script of the mind, that
mind and body are (ultimately) part of a single sign system readable
by the initiated. For Sagestus the human inclination sensibility remains
an omnipresent force: it is an agent of change for the better, effecting
benevolence, imagination, and quick cognition wherever it resides,
and, as such, frequently an organizing as well as an animating presence
in the individual. Sagestus also assumes that human character receives
its distinctive stamp from the kind and degree of its sensibility; as the
key to early character formation,[5] sensibility is also a unifying presence in the mind.

Arbitrary as these claims may seem, they all pretend to the status of
empirical evidence, verifiable observations based on Lavater's new
pseudoscience of physiognomy. In the mid to late eighteenth century
it gains favor among writers of sensibility, probably because it stress-
es, as they do, the importance of the passions in the formation of character, and the superiority of nonverbal signs as the mark of character.
Sagestus teaches Sagesta to search for such signs in her "first impressions," and especially to study the mouth and be attentive to modulations in the voice:

The mouth . . . seems to be the feature where you may trace every kind of
dissimulation, from the simper of vanity, to the fixed smile of the designing villain. Perhaps, the modulations of the voice will still more quickly
give a key to the character than even the turns of the mouth, or the words
that issue from it; often do the tones of unpractised dissemblers give the
lie to their assertions. Many people never speak in an unnatural voice, but
when they are insincere: the phrases not corresponding with the dictates
of the heart, have nothing to keep them in tune. (*Works*, 1.3.199)

Never before or after "Cave of Fancy" does Wollstonecraft rely so studiously on physiognomy, though there is evidence of a residue of belief in it throughout her career. What sets her apart somewhat from other writers of sensibility, who place more importance on the eye (with its tears), the blush, the trembling lip, is her focus on the voice as the truest metonymic representative of the heart.[6] It bears keeping in mind, since one of the distinctive features of Wollstonecraft's prose is an authoritative, if fluctuating, voice—now cool and detached, now bitingly sarcastic, now demonstrably sentimental.

The treasure in the "Cave of Fancy," by general consensus, is Sagestus's definition of sensibility as the affective cognition of a sensitized psyche:

> To give the shortest definition of sensibility, replied the sage, I should say that it is the result of acute senses, finely fashioned nerves, which vibrate at the slightest touch, and convey such clear intelligence to the brain, that it does not require to be arranged by the judgment. Such persons instantly enter into the characters of others, and instinctively discern what will give pain to every human being; their own feelings are so varied that they seem to contain in themselves, not only all the passions of the species, but their various modifications. Exquisite pain and pleasure is their portion; nature wears for them a different aspect than is displayed to common mortals. (*Works*, 1.3.201)

The characteristics outlined here—finely fashioned nerves, instant perception, telepathic empathy, infinite variety of passion, exquisite pain and pleasure—are the ones Wollstonecraft mentions most often when she mentions sensibility, notable above all because they all emphasize internal qualities equally accessible to both men and women so long as they have "acute senses." Sensibility in "Cave of Fancy" still has to do primarily, as it does in *Mary*, with gender-neutral interiority; it is a tactile and affective awareness that arises from beneath the conscious surface of the subject and is also capable, in especially gifted people, of penetrating beneath the surface of the object. Sagestus, of course, has long enjoyed such exceptional perceptive powers; he not only reads life's transcripts from the dead, he commands deceased human spirits in his Cave of Fancy. He is a prophet with second sight whose "hollow eyes, sunk in their orbits, retired from the view of vulgar objects, and turned inwards, overleaped the boundary prescribed to human knowledge" (*Works*, 1.1.191). At the same time, Sagesta's name suggests that she is expected to come to full inheritance of her mentor's wisdom and perspicacity.

More than anything else at this point, Wollstonecraft seems interested in allying sensibility with "instinctive discernment" or "genius," something which for her, as her portrait of Sagestus underlines, is mysterious, with mythic origins and potentially magical effects. She also links sensibility here with virtue, if not with happiness. It is not in itself a virtue, because it is at base a sensory sensitivity, but its presence nurtures virtuous behavior (empathy, benevolence, love) and its absence renders the person subject to all manner of vice—by Sagestus's observations of the dead on the beach, from indolence and obstinacy to vanity and designing villainy.

Once Sagesta understands, by precept, the essence of sensibility, the sage begins to teach her, by example, what it can do in action. For that purpose, he conjures up the spirit of a recently departed young woman, whose life bears a resemblance to the heroine in Wollstonecraft's first novel, *Mary*. After youthful experiences that overexercise her pity, she is embroiled in a hopeless love relationship with a man of sensibility, and at last confined to an unhappy arranged marriage with an older businessman. She and her lover are in such perfect sympathy with one another that they can communicate without words: a glance, a held hand, do just as well: "Our corresponding feelings confounded our very souls; and in many conversations we almost intuitively discerned each other's sentiments; the heart opened itself, not chilled by reserve, nor afraid of misconstruction" (*Works*, 1.3.203).

Since their relationship is already predominantly one of communing spirits, when he dies she finds it easy to continue to think of him and love him until her "voluptuous sorrow" becomes more appealing to her than "every gratification of sense": "Death more firmly united our hearts." Such an attachment necessarily gives her reason to be melancholy, something her husband "attributed to [her] extreme sensibility, and loved [her] the better for possessing qualities he could not comprehend" (*Works*, 1.3.205). In retrospect she realizes—and this is the lesson she tries to convey to Sagesta—that she "neglected many opportunities of being useful, whilst [she] fostered a devouring flame," that she should have contemplated God more, should have learned that "earthly love" is meant to be a preparation for heavenly love. Her final advice, then, is not to abandon sensibility but also not to overindulge it. One should treasure it and use it well to ease suffering in this life and expedite the journey to the next (*Works*, 1.3.206). Although the cautionary tale within the tale focuses on feminine sensibility, and its underlying assumption might be that women stand in greater need of such cautionary tales, nothing in "Cave of Fancy" demands such a conclusion. The moral of the tale, drawn by the speaker-spirit (not Sagestus), is not gender specific: anyone, either man or woman, can fall victim to "voluptuous sorrow" at the loss of a loved one and wish for

Liebestod, and anyone, too, can learn that it is more important to moderate sensibility and its gifts wisely than to be consumed by love.

By the end of the third chapter, Sagestus's valley has become as much a highly resonant mindscape as a landscape. The description of its three regions evokes three states of mind, all emphasized in the literature of sensibility: consciousness (the blazing light of beach and plain); melancholy (the perpetual twilight of the woods); and otherworldliness, or, in prominent instances like *Clarissa* and *Werther*, outright longing for death (the mythic world of the cave). The cave's name and inhabitants, in turn, dramatize an allegory of mental faculties: the only cave dweller conjured up for Sagesta's benefit is a young woman who wastes her life in the fanciful pursuits of sensibility—an inaccessible lover, "treacherous imagination," "voluptuous sorrow," "tumultuous emotions"—but has now seen the error of her ways. The sage's questions and comments, the departed spirit's replies, become Wollstonecraft's psychomachia of reason and sensibility.

The three chapters together, despite their fragmentary state, offer readers a relatively optimistic extended metaphor of mind, one foreshadowing Freud's tripartite mind with its superego, ego, and id, but one finally less alarming in its operation. Wollstonecraft's superego (Sagestus) nurtures and then releases pent up spirits, rather than repressing them. Her id (departed spirits) undergoes constant rejuvenation and frequently "airs" its desires. Her ego (Sagesta) observes, listens, and learns from both in all tranquility and without recourse to psychoanalytic exorcism. The most original feature of Sagestus's landscape of the mind, however, is most certainly its integration within and without, the easy communion among its faculties, and its openness, as well, to the outside world. There are no impassable barriers here between things immortal and mortal, persons male and female, events present and past, nor between observation and introspection, reason and fancy, or sense and sensibility. Protected from any place else by a range of encircling mountains, Sagestus's valley becomes a fictional space where Wollstonecraft can reiterate her belief in certain key myths of sensibility and then sketch out her own revolutionary model of a dynamic mind fueled and formed by that sensibility—one with all its rational, emotional, sensible, and imaginative faculties in complete and constant dialogue with themselves and their world.

This fragment is written with such intensity, such obvious emotional participation, that it seems more like a lyric poem than a tale. In nearly every other place in her writing where Wollstonecraft talks of sensibility, she leaves the impression of ambivalence, of resisting as well as being drawn to it. She seems perpetually to be (as she was, by her own admission, with Rousseau), just "half in love" with it.[7] In

"Cave of Fancy," in contrast, there is a notable absence of such resistance. Wollstonecraft's narrator creates no ironic distance between herself and the story; and neither narrator nor characters seem to notice the pathologies of sensibility that the tale betrays. Sensibility is otherworldly and silent to the point of extreme antisociability: its insights are bought at the price of self–isolation, its affective experience at the cost of suffering. Most alarming is its intimate alliance in this narrative with death: some of those who died had it; those still alive who have it are drawn themselves to the dead, to silence, and to the state of death. Again, as in *Mary*, sensibility subverts active participation in life; perhaps this helps to explain why the tale remains a fragment.

Even so, "Cave of Fancy" remains a significant if sinister idyll in the maelstrom of Wollstonecraft's writings, one that sheds, in its stark simplicity, considerable light not only on the tragic associations sensibility holds for her but on the nature of her fascination with it. "Cave of Fancy" reiterates once more the links Wollstonecraft chooses to forge between sensibility, education, and women. Precisely because she views sensibility as so vital to the development of character and the acquisition of knowledge, she suggests through Sagestus that it is a subject about which educators must speak. And perhaps because she knows the prevalent opinion among her contemporaries is that young women have a greater degree of sensibility, she suggests, again through Sagestus, that learning about it should be Lesson Number One for those young women. This will be a major underlying assumption in the educational treatises that follow "Cave of Fancy" into print.

4
Early Thoughts on Education

> I would have every one try to form an opinion of an author
> themselves, though modesty may restrain them from
> mentioning it. Many are so anxious to have the reputation
> of taste, that they only praise the authors whose merit is
> indisputable. I am sick of hearing of the sublimity of
> Milton, the elegance and harmony of Pope, and the
> original, untaught genius of Shakespear. These cursory
> remarks are made by some who know nothing of nature,
> and could not enter into the spirit of those authors, or
> understand them.
> —"Reading," *Education of Daughters* (*Works*, 4.21)

Persons encountering Wollstonecraft for the first time through her early
books on women's education, *Education of Daughters* (1787), *Original
Stories* (1788), and *The Female Reader* (1789), might find it hard to
believe that she is also the author of the better-known *Mary* (1788) and
Rights of Woman (1792).[1] Different as they are in other respects, the latter two works are certainly impassioned and original. In contrast, the
tone of the pedagogical treatises sounds cool and distant; their authorial voice is generic, nonreflective, and deferential; and their phrases are
stilted and borrowed. For example: "May I venture a conjecture?—I
cannot help thinking, that every human creature has some spark of
goodness, which their long-suffering and benevolent Father gives them
an opportunity of improving, though they may perversely smother it
before they cease to breathe" (*Works*, 4.46). The only passion or questioning in these works seems to be the kind found in the "conjecture,"
directed at undisciplined or nonconformist children, servants, or parents. At the same time, the author accepts without question many contemporary notions of female education, citing freely as authorities male
writers she will take to task in *Rights of Woman*: Lord Chesterfield, John
Gregory (author of *A Father's Legacy to his Daughters* [1774]), Milton,

and Rousseau. Topics in these treatises tumble out in various shapes and sizes, seemingly selected at random, broad next to narrow, philosophical shouldering aside practical, with gaps between; and contradictions often stand side by side unchallenged. Of these, the most significant is the clash between Wollstonecraft's philosophy of education, most completely articulated in *Education of Daughters*, and her recommended pedagogical practice, most evident in *Original Stories*.

In twenty-one brief essays arranged in roughly chronological order, *Education of Daughters* moves from some preliminary steps in the education of infant daughters to selected lessons for young women of marriageable age, among them how to dress, what to read, what to think of love, when to marry, what duties and leisure activities to pursue after marriage. Restrictive though this list may sound to modern ears, it forms a part of Wollstonecraft's most liberal pedagogical treatise. *Education of Daughters* enunciates a relatively permissive ethic of rights for the female pupil and casts sensibility in a major role in the educational process.

She begins her second essay, "Moral Discipline," by citing the two Enlightenment thinkers who contribute most to the theoretical foundation of her views on education: John Locke and Jean-Jacques Rousseau.[2] Indications abound here and elsewhere in her works that she accepts, as a given, Locke's sense-based epistemology; even in the nursery, she notes here, educators can make use of "Mr Locke's system": "Above all, try to teach them [the children] to combine their ideas" (*Works*, 4.9, 11). If her views on education are heavily indebted to Locke, her view of children seems largely derived from Rousseau. She seems to share his reverential attitude towards children as fresh from nature's womb and not yet corrupted by civilization; she pleads throughout this first treatise, in any event, for kindness and understanding in child rearing: "It is only in the years of childhood," she notes in her first essay, "The Nursery," "that the happiness of a human being depends entirely on others—and to embitter those years by needless restraint is cruel. To conciliate affection, affection must be shown, and little proofs of it ought always to be given . . . and they will sink deep into the young mind, and call forth its most amiable propensities" (*Works*, 4.8). Near the end of the treatise, she is still recommending kindness, now in the form of "compassion for those young females who are entering into the world without fixed principles" (*Works*, 4.42).

True to both her adopted mentors, Wollstonecraft emphasizes the gradual, the natural, the experiential, and the individual qualities of a good education.[3] Do not give children too much information too soon, she warns parents, but do guard them against "wrong impressions":

Intellectual improvements, like the growth and formation of the body, must be gradual — yet there is no reason why the mind should lie fallow, while its "frail tenement" is imperceptibly fitting itself for a more reasonable inhabitant. It will not lie fallow; promiscuous seeds will be sown by accident, and they will shoot up with the wheat, and perhaps never be eradicated. (*Works*, 4.10)

Teach by example, she urges teachers, but do not try to devise "fixed rules" for all children in order to "create" in all of them identical minds. Every child is different, every mind already fertile ground before any teacher's arrival:

It may be observed, that I recommend the mind's being put into a proper train, and then left to itself. Fixed rules cannot be given, it must depend on the nature and strength of the understanding; and those who observe it can best tell what kind of cultivation will improve it. The mind is not, cannot be created by the teacher, though it may be cultivated, and its real powers found out. (*Works*, 4.21)

The organic development of the mind, Wollstonecraft implies here and elsewhere, begins at birth; and in that process, the first and best remembered teachers are the senses and sensibility. With this insight in mind, she recommends object lessons for the first lessons of the youngest children, and vivid exemplary tales for slightly older ones:

Children should be permitted to enter into conversation; but it requires great discernment to find out such subjects as will gradually improve them. Animals are the first objects which catch their attention; and I think little stories about them would not only amuse but instruct at the same time, and have the best effect in forming the temper and cultivating the good dispositions of the heart. (*Works*, 4.10)

I do not mean to recommend books of an abstracted or grave cast. There are in our language many, in which instruction and amusement are blended; the Adventurer is of this kind. I mention this book on account of its beautiful allegories and affecting tales, and similar ones may easily be selected. Reason strikes most forcibly when illustrated by the brilliancy of fancy. (*Works*, 4.20–21)

Like *Mary, Education of Daughters* associates sensibility with self-education more than formal education. In a section arguing for delayed matrimony, Wollstonecraft suggests that a young woman's mind "improves itself," even when formal education has been neglected, if only "it has leisure for reflection, and experience to reflect on; but how can this happen when they [young women] are forced to act before they have had time to think, or find that they are unhappily married?" (*Works*, 4.31). Sensibility governs the process of education by experience. Especially for the formation of artistic talent, "sense, taste and sensibility" must all be present (*Works*, 4.18); if they are not, it is useless to force a child into the fine arts. Although this trio of blessings may be perverted, such a "perversion" does not lessen their "intrinsic value" (a point to be kept in mind while reading Wollstonecraft's later sharp criticisms of "false sensibility" [*Works*, 4.18]). She often relies on organic metaphors to describe the autodidactic functions of sensibility. She views sensibility as one of those "instincts which are implanted in us to render the path of duty more pleasant." The role of reason in this mental garden is not to "extirpate" such plants, even though they may, if unchecked, "run wild," but to weed them, prune them, guide their contribution to the personality as a whole (*Works*, 4.7, 30). If the presence of sensibility is a prerequisite to certain kinds of development, the fruit it bears is equally valuable to the world at large: benevolence, that "first, and most amiable virtue" (*Works*, 4.43). In his study of mind metaphors, Kearns suggests that organic language like this implies a view of mind as sentient and at once more autonomous and less passive than its basic Lockean predecessor;[4] but the young Wollstonecraft, although envisioning the mind as a living organism rather than a machine, presents reason as the agent and sensibility as the recipient of actions within that organism.

Even as a passive faculty, however, sensibility can make the difference between wisdom and folly, virtue and vice, sound character or no character at all. "Most women, and men too," Wollstonecraft adds, providing a corrective to Pope, "have no character at all."[5] Only the reflective person has character in the form of "habits" and "fixed principles"; the nonreflective person, in contrast, has a "mind . . . like a wreck drifted about by every squall." And persons of extraordinary sensibility are the most reflective people, because they "suffer more" in response to the "adversity" that promotes reflection: "Adversity is mercifully sent to force us to think" (*Works*, 4.34, 36):

> There are some who delight in observing moral beauty, and their souls sicken when forced to view crimes and follies which could never hurt them. How numerous are the sorrows which reach such bosoms! They may truly be called *human creatures*; on every side they touch their fellow-mortals, and vibrate to the touch. Common humanity points out the important duties of our station; but sensibility (a kind of instinct, strengthened by reflection) can only teach the numberless minute things which give pain or pleasure. (*Works*, 4.36)

In this passage, and once more, Wollstonecraft at least momentarily casts sensibility in the role of active tutor or internal monitor, a rhetorical move that transforms it from a passive propensity into a dynamic force within the mind. While she is working to convince women to be neither remiss nor overfond as wives but to find a golden mean of affection, she urges them to let sensibility be their guide: it is "sufficient for a woman to receive caresses, and not bestow them. She ought to distinguish between fondness and tenderness. The latter is the sweetest cordial of life . . . reserved for particular occasions; to exhilarate the spirits, when depressed by sickness, or lost in sorrow. Sensibility will best instruct." As she concludes her thought, Wollstonecraft defers in passing to the mythic mysteriousness, the inexpressibility, of the many offices of sensibility: "Some delicacies can never be pointed out or described, though they sink deep into the heart, and render the hours of distress supportable" (*Works*, 4.32).

A curious interruption in her argument occurs in *Education of Daughters* after a section on "Temper"; the flow of instructional advice to accompany the progress of the young child stops while Wollstonecraft considers the plight of young women "Fashionably Educated, and Left Without a Fortune." The shift disrupts the temporal continuity of the treatise, and a plaintive tone shatters its tranquil, dispassionate mood. Wollstonecraft takes an actively empathetic view of these young women, essentially overeducated for the lives they are condemned to lead by their economic circumstances; like a sentimental novelist, she suddenly seems to wish her readers would join her in feeling anger and pity: "How earnestly does a mind full of sensibility look for disinterested friendship," but, invariably, the "painted cloud disappears suddenly . . . and what an aching void is left in the heart!" (*Works*, 4.26). The section disquiets and invites speculation about the author, the sentimental, mysteriously private, tone erupts from the cool surface of the treatise. Despite the attempt to exit gracefully from the topic with some platitudes—"Good must ultimately arise from every thing. . . . The main business of our lives is to learn to be virtuous" (*Works*, 4.26 –27)— the problem uncovered remains intractable, unresolved. It alerts the reader to a dawning dissatisfaction on Wollstonecraft's part with either the aims or the end results (or both) of female education; it invites the suspicion of a disjunction between the sentimentalized feminine ideal of the age and her own newly articulated, essentially gender-blind, ethic of rights for the pupil.

Once alerted, moreover, the reader may detect other signs of discontent in the sections of the treatise on love and marriage. Although Wollstonecraft admits there may be no reasoning about the two, she works to demystify both. Love, she suggests somewhat puckishly, is neither irresistible, nor singular, nor best when either purely platonic or wildly passionate: "Love, unsupported by esteem, must soon expire" (*Works*, 4.28–29). Marriage, as a result, should be entered into with caution in maturity: "When a woman's mind has gained some strength, she will in all probability pay more attention to her actions than a girl can be expected to do; and if she thinks seriously, she will chuse for a companion a man of principle" (*Works*, 4.31). In these sections more than any others, the authorial voice has the ring of the later Wollstonecraft's—pointed, acerbic, witty, epigrammatic, irreverent: "Many [young women] are but just returned from a boarding-school, when they are placed at the head of a family, and how fit they are to manage it, I leave the judicious to judge. Can they improve a child's understanding, when they are scarcely out of the state of childhood themselves?" (*Works*, 4.31).

There are no other signs in these early documents, however, that Wollstonecraft disagrees with the prevalent advice given to young women and their educators. She assumes that young women are especially vulnerable to the tyranny of sensibility and the passions, but she also assumes that they will easily and willingly listen to reason, the "heaven-lighted lamp in man" (*Works*, 4.41). Without reflection plus religion, she insists, there can be "no true sentiment" nor any "effectual check to the passions"; and checked, she believes, they must be. If they are not, they will ravage the personality. To forestall this, she recommends socially conservative behavior—submission to authority and the suppression of negative feelings, especially anger—sometimes associated with the notion of sensibility in the 1780s, to be sure, but soon seen by her to be incompatible with her emerging feminist point of view.

The first thing all children need to be taught, she insists in *Thoughts*, is "a strict adherence to truth"; the second, "a proper submission to superiors" (*Works*, 4.11). The word "proper" implies an important qualification: never, either here or later, does she recommend blind allegiance to arbitrary tyranny, and her stated interest as an educator in this treatise is to help young women to think for themselves: to use their own judgment to weigh alternatives and form their own opinions based on observations (see, for example, *Works*, 4.21). Nevertheless, deference is due, Wollstonecraft makes it clear, to all reasonable authorities: the Bible, parents, husbands, teachers, and their internal monitors, conscience and reason: "A mind depressed with a weight of weaknesses can only find comfort in the promises of the Gospel. . . . Reason is indeed the heaven-lighted lamp in man, and may safely be trusted when not entirely depended on" (*Works*, 4.41).

More surprising, perhaps, this future champion for women's rights—including full rights of the heart—here roundly recommends the suppression of feeling. Since the signs of sensibility on the face and in the manner are easily feigned—"it is easier to copy the cast of countenance, than to cultivate the virtues which animate and improve it" (*Works*, 4.14)—those signs should be concealed: "Feeling is ridiculous when affected; and even when felt, ought not to be displayed. It will appear if genuine; but when pushed forward to notice, it is obvious vanity has rivalled sorrow . . ." (*Works*, 4.14). What a face should show, she concludes, is a "well-ordered mind." Of all emotions, anger is most studiously to be avoided—not only not "displayed," but not even entertained. She believes it to be the most destructive and self-destructive of emotions: "There is not a temper in the world which does not need correction, and of course attention." The correctives she suggests are piety, humility, and sensibility, in the guise of "benevolence" or "active virtue" (*Works*, 4.24).

The unencumbered way Wollstonecraft offers these recommendations suggests that she has yet to grapple with many of the self-contradictory implications in the code of sensibility; certainly her interest in women's education has not yet caught feminist fire. Moreover, submission to authority and self-control are not only handicaps to feminist activism but even to two of the more active virtues of sensibility: benevolence and self-realization. Benevolence sometimes necessitates intervention, a behavior hardly in harmony with submission to authority. Self-improvement, consistently prized by Wollstonecraft from the beginning to the end of her career, is also difficult to reconcile with the self-denial implicit in patient submission and passivity. Just how quickly and how far she moves from her position in *Education of Daughters* can be usefully measured by noting her own angry criticism, just five years later, of Dr. Gregory's insistence that young women should be "decorous" and "restrained" in all things:

> The remarks relative to behaviour, though many of them very sensible, I entirely disapprove of, because it appears to me to be beginning, as it were, at the wrong end. A cultivated understanding, and an affectionate heart, will never want starched rules of decorum — something more substantial than seemliness will be the result; and, without understanding, the behaviour here recommended, would be rank affectation. Decorum, indeed, is the one thing needful! — decorum is to supplant nature, and banish all simplicity and variety of character out of the female world. . . . It is this system of dissimulation, throughout the volume, that I despise. Women are always to *seem* to be this and that — yet virtue might apostrophize them, in the words of Hamlet — Seems! I know not seems! — Have that within that passeth show! (*Works*, 5.5.167–68)

•   •   •

Restraint, however, is precisely what the governess in *Original Stories* emphasizes and exercises in the training of her two young aristocratic charges, Caroline and Mary. This second pedagogical work, consisting of a series of vignettes illustrating the practice of teaching, yokes together liberal and conservative, permissive and repressive, teaching strategies. In this work, sensibility is not so much acknowledged as used, then cast aside.

The governess Mrs. Mason seems to be implementing the liberal educational philosophy of the author of *Education of Daughters* as the book opens. Her lessons are invariably experiential and object-centered; and she avoids the rote conning of passages and acquisition of mechanical skills that the preface to the *Female Reader* deplores (*Works*, 4.58–59). In short, she is a Lockean educator who elects to reach her young charges through their sensibilities. Mason seizes every opportunity that arises from a striking experience to tell a memorable story, which then in turn reinforces a moral precept. She chooses her genres carefully, seeming again to follow the advice in *Education of Daughters*. She tells the young girls short, vivid animal stories, anecdotes, and allegories; the older girls are told stories about people closer to their own range of experience (often people they have just met): "History of the Village Schoolmistress," "History of Peggy and her Family," "Visit to a Poor Family in London." Many of these tales appeal to more than one of the faculties of sensibility—pity, fear, imagination, the senses—and their vividness often obviates the need for sermonizing. Here is one of the earliest of those lessons:

> I myself knew a man who had hardened his heart to such a degree, that he found pleasure in tormenting every creature whom he had any power over. I saw him let two guinea-pigs roll down sloping tiles, to see if the fall would kill them. And were they killed? cried Caroline. Certainly; and it is well they were, or he would have found some other mode of torment. When he became a father, he not only neglected to educate his children, and set them a good example, but he taught them to be cruel while he tormented them: the consequence was, that they neglected him when he was old and feeble; and he died in a ditch. (*Works*, 4.373)

The difficulty with Mason's pedagogy may already be clear from this example. Though identified as their "tender friend," Mason is far from tender in her choice of tales or tactics. Many, if not all, of her stories are grisly cautionary tales. The story above is told to encourage the girls to be kind to animals. Another especially vivid one to teach them to control their tempers is the "History of Jane Fretful," who dies an embittered, lonely, unhappy woman after killing her dog and her mother with her ill-humor (*Works*, 4.380–82). Object lessons are equally grim; in one, Caroline, just recovering from a surfeit of fruit, is made to stand by the pig pen to hear a two-page lecture on moderating her appetites. Even before the lecture the child is blushing for shame; the lengthy lecture plus the humiliating object lesson simply bludgeons her with the point (*Works*, 4.399–401). In addition to grisly warnings and personal humiliations, the children are sometimes subjected to withdrawal of affection or approval when they commit an offense; and sometimes they must wait overnight to learn just what that offense has been. This pedagogy of negativism dominates the girls' first months with Mason; only later does she begin to speak in more abstract and positive terms and to offer them some admirable role models besides herself. These are terrorist tactics inconsistent with the recommended child-rearing attitudes in Wollstonecraft's first treatise; they are consistent, however, with Mason's moral rigorism.

Her way of inculcating virtue is to root out every childish inclination that could ever tend in the other direction. She seems to believe that any behavior that is not perfectly right is wrong and, no matter how innocent it may seem, potentially corrupting or dangerous. Mason is a virtual library of stories about dire consequences. Any attempt, she tells them, to conceal the complete truth, whether verbal or visual, is a lie; and no lie, moreover, however tiny or subtle, goes unnoticed by the "Searcher of hearts" (*Works* 4.383). People who lie are punished both in this life and the next: neglected by family, shunned by acquaintances (they have no friends), they are even abandoned by God ("He hates a liar!") (*Works* ,4.385). Other misdemeanors cut the offenders off from the grace of God as well; failure to pray is certainly another—even failure to pray correctly. They must pray regularly, but not mechanically or habitually; Mason pronounces all "devotion . . . mockery and selfishness, which does not improve our moral character" (*Works*, 4.424). A child might well conclude from Mason's lessons that "trifling omissions" (*Works*, 4.409) invariably lead to moral catastrophe: anger to murder (chapter 41), lying to hell (chapter 5), overindulgence to bestial turpitude (chapter 9), procrastination to devastating remorse (chapter 10), idleness to vice, and prodigality to miserliness (chapter 24). Actual catastrophes, in surprising contrast, frequently lead to moral improvements in Mason's fictional universe: disfigurement to wisdom (chapter 7); poverty to generosity and contentment (chapter 8); and physical pain to virtue (chapter 21).

Although Mason's teaching practices are difficult to read as acts of fellow-feeling (Wollstonecraft's biographer Wardle calls her a "heartless virago")[6], Wollstonecraft presents her quite unequivocally as a spokesperson for the ethic of feeling and a woman of feeling herself.

She disciplines the girls when they engage in behavior that would, in time, block the development of their tender passions and their social virtues. She is quite explicit about this: cruelty to animals, she believes, retards the development of fellow-feeling; anger drives out compassion; mockery of others drives out empathy; lies stifle friendship; vanity prohibits the growth of the mind; lack of moderation deters sociability; procrastination or prodigality prevents the exercise of charity. She seems unaware of the disharmony between her severe means and her sentimental ends. The preface acknowledges it, then excuses it as a "cruel necessity" in the present age of vice. Her severity, then, can be read as a critique of Wollstonecraft's age rather than a presentation of the ideal pedagogue:

> The way to render instruction most useful cannot always be adopted; knowledge should be gradually imparted, and flow more from example than teaching: example directly addresses the senses, the first inlets to the heart. . . . But to wish that parents would, themselves, mould the ductile passions, is a chimerical wish, for the present generation have their own passions to combat with, and fastidious pleasures to pursue, neglecting those pointed out by nature: we must therefore pour premature knowledge into the succeeding one; and, teaching virtue, explain the nature of vice. Cruel necessity. (*Works,* 4.359)

Mrs. Mason herself also exemplifies the ethic of feeling she espouses. She exercises her benevolence (the universal love of people that the *Education of Daughters* calls "the first duty," *Works*, 4.30) and practices charity whenever she can; and she has perfected the art of empathy or fellow-feeling. She is never tempted, she tells the girls, to "ridicule . . . personal defects" because she accustomed herself long ago "to think of others, and what they will suffer on all occasions: and this lothness [*sic*] to offend, or even to hurt the feelings of another, is an instantaneous spring which actuates [her] conduct, and makes [her] kindly affected to every thing that breathes" (*Works*, 4.393). Witnessing "harmless mirth" has another effect on Mason: for awhile, she may empathize—"She laughed with the poor whom she had made happy"— but eventually she reverts to the memory of her own sorrows and weeps (*Works*, 4.422). Mason inclines to tears and gloom; she is a woman of melancholy disposition. She generally submerges her disposition in activity or translates it into empathy, but on one evening, in the midst of rural entertainments, she opens her "state of mind" to the girls, as she claims, in order to tell them how she endures it. What follows is a sermonette on the benefits of prayer that just barely escapes the maudlin:

I have been very unfortunate, my young friends; but my griefs are now of a placid kind. Heavy misfortunes have obscured the sun I gazed at when first I entered life; early attachments have been broken; the death of friends I loved has so clouded my days; that neither the beams of prosperity, nor even those of benevolence, can dissipate the gloom; but I am not lost in a thick fog. My state of mind rather resembles the scene before you, it is quiet: I am weaned from the world, but not disgusted; for I can still do good, and in futurity a sun will rise to chear [sic] my heart. Beyond the night of death, I hail the dawn of an eternal day! I mention my state of mind to you, that I may tell you what supports me. . . . Prayer, my children, is the dearest privilege of man, and the support of a feeling heart. (Works, 4.422)

In a subsequent chapter Mason attempts to demonstrate to them the personal benefits of exercising affection, and she reveals the specific cause of her grief. This confession then sets a train of memories in motion that both shifts the mood and alters the conclusion of the chapter to a cry of pain and a self-conscious apology for her "melancholy":

I lost a darling child, said Mrs Mason, smothering a sigh, in the depth of winter: death had before deprived me of her father, and when I lost my child, he died again.

The wintery prospects suiting the temper of my soul, I have sat looking at a wide waste of trackless snow for hours; and the heavy, sullen fog, that the feeble rays of the sun could not pierce, gave me back an image of my mind. I was unhappy, and the sight of dead nature accorded with my feelings —for all was dead to me. . . .

But I am growing melancholy, whilst I am only desirous of pointing out to you how very beneficial charity is; because it enables us to find comfort when all our worldly comforts are blighted: besides, when our bowels yearn to our fellow-creatures, we feel that the love of God dwelleth in us — and then we cannot always go on our way sorrowing. (Works, 4.432, 434)

The narrator of *Original Stories* endorses Mason's pedagogy in the last pages by pointing out both the tender attachment between governess and pupils and the visible signs of improvement in the girls. When Mason takes Caroline and Mary to London and bids them farewell until the following summer, she dissolves into tears of anxious affection: "She took a hand of each, and pressing them tenderly in her own, tears started into her eyes — I tremble for you, my dear girls, for you must now practise by yourselves some of the virtues which I have been endeavouring to inculcate: and I shall anxiously wait for the summer, to see what progress you have made by yourselves" (Works, 4.449). The girls, too, weep at the prospect of "parting with Mrs Mason"; they find it difficult to believe they can do without her, although they demonstrate increased maturity and independence of judgment that will enable them to do so:

The girls were visibly improved; an air of intelligence began to animate Caroline's fine features; and benevolence gave her eyes the humid sparkle which is so beautiful and engaging. The interest that we take in the fate of others attaches them to ourselves; thus Caroline's goodness inspired more affection than her beauty.

Mary's judgment grew every day clearer; or, more properly speaking, she acquired experience; and her lively feelings fixed the conclusions of reason in her mind. (*Works*, 4.440)

Other actions of Mason and the girls throughout the story, however, rise up to testify against this final, official endorsement. Mason is a teacher out of tune with her own professed philosophy: she aims to instill benevolence but more frequently inspires doubt, guilt, or fright; she promises her pupils a gradual, natural learning process through experience and example, but she practices interventionist tactics to influence that process—they unfold, she cuts back, lops off; she preaches that a life of right sensibility leads to tranquility, but she is living proof that feeling can also cripple and cause permanent unhappiness. There is no way to know if Mason gives an accurate picture of Wollstonecraft's private feelings and public demeanor as a governess in Ireland (she apparently felt chastened by the experience); Mason does dramatize rather well, however, an uneasy disjuncture—apparently registered at some level in Wollstonecraft's consciousness—between the psychological quietism celebrated by the ethic of feeling and a degenerate society (one where "vice" prevails) increasingly calling for social activist reform through education reform.

•   •   •

Wollstonecraft is compiler rather than author of *The Female Reader*, though she does include a few contributions of her own in this six-part compendium of instructional readings for young women. Like her other two educational works, this collection aims to "imprint some useful lessons on the mind, and cultivate the taste at the same time"; the recommended method is still to teach by example; and the end result desired is still a child who can both think for herself and express herself in a simple, sincere way: "to infuse a relish for a pure and simple style, by presenting natural and touching descriptions from the Scriptures, Shakspeare, etc. Simplicity and sincerity generally go hand in hand, as both proceed from a love of truth. In subordination to this design, passages varying in style, in verse and prose, have been chosen." If there is a new emphasis here, it is on the importance of fixing "devotional habits in a young mind" (*Works*, 4.55–57).

The selected readings, however, better support the aims of the preface in some areas than in others. The anthology certainly includes a wealth of material to inspire piety: it cites the Bible more frequently than any other book, and the first book is given over entirely to "Devotional Pieces, and Reflections on Religious Objects." Of the dozens of stories, essays, poems, and dialogues here, however, only one addresses the subject of taste directly ("A Definition of Taste," 4.143), although a few others are on related topics (those on music, letter-writing, and dress, for example). All these pieces, of course, might improve the young readers' taste in literature, as the preface assumes. Lesser known instructional authors like Aikin, Barbauld, Chapone, Genlis, Gregory, Lavater, and Trimmer have many more selections included than acknowledged stylists like Johnson, Goldsmith, Shakespeare, and Milton. The selections are, however, all earnest, challenging, and well written; and the young female reader could easily glean essay form as well as syntactical sophistication from the wide variety and number of periodical pieces included from the *Adventurer, Connoisseur, Guardian, Lounger, Mirror, Rambler, Spectator,* and *World.*

The collection, then, might well inspire, with descending frequency, piety, taste, and imagination, but, at the same time, it might not encourage judgment. The reader is seldom given conflicting opinions to consider on a single subject, and the subjects addressed much more often encourage duty than decision-making or discrimination. Readers are invited either to arrange their characters, discarding faults and cultivating virtues (discarding, for example, dissimulation, indolence, temper, and vanity and affectation, and cultivating employment, humility, moderation, obedience, religion, taste, true beauty, and true elegance) or to become more sociable through benevolent employments, cleanliness, filial piety, manners, pity, politeness, social love, tenderness, or justice. If there is an ethic implicit in this book, it is not the ethic of feeling, and certainly not the ethic of the pupil's rights, but rather the ethic of responsibility. In keeping with this emphasis, sensibility as a subject is, for the most part, avoided except to encourage the reader to subdue her sensibility with the practice of religion or to respect only that kind of sensibility that is other-centered and firmly allied to virtuous action or the exercise of conscience. Essentially, Wollstonecraft submerges her interest in the literature of sensibility here, allowing it to find only indirect expression in a few excerpts from Cowper, Thomson, Charlotte Smith, and Young: Cowper's "On Humanity," "On Slavery," "Verses Supposed to be Written by Alexander Selkirk," "The Poet, the Oyster, and Sensitive Plant," and "On Waste of Time"; Thomson's "An Address to the Deity," and "Female Amusements"; and Young's "Love of Fame."

Actually, however, the language of sensibility does not dominate any of these treatises. In *Mary* and "Cave of Fancy," it threatens to escape the uncertain boundaries of fictional characters to permeate the narration and color the narrator's perspective. Not so here. In an unobtrusive way, the ethic of feeling does inform the points of view of the first two treatises: the kindliness of the preceptor in *Education of Daughters* and the public benevolence and private melancholy of Mason in *Original Stories* lend a sentimental cast to each. Generally speaking, however, in these treatises sensibility is talked about less and less until it is, at last, reduced to an afterthought in this third treatise. Its reputation diminishes at the same time: from a child's first and most memorable tutor in the first, to a childhood inclination to be tamed and channeled in the second, to a source of unhappiness, selfishness, and deception in the third:

> That sort of tenderness which makes us useless may indeed be pitied and excused, if owing to natural imbecility; but if it pretends to loveliness and excellence it becomes truly contemptible. ("False Sensibility," by Mrs. Chapone, *Female Reader* [*Works*, 4.135])

> This separation of conscience from feeling is a depravity of the most pernicious sort; it eludes the strongest obligation to rectitude, it blunts the strongest incitement to virtue; when the ties of the first bind the sentiment and not the will; and the rewards of the latter crown not the heart but the imagination. ("False Notions of Sentiment," from the *Lounger, Female Reader* [*Works*, 4.136])

> The noblest minds their virtue prove
> By pity, sympathy, and love:
>
> These, these are feelings truly fine,
> And prove their owner half divine.
>
> His censure reach'd them as he dealt it,
> And each by shrinking shew'd he felt it.
> ("A Fable, The Poet, the Oyster, and Sensitive
> Plant," by Cowper, *Female Reader*
> [*Works*, 4.138])

Sensibility, one could conclude from these treatises, is still the fountainhead of virtues, and may serve well enough to console an occasional overeducated young woman or a governess, but it must be first restrained, then carefully watched and channeled, in order to socialize the child. As an educator Wollstonecraft clearly tries to extricate herself from blind faith in many of her favorite fictions of sensibility; but as the inner contradictions in these treatises suggest, she does so only with partial success.

Part Two
The Test of Reason

5

The Fictions of Sensibility
under Analysis

The subject of female education, consequent manners, and
station in society, appear to him to be of the greatest
consequence in a system of civilization, or progress
towards improvement. Some of his opinions will doubtless
seem singular — for he exclaims against the present mode
of polishing and indulging women, till they become weak
and helpless beings, equally unnerved in body and mind:
and hence infers, that gentleness, or rather the affectation of
sickly feminine sensibility, indiscriminately wears away
not only strength but identity of character.
> —Wollstonecraft's review of *Letters from Barbary*,
> by an English Officer, *Analytical Review*[1]
> (June 1789): 141, *Works*, 7.142

Writings from Wollstonecraft's early years document some unease
with the notion of sensibility and its various doctrines, but an unease
without a clear focus. She occasionally chafes about it but without ever
facing the larger questions of its coherence as a linguistic or value system, or its compatibility with her other preoccupations—key among
them, the shaping of a new feminine ideal. On the contrary, as a young
novelist and pedagogue, she often treats educational reform and sensibility as allies and sees the denigration of sensibility as a large part of
woman's problem. Only when she becomes a regular contributor to
Joseph Johnson's newly formed *Analytical Review* in the late 1780s does
she begin to see sensibility as part of the problem rather than the solution. The *Analytical Review*'s stated purpose is entirely in keeping with
Wollstonecraft's long-standing notion that the aim of education is to
teach people "the exercise of their own reason" (*Rights of Woman*,
Works, 5.179): "to judge for themselves" (1 [May 1788]: 2).[2] She follows that advice herself: her apprenticeship on Johnson's staff constitutes the last stage in her own informal self-education, heightening her

85

critical awareness and her language consciousness, and the first stage in her growing distrust of the literary offspring of sensibility.

In charge of what might be called today the fine arts section, she reviews dozens of sentimental books on the market, gathering information and, as she does, hammering out attitudes that will help to shape her works for the rest of her career.³ Her reviews reveal publicly, for the first time, the restless, probing intellect that emerges privately much earlier and her growing impatience with the clichés of the sentimental tradition. At the same time, however, they also reveal the extent to which the myths and metaphors of sensibility, even if she uses them more self-consciously, continue to structure her ethical as well as her aesthetic judgments. Her views of novels, artists, and style are permeated with the values of sensibility.

Wollstonecraft's many acerbic reviews of sentimental novels make it easy to misconstrue her articles as fragments of one long, fairly sustained attack on sensibility and everything connected with it. She most frequently laments the proliferation of sentimental novels, "the fashionable spawn of the present day" (10 [June 1791]: 218). They seem to her, in addition to being unrealistic and inflammatory, cliché-ridden and mercilessly "dismal." Wollstonecraft praises Charlotte Smith's *Emmeline* for avoiding the all-too-prevalent "drapery of woe": "grief personified, hair freed from confinement to shade feverish cheeks, tottering steps, inarticulate words, and tears ever ready to flow, white gowns, black veils, and graceful attitudes" (1 [July 1788]: 328). Whenever she encounters such displays of dress and demeanor in novels, she dismisses them; the thicker the "drapery of woe," the crisper her dismissal. In a review of *The Self-Tormenter* she complains of the pressure that a "ridiculous display of false sensibility" can place on a novel's probability: characters become "unnatural," situations "strange," language "affected," and plot absurdly fabricated: "for the gentlemen, as well as the ladies, faint, lose their senses, are dying one hour, and dancing with joy the next" (4 [June 1789]: 221).

Such tales occasionally heighten Wollstonecraft's rarely displayed sense of the ridiculous. Her review of *Juliet* regrets, but playfully, the lack of originality in the female followers of Richardson and Sterne: "The lady authors jump over the hedge one after the other, and do not dream of deviating either to the right or left."⁴ The only change they have managed in the formula is to have the heroine's chastity tried with an "insidious sigh" and a "hand . . . gently pressed" rather than by a giant or an abduction (3 [March 1789]: 345). She treats the relentless woe depicted in *Louis and Nina* with comparable light irony, ending her short remarks with a mock tribute to the father of such productions, Laurence Sterne:

In these most *dismal* tales, sentimental to the very marrow, the tender feelings are torn to tatters, and the shreds vain gloriously displayed. Sudden death, everlasting love, methodical madness, bad weather, a breaking heart, putrid body, worn out night cap, etc. etc. Nothing but sentiment! the finely fashioned nerves vibrate to every touch — Alas poor Yorick! If an earthly wight could punish thee for having, in the mere wantonness of unbridled vanity, scattered unseemly weeds amongst the sweet flowers genius had culled, thou wouldst be condemned to review all the sentimental wire-drawn imitations of thy original interesting pages. (4 [June 1789]: 222)

Wollstonecraft's distinction between Sterne and his mindless imitators unlocks an understanding of the nature of her complaint. She objects not to sensibility per se but to its abduction by mediocre writers, and to their reduction of the vibrant antilanguage of sensibility to verbal clichés and plot formulas. Throughout her early works, Wollstonecraft steadily holds sensibility in high esteem, allowing its language(s) to shape her aesthetic and ethical thinking as well as her definition of self. She considers it the vital spark in the human mind, one that fosters genius, character formation, and—that noblest of virtues—benevolence. She sees it primarily as an intellectual propensity; she sees its language as an invaluable aid to self-expression, and an indispensable tool on voyages to the interior. What she encounters in many of the novels she reviews, in contrast, is sex and sensibility, sensibility crystalized into a set of (usually) feminine behaviors and physical characteristics presented as erotic or romantic.[5] The metonyms of sensibility are now taken to be the thing itself; and not only that, they are being made to serve as signs of feminine sensuality. It is this—from her perspective—denigration of sensibility she targets: the "inflammatory" concentration on "drapery," the "false" (exterior) sensibility, the "affected" language, the near exclusive focus on "delicacy" and the physiology of feeling ("Nothing but sentiment! the finely fashioned nerves vibrate to every touch —"). Although she generally maintains both her equanimity and her sense of humor in these reviews, her clever troping of "Alas poor Yorick!" for her own purposes brings into her text some of the sadness as well as the good humor of Tristram Shandy's remark (drawn from Hamlet's melancholy remark): it suggests that she regrets much more than she deplores the burgeoning sentimental novel industry at the century's end.

Wollstonecraft's tone sharpens as she focuses on the possible effects of these "dismal tales." She deplores them not simply because they are bad art but because they constitute an undesirable education for young women readers and potential writers. They promote unhealthy "romantic notions" (1 [July 1788]: 333) that sensibility makes women more attractive and that delicacy makes them more feminine. Such notions

only "give a sanction to the libertine reveries of men" by "strengthen-
ing a male prejudice that makes women systematically weak"; they
"poison the minds" of women. She registers periodic Austen-like
impatience, too, with "lady authors" who swallow this poison without
resistance, and who seem incapable either of independent thought or of
creative originality. Her impatience with the women of her day who
succumb to self-sabotaging myths of sensibility, it should be added, has
not yet erupted into the steady flow of anger so evident in the *Rights of
Woman*. Nevertheless she occasionally strikes a theme and a Swiftian
tone that anticipate her coming polemic phase. A "delicate constitu-
tion," with its signs of "fevers, swoons, and tears," she charges, deprives
the heroine of her dignity (10 [May 1791]: 101–02); and cultivating
sensibility in this sense, that is, "glorying" in "weakness" and "delicacy," deprives women of their adult status, keeps them "overgrown children" (5 [October 1789]: 218).

How distant from the voice of the contemporaneous private letters
this one seems: there, the tone of a William Collins, gentle, meditative,
quietly melancholy; here, the tone of an Alexander Pope, incisive,
impatient, coolly disdainful. Yet even if they disregard her private
voice, those who seek to characterize Wollstonecraft the reviewer as a
satirist of sentiment will have to suppress many of the lengthiest and
most original of her reviews, ones in which she becomes an advocate
for sensibility in a world of libertine pretenders. The most important
of these are two sets of reviews: of Goethe's *Sorrows of Young Werther*
and its English imitators; and of various publications dedicated to
Rousseau's life or works.

Critics have differed over *Werther* from the moment of its publication in 1773, some praising its originality and beauty, others condemning it as a menace to the moral and spiritual well-being of the reading
public. Wollstonecraft takes a sympathetic stand, openly admiring
both the style and the hero of the book. Her own preference for sincerity of expression perhaps explains her praise for Werther's spontaneous, even impulsive, habit of self-expression: she is certain that his
"energy and beauty of language, a uniformity in the extravagancies of
passion that arrests our attention" makes him more credible, more
authentic, more lifelike, gives a "reality to his misery." She discusses
the hero with uncharacteristic enthusiasm, sympathetic assessment
nearly slipping into a cultic participation in his sorrows:

> To pity Werter we must read the original . . . we are affected by his sorrows,
> even while we lament the wanderings of his distempered mind, the sad per-
> version of those talents which might have rendered him a useful and
> respectable being. His ungoverned sensibility would have been, in every

situation, hostile to his peace, finding some unattainable object to pine after. Characters of this kind, like a view of a wild uncultivated country, raise lively emotions in the mind; yet who would wish to fix their constant residence on the most picturesque rock or romantic mountain? The sensations of the moment are confounded with the convictions of reason; and the distinction is only perceived by the consequences. (3 [January 1789]: 73)

Maintaining a precarious balance, this review does not endorse Werther's "ungoverned sensibility," "distempered mind," or wasted talents. It reveals nevertheless that Wollstonecraft is "affected" by Werther's sorrows; she records a fleeting but near complete identification with the hero, a temporary confusion or conflict about how to read the book: "The sensations of the moment are confounded with the convictions of reason." The amiable, pitiable Werther has nearly seduced her, as he certainly does many of her contemporaries, into finding the dark side of sensibility—its solipsism, its suicidal melancholy—heroic. She catches herself just in time, returning to the safety of editorial detachment and a rhetorical question at the last possible minute: "Characters of this kind, like a view of a wild uncultivated country, raise lively emotions in the mind; yet who would wish to fix . . . ?"

She is not so generous to Werther's British women admirers, whose productions she declares "hackneyed" (3 [January 1789]: 73) and saccharine:[6] "The ladies are all so partial to the man, who *could* die for love," Wollstonecraft chuckles in her review of Anne Francis's poem "The Ghost of Charlotte at the Tomb of Werter," "that it appears to be high treason against the laws of romance, to allow Charlotte to live, and bring young Alberts into the world: — true, tender hearted ladies — she ought to have *ran mad*, and died. — It was very indelicate to live to fulfil the duties of life!" (7 [July 1790]: 299–300). She is more contemptuous of the maudlin redundancy of *The Confidential Letters of Albert; from his first Attachment to Charlotte to her Death*: "One death was not sufficient to wind up the tale; probably recollecting the infantine stories of Raw Head and Bloody Bones, horrors are heaped on horrors, and no less than three of the loveliest of their sex, fall a prey to grief, as a sacrifice to the manes of Werter" (6 [April 1790]: 466).

Even more blameworthy than their lack of restraint, Wollstonecraft observes, these followers deviate utterly from Goethe's original; rather than imitating *Werther*, they seem intent instead on imitating sentiment: "in short, this is a *sentimental* fabrication, in which, nature and the characters of the original are so entirely lost sight of, that instead of calling it a caricature it might be termed an ugly mask." Both "caricature" and "ugly mask" are telling terms, of course, pointing to a key concern of Wollstonecraft's here and elsewhere: she deplores the impersonators of sensibility, those who cloak themselves in the "drapery of woe," and, in so doing, threaten to materialize sensibility, to reduce it to a series of external physical signs. In the remainder of her diatribe against *Confidential Letters*, she levels her harshest charges at artificers of feeling: "ludicrous," "unnatural," "ridiculous feelings . . . covered with a sickly veil of artificial sentiment, are as contrary to nature as virtue" (6 [April 1790]: 466 – 67).

Wollstonecraft's attitude to Rousseau, never static and seldom free from ambivalence, is never completely dismissive either.[7] Her first (1788) and last (1792) reviews of his thoughts both insist upon Rousseau's greatness but, at the same time, caution parents to restrict their children's access to him. On the one hand, he is pronounced a "genius" whose thorough acquaintance "with the human heart" should serve as defense enough against his detractors: "A defence of Rousseau appears to us unnecessary — for surely he speaks to the heart, and whoever reading his works can doubt whether he wrote from it — had better take up some other book" (Appendix to 11 [1791]: 528). It is this very acquaintance with the heart, however, that renders Rousseau "improper" for the young; his very "beauties"—the warmth of his passions, the voluptuousness of his pictures—will "tend to lead the opening faculties astray." Let young people first acquire experience and fixed principles: " 'There is a time for all things.' "

Wollstonecraft's half dozen other discussions of Rousseau in the *Analytical Review*, although rarely entirely forgetting his faults, elaborate her notion of genius, sketch out her idea of the best style, air her profound suspicion of Rousseau's detractors, and exhibit a penetrating understanding of the psychology of sensibility. Besides his "alluring" voluptuousness, she pronounces his "paradoxical caprice" to be his other chief defect; but both of these she views as the wildflowers of his genius: "Rousseau's mistake was the mistake of genius, ever eager to trace a well-proportioned system; though vortex whirling round vortex threatened immediate destruction to the airy fabric" (4 [August 1789]: 411; cf. 4 [July 1789]: 360). In passing, Wollstonecraft makes some remarkable claims about genius that call to mind comments made in preceding decades by the *Geniekult*[8] on the continent: she compares it to a "sublime mountain" or the "sun"; she associates it with sensibility, originality, and imperfection of character; and she firmly exempts it from following rules set down for ordinary people:

> The excess of his affection for his fellow creatures, his exquisite sensibility, and that panting after distinction, so characteristic of genius, all contributed to render his conduct strange and inexplicable to little minds; for experience seems to prove, that a man of genius is seldom respected by his

inferiors, if they live within his vortex, nor are his moral virtues allowed to be pure, because he is a rule to himself. (6 [April 1790]: 389)

The mention of "vortex" twice in these passages suggests that Wollstonecraft is at least subliminally aware of the dangers of getting too close to Rousseau; but she nevertheless presents him as admirable. She reserves her contempt for his critics—"little minds," she calls them. Never expect a generous deed of anyone who could be so insensitive as to ridicule Rousseau, she insists:

> Reading the effusions of a warm heart, cold critics have termed them the ravings of a madman. . . . But this is not to be wondered at; people who have but one criterion of excellence, whose minds have a confined range, will ever be intolerant. . . . However . . . he should never expect to see that man do a generous action, who could ridicule Rousseau's interesting account of his feelings and reveries. . . . a description of what has actually passed in a human mind must ever be useful. (6 [April 1790]: 385–86)

In this passage, as so often, Wollstonecraft reveals her bias for interiority, for authors and books that give pictures of the mind and heart. Because Rousseau does this so skillfully, she forgives him his other faults. Enough that his simple prose "finds the nearest way to the heart" (9 [January 1791]: 183). Instead of worrying about defending him, Wollstonecraft works to understand him, and to render him understandable to her readers.

In her long review of Rousseau's *Confessions*, she makes sense of a number of his imputed eccentricities—his attraction to the bovine Therese, his need for solitude, his irascibility, his creative process: all are traceable, she claims, to his "exquisite sensibility." It causes him to "profoundly feel the vices and follies of mankind"; and that in turn, drives him from "the bustle of society" to the calm Therese, or to solitude, where he becomes "himself again" (6 [April 1790]: 389). That solitude, in its turn, however, makes him susceptible to love. His heroine Julie of *Nouvelle Héloïse* is born out of solitary reveries: "His heart having no real object for his imagination to adorn—it quickly created one, and he peopled an ideal world with beings after his own heart." Stimulated to "exaltation of his imagination" by his "new Eloise," "intoxicated with love, without an object," once he meets an attractive woman, he sees "his Julie" in her and invests her "with all the perfections with which he had adorned the idol of his heart." At this point, Wollstonecraft admits, he becomes "the slave of a most violent passion" (390). In this review Wollstonecraft uses the idea of sensibility as a metaphorical key to the operations as well as the development of

a creative mind. It allows her to describe mental processes involving
the lower faculties, the senses, the imagination, and the passions, in a
way that makes them seem, despite their nonrationality, reasonable,
accessible, even predictable.

The values Wollstonecraft champions in her reviews on *Werther* and
Rousseau—values, derivable from the code of sensibility, like sympathy, genius, imagination, passion, originality, and sincerity—operate
covertly throughout many of her pieces for the *Analytical Review*, quietly but firmly revealing her to still be a friend of sensibility.[9] These values, in various combinations or singly, are often cited as the touchstones
of merit for authors, works, styles; their absence is grounds for her condemnation. And occasionally, but often enough to be unmistakable,
Wollstonecraft speaks in these reviews with the voice of sensibility.

The virtues of sensibility redeem, in Wollstonecraft's eyes, a number
of novelists whose productions otherwise might be discounted. Richardson's characters, she believes, are too good to be true, indeed
"scarcely resemble human creatures," but as they gradually open, "we
find them made up of mortal passions, and are affected by those delicate shades and tints which suddenly give a glimpse of the heart" (3
[January 1789]: 68). So, too, Defoe, despite his obvious offenses to the
"fastidious ear," Wollstonecraft defends energetically. She admires the
"simple force of diction," which suggests to her Defoe's "energy of
mind" and sincerity. Emphasized most in her praise, however, are
Defoe's capacities for feelings, for understanding feelings, and for
speaking to the feelings of his readers:

> He appears to be a man of quick feelings and strong discernment, who knew
> the human heart, and did not always view its frailties with a . . . patient coun-
> tenance. . . . his tale comes home to every human bosom . . . both young and
> old. A book, Dr Johnson would say, that is generally read, must have merit:
> and who has not heard of Robinson Crusoe? (8 [October 1790]: 188–89)

Charlotte Smith's "quick sensibility" as a poet of nature also wins Wollstonecraft's praise, though she generally does not like derivative Gothic romances. The more original Gothic novel by Matthew G. Lewis,
The Monk, however, receives warm praise from Wollstonecraft, despite
its contrived double plot and superfluous use of the supernatural, for
marking the "progress of passion" and inspiring sympathy (24 [Octo-
ber 1796]: 403). In the same number, Wollstonecraft nods her approval
to a German novel, *Albert de Nordenshild*, for its "warmth of imagination" and "truth of passion" (404).

The virtues of sensibility, it should be added, are not the only virtues
a work of art can have, according to Wollstonecraft. Other criteria for

excellence in novels, for example, include dramatic plots, probable and exemplary characters, and morally responsible themes like "domestic happiness," "the fatal effects of licentious love," or the "advantage of a good education." What emerges from an overview of her reviews, however, is her double conviction that the best books always endorse at least a few of the virtues of sensibility and that the worst ones—like false Prometheans—steal the language of sensibility to paper over their licentiousness. She abhors the masquerade much more than the lack. For this reason, the novel *Arundel*, for example, is roundly condemned: "Throughout, sensation is termed sensibility; and vice, or rather sensuality, varnished over with a gloss, which the author seems to think virtue" (3 [January 1789]: 69). So, more generally, are all novels written by "young misses" who are "without a knowledge of life, or the human heart": "After talking of the soul of sentiment — double-refined delicacy — how can they, without blushing, own that they have allowed the imaginations to revel in *sensual* love scenes?" (5 [December 1789]: 488). Or how can they pretend to " 'love the offender, yet detest the offence'? This is the varnish of sentiment to hide sensuality" (3 [1789]: 222).

Sensuality masquerading as sensibility is one of the most persistent themes in Wollstonecraft's negative reviews of sentimental fiction. She sees two ways in which the professors of sensibility can go wrong, but the second is the more reprehensible of the two: to be excessive is merely to be guilty of the Aristotelian error of immoderacy; to impersonate or pay lip service to sensibility, however, is to add to immoderacy the Christian fault of hypocrisy. Her terms for these faults are many: excessive sensibility is called "sickly," "romantic," "violent," "unrelieved," "pumped up," "absurd"; impersonated sensibility is called "masquerade," "varnish," "false refinement," "affectation," "fabrication," and "artificial"; and perfunctory sensibility is termed "insipid," or "cant." Altogether they call attention to her continuing valorization of sincerity and her growing sensitivity to style—one of the other recurrent themes of her reviews.[10] It is clear she believes what she had Sagestus urge in "Cave of Fancy": that style is to the written word what facial expression is to the spoken word—the last, best test of the speaker's genuineness, of the truth-value of the utterance.

Wollstonecraft consistently praises originality, simplicity, fervor, spontaneity, even carelessness, wherever she finds them; these, to her, are the signs of true sensibility speaking. An especially clear demonstration of this conviction occurs in her review of her friend Richard Price's controversial *A Discourse on the Love of Our Country*. She praises Price's "animated sentiments of ardent virtue," his "careless dignity," his "simple, unaffected, nay, even negligent style," and his "natural phrases," concluding, "the heart speaks to the heart in an unequivocal language, and the understanding, not bewildered by sophistical arguments, assents." This, she believes, is the language of "sincerity" (5 [December 1789]: 471–72). Wollstonecraft adopts such a style self-consciously in the preface to the *Rights of Woman*; in the *Analytical Review*, authors automatically raise or lower themselves in her estimation depending on how closely they approximate this ideal. Defoe's "simple force of diction" is favored over "studied graces, which may please the fastidious ear; but seldom reach the heart or inform the understanding" (8 [October 1790]: 188). Rousseau's unadorned style is held up as vastly superior to Lord Shaftesbury's "suspicious garb in his affected inflated periods": "His heart was unmoved whilst his head fabricated the lifeless rhapsody, which might be called a non-conductor, so little does it contain of that subtile fluid, which running along Rousseau's lines, finds the nearest way to the heart" (9 [February 1791]: 183).

Little irritates Wollstonecraft more than affectation in style (or in manners, for that matter): she finds it sufficient grounds for rejection of novels, but especially deplores it in education manuals. The "style," she says of the Reverend John Bennett's *Letters to a Young Lady*, "too much resembles the novels he has such a contempt for. Endeavouring to adapt himself to the capacity of females, he sometimes softens his tone into a whine: his friendly, and sometimes rational, precepts are interlarded with pretty periods and absurd epithets." She concludes: "The writer's acquaintance with the human heart seems very bounded, and his taste artificial" (6 [January 1790]: 105). She rejects *Sermons for Children* on similar grounds. She complains about its "disgusting air of affectation": "The tender epithets continually lavished on the *little* ones . . . appear to have no heart in them" (4 [June 1789]: 226).

Wollstonecraft's rejection of preciosity in style could be read as a sign of her kinship to romanticism, but it is also one of the first signs she gives in her writing of that impatience with restraints that will eventually erupt into feminist rebellion and a flagrant disregard for codes of dress, manners, and even, in rare cases, morality. What should be emphasized at this point is its intimate connection with sensibility: it is a rejection born of the perceived necessity to distinguish true sensibility from false, a task nonetheless urgent to her as reviewer because so difficult to perform. And that will be worth remembering later: even in her most caustic documents, even as Wollstonecraft works most furiously to cut through the mystique surrounding sensibility, she is doing so in a deliberately "careless" style she hopes will allow "heart to speak to heart." She will, for a time, rail at sensibility; but she will never succeed in completely rooting it out of her views on life and art.

For all her critical comments in the reviews, too, an increasingly self-conscious commitment to an aesthetic as well as an ethic of sensibility emerges. She still professes belief in its central myths: that people of great sensibility are frequently geniuses, and that people of the greatest sensibility are also people of the greatest virtue. Essentially untroubled in her convictions, Wollstonecraft also now and again speaks in what might be termed the voice of sensibility. It is, it should be added, one of a number of voices she experiments with in the *Analytical Review* behind the safety of her editorial mask—the "phalanx," as she once puts it mischievously, of the editorial "WE" (6 [April 1790]: 385). This voice first becomes audible in a positive review of the Reverend Samuel Stanhope's *Essay on the Causes of the Variety of Complexion and Figure in the Human Species*. She is possibly predisposed to approve of his study since she agrees with his central premise that environment alone produces variety within the human species. But the voice opening the review, like the voice in the review of *Werther*, is not so much a dispassionate commentator as a person of feeling: "An acquaintance with the human heart has ever been thought important and interesting; those who feel lively emotions wish to know if the same string vibrates in another bosom — if they are indeed tied to their species by the strongest of all relations, fellow-feeling — in short, if the world without resembles that within" (2 [December 1788]: 431).

If Wollstonecraft here acknowledges the centrality of fellow-feeling in human relationships, in other reviews she demonstrates her own capacity for it, shifting the editorial mask enough to allow the tone and values of sensibility to shine through. Two more striking examples occur in volume 6. Early in her review of Charles Burney's *General History of Music*, Wollstonecraft worries that his preference for harmony means he has become "like a mere musician, whose heart and tears were not connected, or to use the language of Rousseau, whose ears were *depraved* by harmony." She handles his history very gingerly in general, however, and she admits the reason for her care in the unmitigated language of sensibility. The fact that this history was so many years in the making, she notes, "spreads a gloomy kind of respectability around these ponderous volumes, something like the rust of time . . . and musing over the pages, which cost half a life — modesty and fellow-feeling whispered [to] us, 'touch lightly the labour of years, and respect experience'" (6 [February 1790]: 131).

Later that same year, she criticizes a scandal-mongering biographer for failing to treat his subjects with sufficient respect: "To hold up living characters to public contempt or derision — to look at the human heart with a microscopic eye, and dissect it, while warm with life it trembles under the knife of the inspector — is a cruel, unmanly exertion of talents" (6 [1790]: 578). Her reason for disapproval might be Swift's; she dislikes the personal nature of the exposé, much preferring it when "vices are lashed and individuals spared." The terms in which she expresses her dislike, however—her suspicion that the author is a "Mahometan" libertine, and her image of the trembling heart—identify her as a late-century friend of sensibility.

Wollstonecraft's reviews do not submit sensibility to the test of reason; rather they use reason—in the form of judgment—to distinguish true sensibility from false. They signal her growing suspicion that emancipating women from impossible heroic models may involve a reevaluation of the belief system of sensibility, but she does not yet break with that system. The irritation they evince is still the irritation of one of sensibility's believers.

6
Private and Public Revolutions:
Burke as Catalyst

sentimental varnish over vice.   —*Works*, 5.25

Wollstonecraft's spirited reply to Edmund Burke's *Reflections on the French Revolution, Rights of Men* (1790), attracts the attention of literary reviewers only after she is revealed as its author in the second edition of December 1790. Soon thereafter, they are "scolding away, advising her not to meddle in men's affairs." The *Gentleman's Magazine* finds it "ridiculous" that the rights of men should be asserted by a woman; the *Critical Review* offers "carping criticism—with a chivalrous apology for so addressing a woman." Other less conservative periodicals are more positive in their assessments but their emphases nevertheless suggest that they find the author's sex at least as interesting as her text. The *Analytical Review* (not surprisingly) praises the *Rights of Men* fulsomely, for example, but cannot resist imagining the "chivalrous" Burke's "annoyance at finding his adversary a woman."[1]

Their initial inattention may be excused, however, since Wollstonecraft's treatise represents, from their perspective, just one more entry in the ongoing pamphlet war between proponents and opponents of the revolution underway in France. Sparked the year before by Richard Price's sermon *A Discourse on the Love of Our Country* delivered in commemoration of England's Glorious Revolution of 1688, and in tribute to the revolutionary spirit of the new French National Assembly, the controversy is brought to nearly everyone's attention by Burke's impassioned counterstatement to the Price sermon in 1790. Burke deplores developments in Paris and defends the institutions of monarchy, inherited wealth, and organized religion that he sees being dismantled across the channel. Burke's reply is Wollstonecraft's prompt to enter the fray; and she enters the male sanctuary of politics with éclat, sporting a new bold style so "masculine" that it has won her the reputation among some modern feminists of a male ventriloquist.[2]

Modern students of Wollstonecraft find it difficult to explain her metamorphosis in 1790 from a reflective writer of women's fiction and education treatises to a bold, polemical critic of one of the dominant political figures of her day. In sharp contradistinction to the gentle, "die-away" tones that close the novel *Mary*, or the impartial to lightly ironic tones Wollstonecraft cultivates as a reviewer, her voice in this book is strident and self-confident. Gone is her former celebration of the quiet, self-effacing attitudes of piety, patience, self-denial, and resignation. She now speaks passionately for the radical reforms implemented by the new French National Assembly and just as passionately against Burke's sentimental defense of the Old Régime. Some critics find sufficient reason for the transformation in her new infatuation with the Swiss radical Henry Fuseli;[3] some in her new found admiration for Catherine Macaulay Graham or her longer standing reverence for her friend Richard Price;[4] and some in her galvanization by the French Revolution in the year before.[5]

Her choice of subject matter and her critical stance are undeniably brash, yet the abruptness of Wollstonecraft's transition has been exaggerated. From the beginning of her literary career, she is something of a critic of the status quo. All of her earlier publications include satiric asides, some epigrammatically short, some much longer, on a wide variety of topics. Even in her first, most sentimental novel, she criticizes repressive traditions or customs from arranged marriage to the Roman Catholic clerical system, a stance perfectly in keeping with the counter-cultural bias of the more politically conscious proponents of sensibility.[6] In this sense, her *Rights of Men* can be seen as the natural outgrowth of previous literary activities as sentimental novelist, periodical reviewer, and expert on female education. Her first vindication is essentially an extended, if far from dispassionate, review of Burke's book;[7] beyond that, it returns to a subject of long-standing interest to her: the fictions, uses, and abuses of sensibility. All continuities notwithstanding, however, its "searing"[8] two-pronged attack on sensibility and on Burke himself, the latter very personal, is startlingly uncharacteristic. The incidental satire of *Mary* or the *Analytical* reviews is as far removed in tone and intent from the sustained invective of the *Rights of Men* as Johnson's *Rasselas* and *Rambler* are from Pope's *Dunciad*.

In her opening pages she protests to Burke that she cannot wait to publish her work "till time has wiped away the compassionate tears which you have elaborately laboured to excite," adding, by way of explanation, that sensibility, "the *manie* of the day"[9] (her emphasis), is now treated as a substitute for any other virtue, and its closest psychological associate, compassion, is now aroused "to cover a multitude of vices, whilst justice is left to mourn in sullen silence, and balance truth in vain." In the next breath, she uses sensibility to fault his style: "All your pretty flights arise from your pampered sensibility" (*Works*, 5.7–9). Even more disconcerting than Wollstonecraft's criticism of sensibility, which sometimes carries her so far that she must repudiate long-held beliefs, is her venomous attack on Burke. Her ad hominem arguments weld the loosely organized "Letter" together. She accuses him of antireason ("you have a mortal antipathy to reason") and unreason ("teeming fancy"), of insincerity and hypocrisy, of "rusty, baneful opinions" and Machiavellian politics, of callousness to the plight of the poor ("you seem to consider the poor as only the live stock of an estate") and blind "veneration for rank and riches," of vanity and envy of moral superiors like Dr. Price:[10]

> In reprobating Dr Price's opinions you might have spared the man; and if you had had but half as much reverence for the grey hairs of virtue as for the accidental distinctions of rank, you would not have treated with such indecent familiarity and supercilious contempt, a member of the community whose talents and modest virtues place him high in the scale of moral excellence. I am not accustomed to look up with vulgar awe, even when mental superiority exalts a man above his fellows; but still the sight of a man whose habits are fixed by piety and reason, and whose virtues are consolidated into goodness, commands my homage — and I should touch his errors with a tender hand when I made a parade of my sensibility. (*Works*, 5.18)

Her condemnation of Burke's treatise is equally excoriating: she dismisses his politics, his ethics, and his aesthetics and mocks his style, his structure, and his theoretical assumptions. One moment his "reflections" are compared to those of a Scriblerian dunce ("you foster every emotion till the fumes, mounting to your brain, dispel the sober suggestions of reason"), the next to those of a reactionary Papist or a vain Jean-Jacques Rousseau:[11]

> There appears to be such a mixture of real sensibility and fondly cherished romance in your composition, that the present crisis carries you out of yourself; and since you could not be one of the grand movers, the next *best* thing that dazzled your imagination was to be a conspicuous opposer. Full of yourself, you make as much noise to convince the world that you despise the revolution, as Rousseau did to persuade his contemporaries to let him live in obscurity. (*Works*, 5.44; her emphasis)

If it is hard to believe Elissa Guralnick's claim that these attacks are simply part of a rhetorical strategy to seduce readers into the realm of political controversy,[12] it is equally hard to resist the conjecture that

Wollstonecraft is genuinely angry as she writes her reply. Her words seem to boil over onto the page, everywhere perilously close to transgressive—occasionally even scatological—sarcasm:

> I shall not attempt to follow you through "horse-way and foot-path;" but, attacking the foundation of your opinions, I shall leave the superstructure to find a centre of gravity on which it may lean till some strong blast puffs it into the air; or your teeming fancy, which the ripening judgment of sixty years has not tamed, produces another Chinese erection, to stare, at every turn, the plain country people in the face, who bluntly call such an airy edifice — a folly. (*Works*, 5.9)

What could adequately account for such a level of fury? The usually proffered explanations—new democratic politics, new friends, old friends—hardly seem sufficient causes in themselves to catch her on fire. The grievances against Burke she airs most frequently in *Rights of Men*, and the ones at the heart of her argument, are quite probably at the heart of her anger as well: his choice of language and his presumed sexual politics. She repeatedly returns, with agitation, to what she believes is Burke's misuse of the language of sentiment. She accuses him of usurping it for his own reactionary purposes, of redefining and misappropriating it in the defense of a feudal tyranny that can only arrest the social progress of women. In his *Reflections*, Burke has clearly stung both the habitual woman of sensibility and the emergent feminist in Wollstonecraft.

Through her close reading of Burke's *Reflections*, Wollstonecraft seems to realize fully for the first time that the notions some men attach to sensibility may hold disastrous consequences for women's educational opportunities. Burke's hysteria over the beautiful, endangered queen of France, Marie Antoinette, reminds Wollstonecraft that he equates women and physical beauty both in the *Reflections* and in his earlier treatise on the sublime; and in that equation he implicitly defines women as smooth and fair, but also as sensitive, delicate, little, and weak (*Works*, 5.45). In addition, she is keenly aware of the frequency with which Burke lapses into the language of sentiment—in her words, makes a "parade" of his "sensibility"—when talking of things feminine.[13] What suddenly seems to appall Wollstonecraft is the possibility that Burke's aesthetic together with his sentimental rhetoric will deprive both women and sensibility of any access to virtue and piety and make them mere accessories to libertinism. By convincing women that their supreme duty in life is to be beautiful in order to please men, he might just transform the ethics of feeling into an apology for sensuality. In essence, she charges Burke, he seeks to reduce women to toys, to seduce them into believing that one half of the human species, at least, have not souls; and that Nature, by making women *little, smooth, delicate, fair* creatures, never designed that they should exercise their reason to acquire the virtues that produce opposite, if not contradictory, feelings. The affection they excite, to be uniform and perfect, should not be tinctured with the respect which moral virtues inspire, lest pain should be blended with pleasure, and admiration disturb the soft intimacy of love. This laxity of morals in the female world is certainly more captivating to a libertine imagination than the cold arguments of reason, that give no sex to virtue. (*Works*, 5.45–46)

In this passage, Wollstonecraft betrays profound feelings of exclusion, injustice, and disillusionment as a woman reader of Burke. Like other women writers of her day, she tends to emphasize the intellectual and the emotional facets of sensibility, while contemporary men writers stress the physical and the erotic.[14] She treats sensibility in all of her earlier writings primarily as a psychological entity, yet she also draws on the lexicon of sensibility quite freely and finds Burke's (and Rousseau's) ideal of fragile beauty, at least to some extent, appealing as a metonymic sign of the presence of extraordinary sensitivity, virtue, or intelligence. True, she satirizes the heroine's enervated mother in *Mary* for her "false sensibility"—a combination of irascibility, misplaced tenderness, stupidity, and physical delicacy—but the heroine's friend Ann corresponds rather closely to the Burkean ideal, as does the heroine herself. More important, Wollstonecraft frequently characterizes herself in her private correspondence in Burkean terms: physically and emotionally delicate, weak, and eager to please. Some of Wollstonecraft's anger in this treatise may well stem from the sudden clarity with which she sees the logical consequences of adhering to Burke's feminine ideal. Perhaps she feels herself suddenly denigrated, deprived of soul. Whatever her posthumous critics claim of her, she certainly never aspires to inflame "the libertine imagination."

A second source of disillusionment may well be the wedge Wollstonecraft sees Burke driving between men and women, quite closely related to the wedge he drives between women and strength of mind and body. For a brief, heady moment midcentury, when the ethics of sensibility is newly articulated, women think they see the possibility of new commonalities between men and themselves: the ethics celebrates tenderness, empathy, and benevolence; the aesthetics the natural, the spontaneous; the psychology, sensitivity—surely these inclinations could be shared by men and women, suggesting new possibilities in male-female relationships. What these women writers hope for, as J. M. S. Tompkins puts it, from the "cult of sensibility," is "some measure of approximation in the ethical ideals and emotional sensitiveness of the two sexes."[15]

Wollstonecraft's *Mary* reveals—through her ideal man and woman of feeling, Mary and Henry—that she, too, harbors hopes at the beginning of her career of a new era in relations between the sexes. Her earliest treatise on education, even though ostensibly focusing on the "education of daughters," offers an essentially gender-blind picture of the young child's mind; and it never occurs to her to suggest, there or elsewhere, that women cannot attain virtue and piety because those acquisitions arc "manly," or that men cannot aspire to tenderness, sensibility, compassion, or benevolence because those qualities are "feminine." That would be, in effect, an abrogation of her faith in the magical, reconciling power of sensibility. Something in Burke's *Reflections*, however, seems to convince Wollstonecraft of the naïve folly of her earlier hopes. Her vision of Burke's aesthetic places men and women in separate spheres, in which men have access to virtue but women only to beauty, and in which men's interest in women is solely in their beauty, so that, as a result, women's access to men is solely through the cultivation of that beauty. Burke has turned the sensibility that she has always hoped can become a bridge between men and women into a medieval wall to surround and contain women. That, with such attitudes, Burke chooses to style himself a man of feeling Wollstonecraft clearly finds outrageous.

Burke commits the final outrage, in Wollstonecraft's eyes, of pressing the language of sensibility into the defense of an antiquated, corrupt, and oppressive political structure: "Your tears are reserved," she charges him early in her essay, "very *naturally* considering your character, for the declamation of the theatre, or for the downfall of queens, whose rank alters the nature of folly, and throws a graceful veil over vices that degrade humanity" (*Works*, 5.15). Just in case the queen's rank does not veil her vice sufficiently, Burke's sentimental rhetoric works to complete the cover: "Surely, they indirectly aim at destroying all purity of morals, who poison the very source of virtue, by smearing a sentimental varnish over vice, to hide its natural deformity" (*Works*, 5.25). On other occasions, his rhetoric aims to divert his attention and that of his readers from the deplorable distress of the poor, usually perpetrated by the injustices of the rich: "Your respect for rank has swallowed up the common feelings of humanity" (*Works*, 5.17). Her peroration—quite a piece of sentimental rhetoric itself—summarizes eloquently her charge against Burke on the subject of pressing sensibility into the service of despotism:

> Man preys on man; and you mourn for the idle tapestry that decorated a
> gothic pile, and the dronish bell that summoned the fat priest to prayer.
> You mourn for the empty pageant of a name, when slavery flaps her wing,

and the sick heart retires to die in lonely wilds, far from the abodes of
men. . . . Such misery demands more than tears — I pause to recollect
myself; and smother the contempt I feel rising for your rhetorical flourishes and infantine sensibility. (*Works*, 5.58)

Disclaimers Wollstonecraft uses, even in these moments of "contempt,"
enable her to target the "infantine" perversion of sensibility rather than
sensibility itself, the poisoning "of the very source of virtue," its misuse as rhetorical "varnish." Here as elsewhere, she leaves herself some
maneuvering room to hold onto her faith in the ethics of sensibility.

Maneuvers notwithstanding, Burke's attack on the French Revolution serves as an unwelcome catalyst in Wollstonecraft's intellectual
life: it takes her largely untested faith in sensibility by surprise and
forces her to sift its contradictory values and truth-claims in order to
decide which, if any, she can reaffirm and which she should reject or
deny. Her first impulse is to run for moderate ground and insist, as she
has often before, that sensibility is neither an end in itself nor a sole
means to the desired end of happy, well-educated, and virtuous maturity. It wants the guidance of both reason and morals; indeed, she
claims here, "without fixed principles even goodness of heart is no
security from inconsistency, and mild affectionate sensibility only renders a man more ingeniously cruel . . ." (*Works*, 5.44 – 45).

Despite her bravado, however, in the heat of her argument with Burke
Wollstonecraft sacrifices two of the fictions of sensibility she has most
often lived by and written by: first, the notion that sensibility promotes
intellectual growth in the form of knowledge, wisdom, even genius;
second, the notion that it nurtures virtue. The first underlies all her
early fictions of sensibility but finds perhaps its best articulation in the
"Cave of Fancy," in which persons gifted with keen or "exquisite" sensibility acquire instant knowledge directly from their senses: "Acute
senses, finely fashioned nerves . . . vibrate at the slightest touch, and
convey such clear intelligence to the brain, that it does not require to
be arranged by the judgment. Such persons instantly enter into the
characters of others, and instinctively discern what will give pain"
(*Works*, 1.3.201). Not all persons, of course, are equally endowed with
this special affective cognition, but those who are, are destined to
genius: "The genius that sprouts from a dunghil [*sic*] soon shakes off
the heterogenous mass; those only grovel, who have not power to fly"
(*Works*, 1.2.196).

By the middle of her letter, Wollstonecraft has raised a number of
relatively well-reasoned points in refutation of Burke as she riffles
through his pages: the barbarism of the "real" (Hume's) Middle Ages;
Burke's unaccountable about-face in supporting the American Revo-

lution, then rejecting the French, or in pleading for the monarchs of France, after failing to support either king or queen of England; the utter inappropriateness of his attack on Dr. Price; and the many injustices perpetrated by parents on children in the name of property. Suddenly her progress through his treatise is arrested as she comes face to face with the "empty rhetorical flourishes" in his description of the night that the Parisian mob evicts Louis and Marie from their palace. She feels compelled to cite it (" 'Whilst the royal captives, who followed in the train, were slowly moved along, amidst the horrid yells, and shrilling screams, and frantic dances, and infamous contumelies, and all the unutterable abominations of the furies of hell, in the abused shape of the vilest of women'"), then interrogate its ambiguities ("Probably you mean women who gained a livelihood by selling vegetables or fish, who never had had any advantages of education"), then correct its selective compassion ("the great and small . . . claim our pity"). Finally, apparently thoroughly irritated, she turns her anger on Burke's frequent use of "sentimental jargon," probably not aware that her attack on him will endanger her own belief system:

> Throughout your letter you frequently advert to a sentimental jargon, which has long been current in conversation, and even in books of morals, though it never received the *regal* stamp of reason. A kind of mysterious instinct is *supposed* to reside in the soul, that instantaneously discerns truth, without the tedious labour of ratiocination. This instinct, for I know not what other name to give it, has been termed *common sense*, and more frequently *sensibility*; and, by a kind of *indefeasible* right, it has been *supposed*, for rights of this kind are not easily proved, to reign paramount over the other faculties of the mind, and to be an authority from which there is no appeal.
>
> This subtle magnetic fluid, that runs round the whole circle of society, is not subject to any known rule. . . .
>
> It is to this instinct, without doubt, that you allude, when you talk of the "moral constitution of the heart." To it, I allow, for I consider it as a congregate of sensations and passions, *Poets* must apply, "who have to deal with an audience not yet graduated in the school of the rights of men." They must, it is clear, often cloud the understanding, whilst they move the heart by a kind of mechanical spring; but that "in the theatre the first intuitive glance"[16] of feeling should discriminate the form of truth, and see her fair proportion, I must beg leave to doubt. (*Works*, 5.30 –31)

This passage marks a watershed moment in the evolution of Wollstonecraft's thinking on sensibility. In her efforts to repudiate Burke's appropriation of sentiment for his own reactionary ends, she has actually transformed sensibility from a cognitive-emotive capacity into an emotive-sensory one, and the language she uses suggests that her new faith in reason and revolution compels her to do so. As a subscriber to the importance of "*regal* . . . reason" in improving both individuals and nations, she can no longer pretend that heightened consciousness depends on an inborn "instinct" with "mysterious," even mystical powers, "a kind of instinct," as she defines it in *Education of Daughters*, "strengthened by reflection" (*Works*, 4.36). Nor can she any longer recommend that any human activity, with the possible exception of poetry, should be exempt from reason's restless spirit of inquiry: "In ceasing to enquire," she notes in her defense of Price, "our reason would remain dormant, and delivered up, without a curb, to every impulse of passion. . . . Perhaps the most improving exercise of the mind, confining the argument to the enlargement of the understanding, is the restless enquiries that hover on the boundary, or stretch over the dark abyss of uncertainty" (*Works*, 5.19–20).

Useful as it can be in the hands of poets in leading the uneducated masses to the truth, she concludes, sensibility is neither an automatic shortcut to truth nor an unassailable authority. These claims, she avers, she "must beg leave to doubt," as she does a second tenet she once held to: that virtue, like truth, comes unaided and unbidden to persons of great sensibility ("Softened by tenderness; the soul is disposed to be virtuous," *Mary*, *Works*, 1.24.59). In the *Rights of Men* Wollstonecraft finds herself insisting, as a convert to the desirability of social reform, that virtue, like truth, must be equally accessible to all reasonable people and "not the blind impulse of unerring instinct." It must be teachable, "an acquisition of the individual," and people must be improvable, perfectible, not propelled by "a kind of mechanical spring." "Bastard vice," she adds to push the point, "has often been begotten by the same father [instinct]" (*Works*, 5.31).

If sacrifices of long-held beliefs shake Wollstonecraft's faith in sensibility during her debate with Burke, certain ambiguities dormant in the notion of sensibility also surface at this point to alienate her further from it. Three such ambiguities will haunt Wollstonecraft until the end of her career, entangling her in many a creative evasion. "What is *homo sentimentalus* at his or her best?" she seems compelled to ask herself repeatedly. Private benefactor or public activist? Liberated or restrained? Sentimental or sensual?

"To endeavour to make unhappy men resigned to their fate," Wollstonecraft insists near the end of her argument with Burke, "is the tender endeavour of short-sighted benevolence, of transient yearnings of humanity; but to labour to increase human happiness by extirpating error, is a masculine godlike affection" (*Works*, 5.53). With these words she clarifies a shortcoming in the ethics of sensibility to which she has hitherto only registered vague discontent: its uneasy alliance with sta-

tus quo politics, and its corresponding emphasis on individual reformation rather than system reform.

The distinguishing feature of most characters and persons of sensibility throughout the century is their capacity for a kind of apolitical
sympathy called "fellow-feeling," their ability to "instantly enter into
the characters of others, and instinctively discern what will give pain
to every human being" ("Cave of Fancy," *Works*, 1.3.201). Although
they engage in private charity, they rarely think of altering the political and socioeconomic systems that make such charity necessary. They
may, of course, and often do indulge in a degree of personal rebellion
by refusing to honor unjust laws or customs, or to adhere to problematic values. But sensibility is understood primarily, especially in England, as an ethic of interiority, of attitude adjustment rather than action;
and the literature of sensibility remains essentially a literature of
retirement, of acquiescence, of non-engagement.

Wollstonecraft's early letters make it sufficiently clear that she
understands this stance and, at least at first, approves of it. Her "res-
cue" of her sister Eliza, for example, represents a courageous act that
impels her to risk personal reputation to alleviate suffering, but without publicly challenging the legal system that allows such suffering to
take place and even condones it. Her first heroine Mary, too, engages
in such activities, *quietly* rebelling against the conventional role of wife
to serve her friends and help the poor, but without ever challenging
head-on the myriad social practices (to name a few, abuses of patriarchal authority, arranged marriages, the grand tour, the exclusion of
women from the intellectual and public spheres, the interdict on divorce)
that entrap her.

Just audible, in these early years, are Wollstonecraft's murmurs of
discontent about the ephemeral nature of acts of private charity. She can
see that sympathy and charity do not solve major problems, but only
offer temporary relief from the symptoms of those problems. One
woman's face in the "Cave of Fancy," for example, is said to exhibit
"compassion that wanted activity"; it is "sincere, though it only embel-
lished her face, or produced casual acts of charity when a moderate alms
could relieve present distress" (*Works*, 1.2.197). The heroine Mary wonders more than once how best to "exercise" her "faculties" (*Works*,
1.22.54); and she weeps helplessly, on her return to London, for "a world
in ruins" before turning to the aid of individual sufferers. Only in the
Rights of Men, however, does Wollstonecraft clearly align herself with
a new activist ethic, to insist that the best form sympathy can take is
social reform to promote increased good for the greatest possible number. "We ought," she concludes, "to beware of confounding mechanical
instinctive sensations with emotions that reason deepens, and justly

terms the feelings of *humanity*. This word discriminates the active exertions of virtue from the vague declamation of sensibility" (*Works*, 5.53).

It is, in fact, the "vague declamation of sensibility" that entangles Wollstonecraft in a second ambiguity, this one having to do with the psychological rather than the social impact of cultivating sensibility. The early Wollstonecraft trusts its language implicitly and finds it liberating: it enables her to feel as well as think, to articulate those feelings and thoughts, and also to distinguish herself from other people of lesser feelings. Wollstonecraft's reading of Burke, however, casts doubt on both the trustworthiness and the safety of that language.

To its claim to authority, she acknowledges ruefully in *Rights of Men*, "there is no appeal," as it is "not subject to any known rule." Twentieth-century historians of philosophy have corroborated her observation: the notion of sensibility lacks any objective criterion for its truth claims and its assertions of excellence; for an objective standard it substitutes a "faculty."[17] Unfortunately, this also renders its language readily adaptable to various rhetorical purposes, and any or all sides of a given vexed question. Wollstonecraft's attack on Burke's sentimental presentation of Marie Antoinette in the first *Vindication* makes very evident her fear that women will be especially endangered by Burke's language of vague, stereotyped superlatives, since they are used to being guided unthinkingly by the arbitrary directives of others: "Ladies may have read your enquiry concerning the origin of our ideas of the Sublime and Beautiful," Wollstonecraft worries, almost foreseeing her culture's later problems with anorexia, "and, convinced by your arguments, may have laboured to be pretty, by counterfeiting weakness" (*Works*, 5.45). If the practical effect of the language of sensibility is to reduce women to intellectual, emotional, or physical infantilism, then Wollstonecraft wants nothing to do with it.

Finally, in the *Rights of Men* Wollstonecraft is forced to confront the essential dualism of the term "sensibility." Does it denote, in the first place, a condition of mind or of body? Although by the late eighteenth century, its dominant meanings are cognitive ("consciousness") or emotive ("tender or fine feelings"), and these are the ones the early Wollstonecraft prefers, "sensibility" is derived from the word "sense" (Latin *sentire*), a word that first denotes physical feelings or faculties of feeling.

Of all the eighteenth-century writers associated with sensibility, Sterne understands best the essential ambiguity of the term; Tristram's and Yorick's opinions hover on the boundary between the cognitive-emotive and sensual frequently, insisting on the one but persistently implying, and revelling in, the other. Wollstonecraft sees the recurring connection between sensibility and sensuality just as readily as Sterne, but, as her hostile reaction to Burke's sensationist aesthetic reveals, it troubles her greatly. She tends to view physicality not as a latent implication of the metaphor "sensibility," but as a male corruption of it;[18] her position is probably most succinctly stated in the fragment "On Poetry": "The same sensibility, or quickness of senses, which makes a man relish the tranquil scenes of nature, when sensation, rather than reason, imparts delight, frequently makes a libertine of him," with the inference, "The most valuable things are liable to the greatest perversion" (*Works*, 7.11). While she sees the sense in sensibility, in other words, she prefers to deny it, to dismiss it, as she does in her first *Vindication*, as masculine sensuality, and to insist, instead, on the ways that sensibility enhances psychic self-realization.

As if she senses how much she has sacrificed of her former faith in this encounter with Burke, Wollstonecraft pays a warm, farewell tribute to "the feelings of the heart" in *Rights of Men* in metaphoric hyperboles borrowed from the religious realm, restating her conviction that feelings are an indispensable part of the complete and balanced psyche: "Sacred be the feelings of the heart! concentred in a glowing flame, they become the sun of life; and, without his invigorating impregnation, reason would probably lie in helpless inactivity, and never bring forth her only legitimate offspring — virtue" (*Works*, 5.31). Here, in a daring inversion of Burke's feminization of sensibility, she makes the feelings masculine and reason feminine. For her the feelings become the impregnating or dynamic principle in the mind, its prime mover, while reason plays the maternal role of bearer and nurturer of the virtue begotten of sensibility. Her metaphor allows her to embrace both reason and the feelings: she can assume that "feminine" reason is her own, and she can, at the same time, aspire to "manly" sensibility, an aspiration that comes naturally to her. It also allows her to erase from her mind, if momentarily, Burke's banishment of sensibility to his own constrictive feminine ideal, and to tweak his ear, as she does so often in this essay, with the sound of his own words but with the message scrambled to suit herself.

By now Wollstonecraft is definitely of two minds about sensibility,[19] an ambivalence she will feel, at least occasionally, for the rest of her life. In the *Rights of Men* she turns her own spirit of "restless enquiry" against it and debunks many of the notions attached to it that she has previously held sacred. Ironically enough, as her critics frequently remark, she is unable or unwilling to renounce the language of sensibility herself for value articulation, or to argue against Burke's rhetoric of sentiment without resorting to a similar rhetoric herself.[20] Did the end seem to her to justify the means?

A number of emancipatory rhetorical strategies have recently been discovered at work in *Rights of Woman*, all designed to break the silence that Rousseau's *Émile* imposes on women readers, to gain equality with Rousseau, even superiority over him, by engaging him in textual dialogue, putting his name and words "in circulation" in a woman's text.[21] Evidence suggests that Wollstonecraft first practices these strategies on Burke in *Rights of Men*: she catches him by surprise, for example, by troping reason as feminine and feeling as masculine; she appropriates his language, then recontextualizes it to lay bare its biases; she challenges, reformulates, and interrogates his ideas at every turn; she renders him guilty, indirectly, by analogy; she interrupts him, lectures him, frequently silences him by refusing to cite him, ultimately reducing him to the mute inferior he wishes woman to be. On this strategic level, *Rights of Men* can certainly be said to succeed, even if, as an even-handed, neatly organized review of Burke's *Reflections*, it fails.[22]

Actually, Wollstonecraft's two vindications have much in common, not only in rhetorical strategies, militant tone, and title, but also in substance, as a comparison of satiric targets and espoused ideals easily reveals. In both treatises, she deplores deference to "rusty, baneful opinions" (5.9; cf. "moss-covered opinions," *Rights of Woman*, 5.5.182); blind reverence for the "rust of antiquity," either traditions or institutions (5.10; cf. *Rights of Woman*, 5.1.84), or inherited wealth (5.10 –11; cf. *Rights of Woman*, 5.1.82 and chap. 11); men's misuse of the languages of sensibility to seduce women into postures of weakness or submission (5.45– 48; cf. *Rights of Woman*, chap. 5); and the insistence on separate sexual virtues as well as separate spheres for men and women (5.45– 46):

> I wish to sum up what I have said in a few words, for I here throw down my gauntlet, and deny the existence of sexual virtues, not excepting modesty. For man and woman, truth, if I understand the meaning of the word, must be the same; yet [for] the fanciful female character, so prettily drawn by poets and novelists, demanding the sacrifice of truth and sincerity, virtue becomes a relative idea, having no other foundation than utility, and of that utility men pretend arbitrarily to judge, shaping it to their own convenience. (*Rights of Woman, Works*, 5.3.120)

In both treatises she advocates Locke's ideas of knowledge acquisition, education, and liberty (5.9; cf. *Rights of Woman*, 5.1.81); the integration and cooperation of head and heart in the mature, thinking individual (5.8; cf. *Rights of Woman*, 5.4.135); and the crucial importance of education—and for women, education reform—to the future health and welfare of the nation (5.11; cf. *Rights of Woman*, 5.2.105). As a logical consequence of her notions of virtue and education, she advocates early coeducation: "Were boys and girls permitted to pursue the same studies together, those graceful decencies might early be inculcated which produce modesty without those sexual distinctions that taint the mind" (5.12.237).

Even a bare list of chapter titles in the *Rights of Woman* reveals to what extent it represents a culmination of Wollstonecraft's thought to 1792; but more particularly, a continuation of her recently declared war on men, their language, and their institutions—all of which she considers responsible for the current "state of degradation to which woman is reduced" (chap. 4). The title of chapter 1 recalls Wollstonecraft's firm theoretical grounding in the epistemology and political theory of Locke ("The rights and involved duties of mankind considered"); chapter titles 2 and 3 recall her struggle with men over the right to redefine the feminine ideal ("The prevailing opinion of a sexual character discussed"; "The same subject considered"); the title of chapter 5 returns to her anger, first leveled at Burke, at the theoretical exclusion of women from a life of reason or virtue by many leading male authors ("Animadversions on some of the writers who have rendered women objects of pity, bordering on contempt"); chapter titles 6 and 12 reiterate her determination to argue for expanded educational opportunities for women ("The effect which an early association of ideas has upon character"; "On national education"); chapter titles 7 and 8 promise discussion of virtue as a gender-neutral ideal ("Modesty—Comprehensively considered, and not as a sexual virtue"; "Morality undermined by sexual notions of the importance of a good reputation"). Altogether these show that the "rights of woman" that Wollstonecraft so vigorously defends are modest by twentieth-century standards (not that, even yet, all her aims have been fully realized). They do not include "equality" (see her introduction to *Rights of Woman* 5.74 for her disclaimer on this subject); and they most certainly do not include equality before the law or equal economic opportunity. They are, quite simply, the rights to enough liberty to "unfold the faculties" (5.74); that is, to gain sufficient knowledge to develop virtue and understanding in order to become reasonable, as well as loving, daughters, sisters, wives, and mothers:

> The education of women has, of late, been more attended to than formerly; yet they are still reckoned a frivolous sex, and ridiculed or pitied by the writers who endeavour by satire or instruction to improve them. It is acknowledged that they spend many of the first years of their lives in acquiring a smattering of accomplishments; meanwhile strength of body and mind are

sacrified to libertine notions of beauty, to the desire of establishing themselves, — the only way women can rise in the world, — by marriage. And
this desire making mere animals of them, when they marry they act as such
children may be expected to act: — they dress; they paint, and nickname
God's creatures. — Surely these weak beings are only fit for a seraglio! Can
they be expected to govern a family with judgment, or take care of the poor
babes whom they bring into the world? (*Works*, 5.76)

Some of these ideas are with Wollstonecraft from the beginning of her
career; others, however, are either born or radicalized by the French
Revolution and the controversies it inspired: her new understanding of
sensibility and the negative power of its language; her new conviction
that whatever progress the world is witnessing in the age of revolutions,
women are losing ground at home; her new, profound disillusionment
with many of the members of the male literary community she once
admired; and her accompanying sense of urgency about the need to
redefine woman and reform her education—all these are clarified during her literary struggle with Burke.

Needless to say, then, although the *Rights of Men* receives relatively
little critical attention, as an episode in Wollstonecraft's continuing
struggle with the language of sensibility it is invaluable. It yields up
glimpses of past, present, and future concerns: the panegyric to "feelings" cited above is the last to appear in her works for a half-dozen
years; the scolding of Burke for his misuse of sensibility, on the other
hand, is a preview of the angry criticism of Rousseau and others to be
found in her next *Vindication*. All in all, *Rights of Men* dramatizes a
woman in transition, struggling to reconcile her own convictions with
those of a rapidly changing world, and to steer clear of certain shortcomings and ideological ambiguities in the notion of sensibility that the
French Revolution on the one hand, and anti-Jacobins like Burke on the
other, make her doubly, and acutely, aware of.

7

The Rights of Woman and
the Wrongs of Sensibility

> Few men have risen to any great eminence in learning, who
> have not received something like a regular education. Why
> are women expected to surmount difficulties that men are
> not equal to?   —"Hints" (*Works*, 5.271)

Wollstonecraft criticism often leaves the impression that Wollstonecraft's *Rights of Woman* (1792) is famous in spite of itself: that it is rambling, unclear, repetitive, and torn apart by its contradictions,[1] chief
among them, its incompatible "noisy rationalism" and passionate outbursts; "the reader," laments a sympathetic Wardle, "is left breathless
and bewildered."[2] Actually, *Rights of Woman* is far from an inchoate
document. In essence, it is an extended problem-solution essay: it presents a difficulty, ferrets out its causes, and muses over its effects, then
proposes a series of solutions. The problem, stated succinctly in the
introduction, then illustrated in chapter 4, is the current "state of degradation to which woman is reduced." Wollstonecraft believes, even
though the world may be progressing, that women have actually declined
physically, mentally, and spiritually; this has provoked in her "the most
melancholy emotions of sorrowful indignation" and impelled her to
pick up her pen. Her ultimate aim in doing so goes beyond pure analysis: she would like to persuade her contemporaries, men and women
(she specifically addresses both genders in her introduction), to initiate reforms necessary to remedy this deplorable state of affairs (introduction to *Rights of Woman, Works,* 5.73–75).

The causes, laid out in chapters 2 through 9, fall into three categories:
education, other institutions, and opinions. Wollstonecraft believes that
education fails women by its neglect as well as its aims. In chapter 1 she
identifies the acquisition of "reason, virtue, and knowledge" in order to

achieve "the perfection of our nature and capability of happiness" chief among "the rights and duties of man" (*Works*, 5.81); but in chapter 4 she must admit that all of these rights have thus far been denied to the majority of women. She begins with the chapter's central assumption: "The stamen of immortality . . . is the perfectibility of human reason . . . Yet outwardly ornamented with elaborate care, and so adorned to delight man, 'that with honour he may love' [this from Milton], the soul of woman is not allowed to have this distinction, and man, ever placed between her and reason, she is always represented as only created to see through a gross medium, and to take things on trust" (*Works*, 5.4.122).

"Civil" and "political" institutions are in the second category of causes: the public boarding school, limited occupations for women, the marriage market, the class system, and limited representational government. These institutions, essentially carrying on what women's education begins, tend to delimit a woman's opportunities still more: they narrow her focus to the domestic sphere, which does not challenge her to unfold her higher faculties. In the third category of causes— most remote but for Wollstonecraft nevertheless most powerful—are the antiquated opinions that help to shape an intolerable (she calls it, at various times, Chinese, "Mahometan," and Egyptian) feminine ideal.

The kind of woman created by these forces, Wollstonecraft argues, adversely affects not only her own personal health and well-being but that of her family and even her nation. She is fickle, selfish, superficial, inept (chapter 4), superstitious, sentimental, materialistic, and ignorant (chapter 13). She frequently drives her husband to prostitutes and burdens the society with ill-disciplined, poorly educated children. To change this "deplorable" state, people must, Wollstonecraft concludes in chapters 10 to 13, eradicate the causes: change the aims of female education; reform the social and political institutions that oppress them; and, most important, change "moss-covered opinions."

There is without question a highly analytical mind at work structuring the argument in *Rights of Woman*. But there is also another recursive structure at work within each of the chapters of the treatise, one more reminiscent of a mystery novel, in which Wollstonecraft, as both chief investigator ("vindicator") and victim ("woman"), is continually forced to return to the scene of a crime because it is both unresolved and ongoing, a kind of serial crime: the denial of women's rights. What is worse, the culprit is known, like Holmes's antagonist Moriarty, to be an old and elusive enemy; and his accessory is a long-time friend of the victim. The culprit is man; and his accessory is none other than sensibility. Man uses the notion or the language of sensibility to flatter woman into a posture of weakness, then declares her weak by nature (or according to God's will) and accordingly denies her access to "manly" pursuits for a strong mind and body. It is woman's first recorded story, Eve's, as told by the ancient Hebrews; and, in the *Rights of Woman*, it threatens to become her only story.

This dramatic complex of ideas suggests the outlines of a new, dark fiction of sensibility in the making that diametrically opposes the more comforting fictions of *Mary* and "Cave of Fancy." In this new antifiction of sensibility, women are betrayed from without and within; their dearest intimates (husbands, lovers, hearts) become their most insidious enemies. Clearly, if Wollstonecraft still harbors a deep, lifelong faith in the notion of sensibility, then her *Rights of Woman* represents the moment of greatest crisis in that faith. In the *Rights of Men* she questions a few of her assumptions about sensibility; here she tries to disentangle herself entirely from the notion: she works energetically to demythologize it, to demystify its causes, and to expose its effects on women.

One of the first telling signs of this change of mind is her change in choice of idiolects of sensibility.[3] In *Rights of Woman*, she studiously avoids the soft, sentimental rhetoric that makes her cringe as she reads Burke's *Reflections*; she reaches for a firmer, bolder vocabulary and syntax to support her arguments: "Dismissing . . . those pretty feminine phrases, which the men condescendingly use to soften our slavish dependence, and despising that weak elegancy of mind, exquisite sensibility, and sweet docility of manners, supposed to be the sexual characteristics of the weaker vessel, I wish to shew that elegance is inferior to virtue . . ." (*Works*, 5.75). Moreover, when she speaks of sensibility, she no longer uses the language of the moralists or the aestheticians of sensibility. Rather she relies on the language and presuppositions of the physiologists; and her discussions of young women in the throes of sensibility frequently read like the diagnoses of some midcentury physician describing "hysterical" female patients:[4]

> Their senses are inflamed, and their understandings neglected, consequently they become the prey of their senses, delicately termed sensibility, and are blown about by every momentary gust of feeling. Civilized women are, therefore, so weakened by false refinement, that, respecting morals, their condition is much below what it would be were they left in a state nearer to nature. Ever restless and anxious, their over exercised sensibility not only renders them uncomfortable themselves, but troublesome, to use a soft phrase, to others. All their thoughts turn on things calculated to excite emotion; and feeling, when they should reason, their conduct is unstable, and their opinions are wavering — not the wavering produced by deliberation or progressive views, but by contradictory emotions. (*Works*, 5.4.129–30)

A more perfect denial of her former advocacy of sensibility hardly seems possible. In her earlier publications, Wollstonecraft equates sensibility with an awareness so heightened it is almost the equivalent of a sixth sense, one that renders its initiates better, wiser, and, however fleetingly, happier. Here she seems to equate sensibility, in contrast, only with unalloyed misery, and mental, physical, and moral instability. Images of debilitating disease abound: fever, fragility, and consumption endanger oversensitized bodies. Minds are prey, as well, to a long list of ills summed up in the phrase "madness and folly" (*Works*, 5.4.130): mood swings, lack of rationality, lack of convictions, obsessive preoccupation with the passion of love and absurd "metaphysical notions" on that subject culled from "stupid novelists." The exclusion of women from the public sphere by "political and civil oppression" renders sensibility an even greater danger: "Sentiments become events, and reflection deepens what it should, and would have effaced, if the understanding had been allowed to take a wider range" (*Works*, 5.13.256).

Although such women may be alluring fiancées, they will certainly not, Wollstonecraft predicts, be satisfactory wives. They will neglect their duties (*Works*, 5.4.129) and be unfit mothers and teachers, subjecting children alternately to "tyranny and indulgence," the "extremes that people of sensibility alternately fall into" (*Works*, 5.4.137). They may even turn to vice—and why not, Wollstonecraft muses; only their senses and their passions have been exercised. In training only for sensuality, they make better mistresses than wives precisely because they have been deprived of the education that could give them any other kind of aim in life: "Without knowledge there can be no morality!" (*Works*, 5.4.132).

Coming from Wollstonecraft, this materialization of sensibility is an unambiguous signal of her desire to repudiate it. In her earlier works, she invariably dismisses the physical implications of the metaphor "sensibility" as mere sensualism or vice. In saying in the *Rights of Woman*, in the spirit of Hobbes, that sensibility is, in effect, all matter and motion, she certainly intends to dismiss it as well:

And what is sensibility? "Quickness of sensation; quickness of perception; delicacy." Thus is it defined by Dr. Johnson; and the definition gives me no other idea than of the most exquisitely polished instinct. I discern not a trace of the image of God in either sensation or matter. Refined seventy times seven, they are still material; intellect dwells not there; nor will fire ever make lead gold! (*Works*, 5.4.132)

It would be foolhardy indeed to attempt to prove that this rift between Wollstonecraft and sensibility is an illusion. It is not. Her growing radical political convictions have eroded her early faith in sensibility. She has become increasingly convinced that, in order to effect the first revolution she recommends here, "a revolution in female manners" (*Works*, 5.3.114), women's education must be radically reformed to include rigorous intellectual, physical, and ethical training; and she feels she must downplay the importance of sensibility in that training:

> My own sex, I hope, will excuse me, if I treat them like rational creatures. . . . I earnestly wish to point out in what true dignity and human happiness consists — I wish to persuade women to endeavour to acquire strength, both of mind and body, and to convince them that the soft phrases, susceptibility of heart, delicacy of sentiment, and refinement of taste, are almost synonymous with epithets of weakness, and that those beings who are only the objects of pity and that kind of love, which has been termed its sister, will soon become objects of contempt. (*Works*, 5.75)

She insists that sensibility is not a magical human inclination but essentially a paper construct, one of several "insipid" virtues—others are decorum, compliance, meekness, mildness, amiableness, ornamental accomplishments—that men have set aside for women to excel in, all of which cramp their bodies, minds, and hearts, and stifle their attempts to "unfold" their faculties and discover their own uniquenesses. Essentially, she argues, such virtues add up to one utterly passive character, or, even worse, to the absence of any character at all:

> Men are allowed by moralists to cultivate, as Nature directs, different qualities, and assume the different characters, that the same passions, modified almost to infinity, give to each individual. A virtuous man may have a choleric or a sanguine constitution, be gay or grave, unreproved; be firm till he is almost overbearing, or, weakly submissive, have no will or opinion of his own; but all women are to be levelled, by meekness and docility, into one character of yielding softness and gentle compliance. (*Works*, 5.5.2.165)

Virtue, she insists (as she does in *Rights of Men*), should be identical for men and women, should be sexless: "I wish to . . . here throw down my gauntlet, and deny the existence of sexual virtues, not excepting modesty" (*Works*, 5.3.120).

As the above passages should suggest, Wollstonecraft activates to her advantage the new language consciousness first revealed in her reading of Burke's *Reflections*. That language consciousness, in fact, gives her *Rights of Woman* its most consistent and unifying theme: the power of mind over matter, the power of language to structure the minds and the realities of the people who speak it. She grounds her hypothesis in her interpretation of Locke's notion of the early association of ideas:

> There is an habitual association of ideas, that grows "with our growth,"[5] which has a great effect on the moral character of mankind; and by which

a turn is given to the mind that commonly remains throughout life. So ductile is the understanding, and yet so stubborn, that the associations which depend on adventitious circumstances, during the period that the body takes to arrive at maturity, can seldom be disentangled by reason. One idea calls up another, its old associate, and memory, faithful to the first impressions, particularly when the intellectual powers are not employed to cool our sensations, retraces them with mechanical exactness.

This habitual slavery, to first impressions, has a more baneful effect on the female than the male character, because business and other dry employments of the understanding, tend to deaden feelings and break associations that do violence to reason. But females, who are made women of when they are mere children, and brought back to childhood when they ought to leave the go-cart for ever, have not sufficient strength of mind to efface the superinductions of art that have smothered nature. (*Works*, 5.6.186)

Any antiquated opinions in circulation among adults are sure to find their way into the minds of at least some children as ineradicable "first impressions," thus perpetuating the chain of errors about men, women, and virtue. In concert with this conviction, Wollstonecraft argues for the absolute necessity of a second revolution: the isolation and overthrow of particularly "moss-covered" opinions (*Works*, 5.5.182).

In this process, Wollstonecraft often targets the language of sensibility that men reserve for their conversation with and about women. She speaks with keen awareness of its capacity to first mesmerize, then seduce and deprave, its listeners; and with special conviction of its power to shape ideas, determine actions, even enslave. Her tropes reinforce the notion that words can seduce, structure, and enthrall the minds of women. In a first forecast of the central metaphor of her last novel *Maria*, Wollstonecraft fills *Rights of Woman* with memorable images of confinement and restraint. She calls women slaves and describes them, from time to time, as bound, mind-shackled, chained, caged. "Confined then in cages like the feathered race," she laments, "they have nothing to do but to plume themselves, and stalk with mock majesty from perch to perch. It is true they are provided with food and raiment, for which they neither toil nor spin; but health, liberty, and virtue, are given in exchange" (*Works*, 5.4.125). Eventually, she fears, women will become so perfectly accustomed to this comfortable confinement that they will become their own jailers; more poignantly and specifically (in a passage reminiscent of Rilke's evocative poem "The Panther," but also of Irigaray's claim that women are outside the symbolic order, hence tongue-tied and body-bound), their bodies serve as the prisons of their minds:[6] "Taught from their infancy that beauty is woman's sceptre, the mind shapes itself to the body, and, roaming round its gilt cage, only seeks to adorn its prison" (*Works*, 5.3.113). At this point, Wollstonecraft believes, women become dehumanized; she gives them the appellation "mere dolls" (*Works*, 5.9.216).

Chapters 2, 3, 4, and 5 wrestle with various men (and a few women) of letters and their "prevailing opinions" about women. They constitute the rhetorical heart of her *Rights of Woman* where she charges the culprits, interrogates them, and harangues her reader-jury. For Wollstonecraft the three most reprehensible of the prevalent opinions are the belief that women do not have enough strength of mind to attain understanding and virtue; the belief that they are "created rather to feel than reason" (*Works*, 5.4.131); and the belief that their sole function in life is to please men. Wollstonecraft wishes to brush these beliefs aside; she believes them to be mere fictions, figments of the overheated male imagination. Cognizant, however, that they have attained the status of myths, she first arraigns two prominent mythmakers: Moses and Milton. She introduces Moses' story of Eden as a "poetical" fabrication; then in a breathtakingly irreverent reversal, she suggests that the story itself, rather than Eve, is the source of all woman's woes. How, her lightly mocking tone seems to suggest here, have women been duped for so long?

> Probably the prevailing opinion, that woman was created for man, may have taken its rise from Moses's poetical story; yet, as very few, it is presumed, who have bestowed any serious thought on the subject, ever supposed that Eve was, literally speaking, one of Adam's ribs, the deduction must be allowed to fall to the ground; or, only be so far admitted as it proves that man, from the remotest antiquity, found it convenient to exert his strength to subjugate his companion, and his invention to shew that she ought to have her neck bent under the yoke. (*Works*, 5.2.95)

Some of her contemporaries would view such remarks as double blasphemy—once against God's authorship of the Bible, once against the truth-value of its words—something Wollstonecraft must have known. For the cause of women's rights, however, she is prepared to rattle her chains at the foot of all thrones, divine and human; she already demonstrates as much in chapter 1 by "attacking the sacred majesty of Kings" (*Works*, 5.1.86). If kings and holy scriptures may be doubted, then men like Milton may be doubted all the more easily; in this context, his *Paradise Lost* becomes one poetical fiction based on another:

> Women are told from their infancy . . . that a little knowledge of human weakness, justly termed cunning, softness or temper, *outward* obedience, and a scrupulous attention to a puerile kind of propriety, will obtain for them the protection of man; and should they be beautiful, every thing else is needless, for, at least, twenty years of their lives.

Thus Milton describes our first frail mother; though when he tells us that women are formed for softness and sweet attractive grace, I cannot comprehend his meaning, unless, in the true Mahometan strain, he meant to deprive us of souls, and insinuate that we were beings only designed by sweet attractive grace, and docile blind obedience, to gratify the senses of man when he can no longer soar on the wing of contemplation. (*Works*, 5.2.88)

Milton, under this kind of scrutiny, fares no better than Burke does in *Rights of Men*: both are viewed as apologists for an old order that insists upon the subjugation of woman to man's authority, and beyond that, as sensualists in the guise of sympathetic, admiring sentimentalists.

Wollstonecraft's favorite epithet for such opinions—"Mahometan"— easily conveys her feelings that they are ridiculously out of place in late eighteenth-century England; perhaps this explains why she spends so much time on contemporary authors, especially Rousseau and his followers. She also loads her critical remarks on them with more sarcasm; they, she must believe, ought to know better. She views Rousseau[7] as a major adversary, pointing out her differences with him frequently (in chapters 1, 2, 3, and 5), and characterizing her entire argument in chapter 1, in relationship to his views on civilization: "Rousseau exerts himself to prove that all *was* right originally: a crowd of authors that all *is* now right: and I, that all will *be* right" (*Works*, 5.1.84). For several pages in chapter 5, she allows Rousseau to speak about the education of women from *Émile* without interruption; but she soon begins to break in, with increasing frequency and irritation, challenging a claim, protesting an obvious injustice, pointing to a particularly amazing instance of his blindness:

"The life of a modest women is reduced, by our absurd institutions, to a perpetual conflict with herself: not but it is just that this sex should partake of the sufferings which arise from those evils it hath caused us."

And why is the life of a modest woman a perpetual conflict? I should answer, that this very system of education makes it so. . . . when sensibility is nurtured at the expence [*sic*] of the understanding, such weak beings must be restrained by arbitrary means, and be subjected to continual conflicts. . . .

"A state of dependence being natural to the sex, they perceive themselves formed for obedience."

This is begging the question; for servitude not only debases the individual, but its effects seem to be transmitted to posterity. Considering the length of time that women have been dependent, is it surprising that some of them hug their chains, and fawn like the spaniel? . . .

"For the same reason," adds Rousseau, "women have, or ought to have, but little liberty; they are apt to indulge themselves excessively in what is allowed them. Addicted in every thing to extremes, they are even more transported at their diversions than boys."

The answer to this is very simple. Slaves and mobs have always indulged themselves in the same excesses, when once they broke loose from authority. — The bent bow recoils with violence, when the hand is suddenly relaxed that forcibly held it; and sensibility, the play-thing of outward circumstances, must be subjected to authority, or moderated by reason. (*Works*, 5.5.152)

Rousseau, although perceived by many to be an innovator in his day, is seen by Wollstonecraft as a mere perpetuator of the old patriarchal, sensualist fictions about women:

Absolute, uncontroverted authority, it seems, must subsist somewhere: but is not this a direct and exclusive appropriation of reason? The *rights* of humanity have been thus confined to the male line from Adam downwards. Rousseau would carry his male aristocracy still further, for he insinuates, that he should not blame those, who contend for leaving woman in a state of the most profound ignorance, if it were not necessary in order to preserve her chastity . . . to give her a little knowledge of men. (*Works*, 5.5.157)

At last sensibility, however, rather than Rousseau, is held responsible for his outrageous ideas: "But all Rousseau's errors in reasoning arose from sensibility, and sensibility to their charms women are very ready to forgive!"; "But peace to his manes! I war not with his ashes, but his opinions. I war only with the sensibility that led him to degrade a woman by making her the slave of love" (*Works*, 5.5.160 – 61).

Wollstonecraft may be at her rhetorical best in chapter 5, "Animadversions on some of the writers who have rendered women objects of pity, bordering on contempt," as she dissects Fordyce's "lover-like phrases of pumped up passion" to expose the dearth of reason or humanity in his sermon directives to women (*Works*, 5.5.162–66). Her lines fairly bristle with her keen sense of his misappropriation of the language of sentiment; she calls his style "sentimental rant" and a "parade of sensibility." Why must women, she asks, "be cajoled into virtue by artful flattery and sexual compliments," by "lullaby strains of condescending endearment"? Perhaps he assumes that they can only be addressed this way because they are creatures without reason: "It moves my gall to hear a preacher descanting on dress and needlework: and still more, to hear him address the *British fair, the fairest of the fair*, as if they had only feelings." Wollstonecraft twice calls attention to Fordyce's profession, implying both times that his language is worthy neither of him nor of the women he addresses:

Idle, empty words! What can such delusive flattery lead to, but vanity and folly? The lover, it is true, has a poetical license to exalt his mistress; his reason is the bubble of his passion . . . and happy would it be for women, if they were only flattered by the men who loved them; I mean, who love the individual, not the sex; but should a grave preacher interlard his discourses with such fooleries? . . . In sermons or novels, however, voluptuousness is always true to its text.

In addition to equating Fordyce's hyperbolism with indecorum, Wollstonecraft aligns it with hypocrisy or insincerity. Such "florid appeals" can only spring, she speculates, from "cold artificial feelings": "This is not the language of the heart, nor will it ever reach it, though the ear may be tickled." Underlying her disapproval is her additional conviction that, in Fordyce's case, medium and message are one, and that together they will have a devastating effect on any young woman, stifling both her spirit and her intellect, and erasing her individual uniqueness: "These discourses are written in such an affected style, that were it only on that account, and had I nothing to object against his *mellifluous* precepts, I should not allow girls to peruse them, unless I designed to hunt every spark of nature out of their composition, melting every human quality into female meekness and artificial grace."

What galls Wollstonecraft most about Fordyce's sermons is their underlying notion of the ideal woman, something that emerges—to her dismay—in fragmentary assumptions he makes in passing, and something that is poles apart from hers. He assumes women will wish to attain physical gracefulness, while Wollstonecraft emphasizes the important of "mental grace," "the expression of the mind"; he advises women against any strenuous physical exercise that would render their "tones" or "figures," their "airs" or "deportment," masculine, while she longs to see women "robust" in body and mind; he assumes women must be addressed like irrational children, while she pleads to have them "taught to respect themselves as rational creatures"; he assumes the dependence, she longs for the independence of women's minds (let them learn to "walk without leading-strings"); he assumes that all good women will aspire to the same few virtues, while she wishes that women, like men, may be allowed to "cultivate, as Nature directs, different qualities, and assume the different characters, that the same passions, modified almost to infinity, give to each individual"; he assumes women's greatest desire is to conquer men, but she does not "wish them to have power over men; but over themselves" (5.4.131).

She is particularly dismayed to see him equate female excellence and the "angelic." She quotes his recommendation that women cultivate piety (something she would, under other circumstances, most certainly agree to): " 'Never, perhaps, does a fine woman strike more deeply, than when, composed into pious recollection . . . she assumes, without knowing it, superior dignity and new graces; so that the beauties of holiness seem to radiate about her, and the by-standers are almost induced to fancy her already worshipping amongst her kindred angels!' " After quoting him, however, she dives for—and critiques— the implications of his comments for the feminine ideal: "Why are women to be thus bred up with a desire of conquest? the very word, used in this sense, gives me a sickly qualm! Do religion and virtue offer no stronger motives, no brighter reward? Must they always be debased by being made to consider the sex of their companions? Must they be taught always to be pleasing? . . . Why are girls to be told that they resemble angels; but to sink them below women?"

Wollstonecraft summarizes her grievances against Fordyce by floating a final passage from his sermons in her own caustic solution. She leads into the following passage from him with a metaphor of repression: "Is not the following portrait—the portrait of a house slave?"

> "I am astonished at the folly of many women, who are still reproaching their husbands for leaving them alone, for . . . treating them with this and the other mark of disregard or indifference; when, to speak the truth, they have themselves in a great measure to blame. Not that I would justify the men in any thing wrong on their part. But had you behaved to them with more *respectful observance*, and a more *equal tenderness*; *studying their humors, overlooking their mistakes, submitting to their opinions* in matters indifferent, passing by little instances of unevenness, caprice, or passion, giving soft answers to hasty words, complaining as seldom as possible, and making it your daily care to relieve their anxieties and prevent their wishes, to enliven the hour of dullness, and call up the ideas of felicity: had you pursued this conduct, I doubt not but you would have maintained and even increased their esteem, so far as to have secured every degree of influence that could conduce to their virtue, or your mutual satisfaction; and your house might at this day have been the abode of domestic bliss."

Her exit from the discussion of Fordyce highlights once more her own worst fears about such a feminine ideal—that it would essentially dehumanize women, discourage them from developing either their most precious faculties (head and heart) or their special uniquenesses, and drown them instead in demeaning, self-erasing solicitude for every whim of the men in their lives: "Such a woman ought to be an angel — or she is an ass — for I discern not a trace of the human character, neither reason nor passion in this domestic drudge, whose being is absorbed in that of a tyrant's."

Wollstonecraft exhorts in the same chapter, "Let us, my dear contemporaries, arise above such narrow prejudices" (*Works*, 5.5.161). Let us cast aside, she might have said, all these fictions of sensibility, for through her word choice she implicates sensibility in most, if not all, of them. In chapters 7 through 12 she tests her own ability to establish new, unbiased truths about her sex: she redefines various sexual virtues as sexless ones, urging men and women at the same time to follow the same ethical code; she suggests concrete reforms in the education of women; and she pleads for a greater inclusion of women in public life.

Boys acquire "nasty indecent tricks," even "vices," when they go to all-male boarding schools and "pig together in the same bedchamber." Train boys and girls together in day schools instead and their differences will diminish while their virtues grow, and grow more and more alike (*Works*, 5.12.236–37). Such retraining must, of necessity, precede any genuine reform in women's rights; women's lot will never improve substantively until men give up their notion of double ethical standards for the two sexes:

> Till men are more chaste women will be immodest. . . . Modesty must be equally cultivated by both sexes, or it will ever remain a sickly hot-house plant, whilst the affectation of it, the fig leaf borrowed by wantonness, may give a zest to voluptuous enjoyments. (*Works*, 5.8.196)

> But, in proportion as this regard for the reputation of chastity is prized by women, it is despised by men: and the two extremes are equally destructive to morality. (*Works*, 5.8.207)

Once this process of coming together has begun, women will be freer to be seen in public; perhaps they may be allowed to study gardening, literature, experimental philosophy (*Works*, 5.4.144), medicine or anatomy (*Works*, 5.2.249), or to go into a greater variety of businesses for themselves (*Works*, 5.9.218–19). Hers is a bold, if sketchy, new plan for women's role in the society, one relying, above all else, on women cultivating sufficient reason to rein in their feelings.

The intensity of her attack on sensibility, of course, can be read as symptomatic of her difficulty with letting it go. In her private correspondence written at the same time as *Rights of Woman* she does not divorce herself as cleanly from the language of her youthful fictions; it is clearly too inextricably interwoven with her sense of the value, uniqueness, and obligations of her selfhood. Two letters written in January and February, just as the *Rights of Woman* goes to press, show Wollstonecraft still measuring her own worth and the strengths and weaknesses of others by the presence or absence of benevolence or sensibility. A letter to Fanny's brother George Blood finds Wollstonecraft immersed as usual in taking care of her family and friends, praising one person for his "humanity," another for her "affectionate heart," and complaining of "hurt" from a third. A letter to Everina worries about a little ward Ann, whom she has recently taken into her own home:

> I discovered that she has been stealing sugar out of my closet constantly, and the artful way she managed it, not to mention the lies, really vexes me— She is undoubtedly very much improved and my visitors think her a fine girl—yet I have long been convinced that she will never be the kind of child I should love with all my heart. She has great *animal* spirits and quick feelings, but I shall be much mistaken if she have any considerable portion of sensibility when she grows up. (*Collected Letters*, p. 209)[8]

This voice of sensibility takes speaking turns with the "noisy rationalist" voice of *Rights of Woman*. Its presence sometimes tempts modern critics to fault Wollstonecraft either for immaturity (for continuing in adolescent emotionalism) or for hypocrisy (for preaching reason and practicing sensibility);[9] but neither does sufficient justice to Wollstonecraft's double-voiced discourse, which is, when viewed in the context of her century rather than her person, a generally successful contribution to the eighteenth-century literary tradition of impassioned polemics in the name of reason. Its presence, of course, signals a double allegiance in her psyche to head and to heart; but, curiously enough, although she rails against the "sentimental cant" of the likes of Dr. Fordyce, her own two voices, for the most part, work in harmony. A "melancholy," "indignant" voice of sensibility, for example, identifies the problem in the introduction, then the voice of inductive reason enters to analyze both its causes and its effects: "I have turned over various books . . . what has been the result? — a profound conviction that the neglected education of my fellow-creatures is the grand source of the misery I deplore." More often, the voice of reason announces a plan to carry something out, then the voice of sensibility seizes the pen to ensure that the plan is carried out persuasively. Chapter 1 may serve as a paradigm of this polyvocal teamwork.

The chapter begins with the quiet promise of a systematic "search" for "the most simple truths" about man's "rights and duties," with "plain questions," and equally plain "reasoning." Then, to this end, it establishes three axioms: that reason is man's claim to "pre-eminence over the brute creation," that virtue "exalts one being above another," and that the passions enable people to gain through experience "a degree of knowledge denied to the brutes." Unfortunately, reason is not yet free; rather it is held in thrall by "deeply rooted prejudices," which it then busies itself "to justify" (*Works*, 5.1.81). Reason in the service of unreason then becomes her theme, and she chooses for an example Rousseau's belief that civilization corrupts, that "a state of nature is preferable to civilization" (*Works*, 5.1.83). He should have looked at civilization, she suggests, more analytically; had he done so, instead of celebrating "barbarism," he might have seen that monarchy and hierarchy, rather than civilization per se, are responsible for most of the world's ills.

As she begins to develop this latter hypothesis, however, questions give way to exclamations, axioms to metaphors, and reasoning to railing; by the end of the chapter, a telling slip of the pen reveals that the voice of sensibility is in command. Monarchies she pronounces madness; hierarchies, dangerous to morality; monarchies and hierarchies together she compares to a "baneful lurking gangrene" that infects the fabric of the society, concluding: "It is the pestiferous purple which renders the progress of civilization a curse, and warps the understanding, *till men of sensibility doubt whether the expansion of intellect produces a greater portion of happiness or misery*" (*Works*, 5.1.87; emphasis mine).

First among the sensibility-inspired values evoked by the voice of sensibility in *Rights of Woman* is a continuing preference for spontaneous prose over polished periods.

> I shall disdain to cull my phrases or polish my style; — I aim at being useful, and sincerity will render me unaffected; for wishing rather to persuade by the force of my arguments, than dazzle by the elegance of my language, I shall not waste my time in rounding periods, or in fabricating the turgid bombast of artificial feelings, which, coming from the head, never reach the heart. (*Works*, 5.75–76)

Wollstonecraft's aim in writing here has not changed from that of her first letters to Jane Arden. She wishes to speak heart to heart; and to do so, she proposes to leave the head out of the process by speaking spontaneously and making no attempts to polish or embellish that spontaneous expression. Flamboyantly calling attention to itself, her style inscribes in all of her texts the affective communicative ideal of the antilanguage of sensibility. And early reviews of her work suggest that the strategy is successful from the beginning; whether positive or negative, they usually understand her style as the effect of language under pressure to convey passionate thought: detractors speak of her "rhapsodical bombast," admirers of her "impressive," "flowing," "bold" language.[10]

Three other earlier values that emerge in the *Rights of Woman*—and are defended—are central tenets of sensibility. First, a preference for the kind of education that allows a child to "unfold" naturally, to integrate head and heart, to interact with environment; second, a preference for friendship over romantic love, for affection and esteem over passion, especially in male-female relationships, and even in marriage; and third, a preference for the social virtues over the "manly" virtues for men as well as women. Although the *Rights of Woman* fairly shouts about its rupture with the past, and even with its author's own past, its ideas about education, based in Locke and his trust in human sensibility, represent no change since her earliest education treatise, *Education of Daughters*. She still believes that education should be gradual, natural (organic metaphors dominate its discussion), and noninterventionist, and that its primary aims should be to develop a person's full potential rather than to mold that person to a preexisting ideal, and to balance the demands, yet sustain the integrity, of both head and heart:

> I am, indeed, persuaded that the heart, as well as the understanding, is opened by cultivation; and by, which may not appear so clear, strengthening the organs; I am not now talking of momentary flashes of sensibility, but of affections. And, perhaps, in the education of both sexes, the most difficult task is so to adjust instruction as not to narrow the understanding, whilst the heart is warmed by the generous juices of spring, just raised by the electric fermentation of the season; nor to dry up the feelings by employing the mind in investigations remote from life. (*Works*, 5.4.135)

Despite the suspicious glance cast at "the momentary flashes of sensibility," the balanced psyche described here is an ideal championed by the literature of sensibility, as is the notion of a sexually neutral zone of virtues where men and women can live together in amity.

Wollstonecraft's expressed preference for friendship over romantic love in *Rights of Woman* is another reiteration of values long held and inspired by sensibility. She treats the subject of romantic love, in a manner reminiscent of her earlier discussion in *Education of Daughters* (*Works*, 1.4.28–30), gingerly, even humorously, yet she returns to it fairly often because only its replacement by a more reasonable model of male-female relationships will provide women with the kind of emotional–intellectual environment they need to grow:

> To speak disrespectfully of love is, I know, high treason against sentiment and fine feelings; but I wish to speak the simple language of truth, and rather to address the head than the heart. To endeavour to reason love out of the world, would be to out Quixote Cervantes, and equally offend against common sense; but an endeavour to restrain this tumultuous passion, and to prove that it should not be allowed to dethrone superior powers, or to usurp the sceptre which the understanding should ever coolly wield, appears less wild. . . . This passion, naturally increased by suspense and difficulties, draws the mind out of its accustomed state, and exalts the affections; but the security of marriage, allowing the fever of love to subside, a

healthy temperature is thought insipid, only by those who have not sufficient intellect to substitute the calm tenderness of friendship, the confidence of respect, instead of blind admiration, and the sensual emotions of
fondness. (*Works,* 5.2.96, 99)

If mature love pays special attention to one of the social virtues, tenderness, education should pay attention to them all. She prefers a
national system of day schools rather than boarding schools for children because the latter deaden "all the social affections," "dry up the
generous juices of the heart," and sow vices where there should be
virtues (*Works*, 5.12.236). In such lines, she espouses once more the
midcentury ethic of sensibility.

It should be abundantly clear from these examples that the tone of
the *Rights of Woman* is far from dispassionate. Wollstonecraft here
laments and dreams, pities and rails, in a voice as emotionally tinged
as Werther's. Her treatise begins, as noted above, with "melancholy
emotions of sorrowful indignation" and ends with an idyllic vision of
hope: "Let woman share the rights and she will emulate the virtues of
man, for she must grow more perfect when emancipated . . . " (*Works*,
5.73; 5.13.266). In between Wollstonecraft shifts[11] constantly from one
of these tones to another, with only temporary rests in a neutral state
of objectivity. Anger, of course, dominates nearly every chapter; hope
gains expression often, but much less often. Melancholy Wollstonecraft
holds generally in abeyance; but twice she strikes a note of compassion for her "fallen" sisters: "What can be a more melancholy sight to
a thinking mind, than to look into the numerous carriages that drive
helter-skelter about this metropolis in a morning full of pale-faced
creatures who are flying from themselves. I have often wished, with
Dr Johnson, to place some of them in a little shop with half a dozen
children looking up to their languid countenances for support" (*Works*,
5.9.217; cf. 5.4.190).

This could hardly be termed a full range of tones, but it is, nevertheless, a telling range. It is the range and distinctive feature, according to the eighteenth-century German aesthetician, poet, and play-
wright Friedrich Schiller, of all the sentimental writers of the age.
Dismayed by their sense of alienation from the reality they inhabit, they
respond in three habitual ways—longing for things as they were, anger
at things as they are, and hope for things as they might be—which translate, when they write, into three poetic genres: elegy, satire, and idyll.
Wollstonecraft's emotional range would bear a perfect resemblance to
that of Schiller's model sentimental poet in *Naive und sentimentalische
Dichtung* except that, as she promises she will in chapter 1, she avoids
nostalgia.[12] Contrary to claims that have been made about Woll-

stonecraft's aim in the *Rights of Woman*, however, she never promises to avoid passion in her treatise,[13] nor, for that matter, to espouse in some exclusive, narrow way the cause of reason. She believes that reason, in its pursuits, should be enlivened by passion, and that passion, in its transports, should be guided by reason; and her vindication, with its volatile fluctuation in tone and its impassioned reasoning, dramatizes those convictions.

As a result of its multiple allegiances and volatile tone, Wollstonecraft's persona in *Rights of Woman* has been, and will undoubtedly remain, something of an enigma. Complex and mercurial, it defies categorization or easy analysis. One feature it retains from chapter to chapter, however, is a stance of authority rare among women writers of the century, even in the 1790s. Wollstonecraft seems to assume she has unimpeachable moral and intellectual superiority over her subjects; in addition, she frequently confronts those subjects like an angry prophet, now denouncing past or present practices, now envisioning a future sweetened by radical reform, now one embittered by continuing oppression. Her prophetic persona emerges most frequently in her perorations to chapters and is especially visible in the last lines of the treatise:

> Asserting the rights which women in common with men ought to contend for, I have not attempted to extenuate their faults; but to prove them to be the natural consequence of their education and station in society. If so, it is reasonable to suppose that they will change their character, and correct their vices and follies, when they are allowed to be free in a physical, moral, and civil sense.
>
> Let woman share the rights and she will emulate the virtues of man, for she must grow more perfect when emancipated, or justify the authority that chains such a weak being to her duty .— If the latter, it will be expedient to open a fresh trade with Russia for whips; a present which a father should always make to his son-in-law on his wedding day, that a husband may keep his whole family in order by the same means. . . .
>
> Be just then, O ye men of understanding! and mark not more severely what women do amiss, than the vicious tricks of the horse or the ass for whom ye provide provender — and allow her the privileges of ignorance, to whom ye deny the rights of reason, or ye will be worse than Egyptian task-masters, expecting virtue where nature has not given understanding. (*Works*, 5.13.266)

Almost no group escapes her occasional censure: kings, aristocrats, soldiers, the middle class, the clergy, men and women of letters: "Women, in general, as well as the rich of both sexes, have acquired all the follies and vices of civilization, and missed the useful fruit" (*Works*, 5.4.129).

Gary Kelly believes that this authoritative stance comes to Wollstonecraft from the rhetorical tradition of the *vir bonus, dicendi peritus* (a good man skilled in speaking).[14] Mary Wilson Carpenter, on the other hand, believes her stance is a deliberate feminist rhetorical construct, a sibylline prophetic stance to counter the male prophetic tradition from Moses to Rousseau, to disrupt its language and rational discourse with cryptic messages of her own making.[15] But the possibility cannot be ruled out that Wollstonecraft believes she has the authority to speak out for women, not because of her virtue or her gender but because she has manifold feelings about the cause of women. And if she is assuming, as she writes, that her anger, her melancholy, or her idyllic hope—her sentiments—legitimate her message, lend it some natural authority, then she is making the assumption of a devotee of sensibility. In this stance, as in her variable style, tones, voices and values, she lags behind herself, embracing some new ideas for the future but remaining, in other respects, a prisoner of her own past, a lagging behind that produces a document of most instructive complexity.

Part Three
Affirmation and Transformation

8

The Test of the Revolution

> Before she left Neuilly, she happened one day to enter Paris
> on foot . . . when an execution, attended with some peculiar
> aggravations, had just taken place, and the blood of the
> guillotine appeared fresh upon the pavement. The
> emotions of her soul burst forth in indignant exclamations,
> while a prudent bystander warned her of her danger, and
> intreated her to hasten and hide her discontents. She
> described to me, more than once, the anguish she felt at
> hearing of the death of Brissot, Vergniaud, and the twenty
> deputies, as one of the most intolerable sensations she had
> ever experienced.   —*Memoirs*, p. 77

The value of *French Revolution* (1794) lies not so much in its rehearsal
of the early events of the Revolution, which is a "compound of various
earlier accounts," as in its interpretation of those events, something for
which Wollstonecraft could draw upon her own powers of observation
and reflection.[1] Many of the contemporary reviews notice that it is
more than a chronicle, but also more than subjective opinion: the sympathetic *Critical Review* and *Monthly Review* call it a critique rather than
a history, while the antagonistic *British Critic* accuses Wollstonecraft
of borrowing her facts from the *New Annual Register*, which, for its part,
remains diplomatically silent about possible sources of Wollstonecraft's
facts, but pronounces its style "impressive" and its reflections judicious, proof positive of a "vigorous and well-informed mind."[2] As might
be expected, the treatise takes up again Wollstonecraft's debate with
Burke in *Rights of Men*, this time defending the Revolution in principle,
even in the face of the Terror, by blaming its excesses on a character
flaw of the French people. Ironically enough, while Burke's impassioned reflections on the Revolution strengthen Wollstonecraft's commitment to reason and alienate her from her lifelong belief in sensibility, her firsthand observation of the Revolution in the name of reason

causes her to temper her faith in reason, and to restore a measure of her faith, if now subdued, in sensibility.

Wollstonecraft leaves England for Paris in December of 1792, not returning until April of 1795; and in these months she experiences two traumas, one public, the other private. Plunged into a bittersweet affair with American businessman Gilbert Imlay, then forced to lengthen her stay despite his unaccountable departure because of the wartime embargo against France, she is compelled to witness the beginning of the Reign of Terror: the disregard of women's rights, the arrest and execution of the king and queen, the transformation of Notre Dame into a "temple of reason," the internment of English and German friends, and the slaughter of the French aristocracy and the liberal wing of the revolutionary movement. Privately and publicly disillusioned, she begins to reassess the roots and the fruits of this "stupendous" historical event (*Works*, 6.6). The resulting document, *French Revolution*, written in radical isolation (and very probably, too, in a state of heightened awareness provoked by private and public tensions), offers her readers a thoughtful reconsideration of her whole belief system. It puts sensibility and reason in a much larger context and builds a place for both in past and present—in the whole of human history as well as the individual human psyche.

Still an ardent egalitarian, she continues to plead for social and economic reforms that will foster equality among marital partners and citizens (*Works*, 6.147–48), and defends political reforms that will eliminate a monarchy of "monsters; deprived by their station of humanity, and even sympathy" (*Works*, 6.30). Also still an ardent libertarian, she longs to see the French people "truly free" but realizes that freedom depends on a reformation in attitudes still not achieved, not even in the new regime:

> Weeping — scarcely conscious that I weep, O France! over the vestiges of thy former oppression . . . I tremble, lest I should meet some unfortunate being, fleeing from the despotism of licentious freedom, hearing the snap of the *guillotine* at his heels; merely because he was once noble. . . . Down fell the temple of despotism; but—despotism has not been buried in it's [*sic*] ruins! — Unhappy country! — when will thy children cease to tear thy bosom? — When will a change of opinion, producing a change of morals, render thee truly free? (*Works*, 6.85)

The French Terror presents Wollstonecraft, as it does many other of the English Jacobins, however, with quite a challenge:[3] to present the unfolding Revolution in a fair light without inadvertently defending the guillotine. With the snap of the guillotine in her ears, she recruits sensibility as an ally in her struggle to encourage in her readers some degree of sympathy for the French experiment. By striking the stance of a reasonable observer of considerable feeling, she encourages her readers to look with her beyond the immediate Reign of Terror to larger, longer lasting benefits:

> The rapid changes, the violent, the base, and nefarious assassinations, which have clouded the vivid prospect that began to spread a ray of joy and gladness over the gloomy horizon of oppression, cannot fail to chill the sympathizing bosom, and palsy intellectual vigour. To sketch these vicissitudes is a task so arduous and melancholy, that, with a heart trembling to the touches of nature, it becomes necessary to guard against the erroneous inferences of sensibility; and reason beaming on the grand theatre of political changes, can prove the only sure guide to direct us to a favourable or just conclusion. (*Works*, 6.6)

At first this passage may seem simply to repeat the claims that sensibility has nothing, and that reason has everything, to do with a "just conclusion" to the "grand" drama "of political change." A new rhetorical stance, however, distinguishes this passage from analogous ones in her previous two books. The polemicist in the two vindications expresses frequent disdain for sensibility. The speaker of *French Revolution*, much more objectively, takes a middle way. She acknowledges allegiance to the superior capacity of reason to ward off error, but she also speaks convincingly, without a trace of irony, about the responses of the "sympathizing bosom." This passage gives us a fair forecast of what is to come in *French Revolution*: from now on, while Wollstonecraft keeps a safe distance between herself and sensibility's shortcomings, she does not try to banish it either from her text or her subtext.

The surest sign of some restored faith in sensibility is Wollstonecraft's cautious return to the language of the ethics of sensibility. "Heart," "feelings," "benevolent complacency," "social affections," "humanity," "sympathy," and "domestic sympathy" are terms Wollstonecraft uses positively here, even if she does pair them frequently with opposites designed to narrow the range of true sensibility, and to distinguish the genuine followers of sensibility from the Pharisees. The distinctions she draws are tenuous, relying on the limited and redundant vocabulary of sensibility, yet they are made clearer by the use of telling descriptors. Better to have "sensibility," she suggests from time to time, than "false refinement," "physical sensibility," or "sensuality"; better to have an "expanding heart" than "refining senses"; better to have "feelings of the soul" than "transient sympathies of the heart"; better to have the "humanity of a cultivated understanding" than the "tenderness of sympathy." Despite the seeming interchangeability of phrases in such pronouncements—giving the disturbing impression of a verbal shell game in which the terms like "heart," "sensibility," or "sympathy" might turn up anywhere—the pairs point towards a new variation on an old distinction Wollstonecraft is crafting between true sensibility and its counterfeits. Her new "true sensibility" is capable of detachment both from the self and from the "fleeting" impulses of the moment. This kind of sensibility, she suggests in a quick review of the rise of modern civilization, transforms the isolated savage into a willing member of human society: "His soul also warmed by sympathy, feeling for the distresses of his fellow creatures, and particularly for the helpless state of decrepit age; he begins to contemplate, as desirable, associations of men, to prevent . . . loneliness and solitude. Hence little communities living together in the bonds of friendship . . . mark the origin of society . . . tribes growing into nations . . ." (*Works*, 6.146). Elsewhere she adds the suggestion that true sensibility also originates true patriotism: "For what is patriotism but the expansion of domestic sympathy, rendered permanent by principle?" (*Works*, 6.54).

False sensibility, in contrast, preoccupied with the needs of the self and buffeted by the ever-changing impulses of the present moment, is incapable of detachment. It manifests itself often, but not always, as unprincipled sensuality: "The french, by the continual gratification of their senses, stifle the reveries of their imagination, which always requires to be acted upon by outward objects; and seldom reflecting on their feelings, their sensations are ever lively and transitory" (*Works*, 6.25). Sometimes, however, it disguises itself as true sensibility: participating in acts of charity, sympathy, or patriotism, only distinguishable from genuine sensibility by its motive—private gain—or its effect: "refining the senses at the expence [*sic*] of the heart" (*Works*, 6.24).

The distinction between sensibility and its counterfeits is not, of course, new either to the period, to women authors of the period, or to Wollstonecraft. It is implicit in her earlier works in one of two guises. One guise is the distinction between sensibility and sensuality that she uses to the detriment of men, especially in her private letters and in both vindications. The other guise is the distinction between sensibility and delicacy she makes to the detriment of women in her early fiction, the *Analytical* reviews, and the *Rights of Woman*. In *French Revolution*, however, Wollstonecraft extends the distinction to apply to questions of national identity and successful political measures, commenting on the French court, the National Assembly, the army, the Parisian citizenry, and the mob, and, beyond that, even on the past, present, and future of human civilization. It has at this point become her metaphoric-mythic distinction for all seasons, enabling her to make sense of the world outside and, for the first time perhaps since *Mary*, to integrate her own longest-held values with her newest convictions.

The Reign of Terror in France, Wollstonecraft insists, is not an inevitable result of historical process itself but an unfortunate outgrowth of the character of the people participating in the Revolution. She believes the French are, like the heroines in so many novels of sentiment (and indeed, like the mother in *Mary* and like Maria in *The Wrongs of Woman*), victims of a false sensibility that has arrested their development. They are slaves to the self and to the moment:

> The *refinement of the senses*, by producing a *susceptibility of temper*, which from it's [*sic*] capriciousness leaves no time for reflection, interdicts the exercise of judgment. The lively effusions of mind, characteristically peculiar to the french, are as violent as the impressions are transitory: and their *benevolence* evaporating in *sudden gusts of sympathy*, they become cold in the same proportion as their *emotions are quick*, and the combinations of their fancy brilliant. People who are carried away by the *enthusiasm of the moment*, are most frequently *betrayed by their imagination*, and commit some errour, the conviction of which not only damps their heroism, but *relaxes the nerve* of common exertions. Freedom is a solid good, that requires to be treated with reverence and respect. — But, whilst an effeminate race of heroes are contending for her smiles, with all the blandishments of gallantry, it is to their more vigorous and natural posterity, that she will consign herself with all the mild effulgence of artless charms. (*Works*, 6.213, emphasis mine)

This characterization of the French as a people of unusually acute sensibilities suggests reasons enough for the temporary bloody detour of their revolution, yet does so without excessive condemnation. Their imputed lack of judgment, their tendencies to be "carried away by the enthusiasm of the moment" or "betrayed by their imagination," and their "effeminate" lack of heroism are all dutifully noted as potential causes for the Terror but finally dismissed as contributory rather than necessary causes. At last, the French are presented as passive agents at the mercy of powerful cultural forces they do not understand. The tone of the passage can remain quiet, almost sympathetic or forgiving, and the reader can indulge this whimsical people for their "lively effusions of mind," their "sudden gusts of sympathy," their "brilliant fancy," and their "gallantry," and wait patiently for the dawning of a new (progressive) age bringing with it a new improved species, a "more vigorous and natural posterity." The same cultural institutions that help to form their minds finally derail their Revolution: their form of government, the teachings of their church:, even their language and literature. Change the institutions, Wollstonecraft believes, and this highly responsive people will change with them.

The French have "arrived, through the vices of their government, at that degree of false refinement, which makes every man, in his own eyes, the centre of the world; and when this gross selfishness, this complete depravity, prevails in a nation, an absolute change must take place; because the members of it have lost the cement of humanity which kept them together" (*Works*, 6.62). By "cement of humanity," Wollstonecraft means Adam Smith's "social affections," the kinds of fellow-feeling that the French monarchs have stifled both in themselves and in their people through their tyranny. Tyranny chokes "at the source" the "spontaneous flow of . . . feelings" that ordinarily "fertilized" people's minds (*Works*, 6.17). The gardening metaphors in the last passage signal a return to her youthful convictions that the feelings are organic, deep-seated, and natural, and enable (fertilize) people's minds to grow. The problem is not with them but with environmental factors that interact with them.

Wollstonecraft also believes that the mythmaking of the church has retarded the intellectual development of the French people. "All the notions drawn from the wild traditions of original sin: the eating of the apple, the theft of Prometheus, the opening of Pandora's box, and the other fables, too tedious to enumerate, on which priests have erected their tremendous structures of imposition, to persuade us, that we are naturally inclined to evil" have impeded the "expansion of the human heart" (*Works*, 6.21–22). Likewise, representations of vice on the stage have also contributed to "destroying the social affections" (*Works*, 6.54), a process expedited, she speculates, by the impediments of the French language itself.

That language has, as it turns out, very much in common with Burke's language in his *Reflections*. It is a language of "copious" and "hackneyed sentiments" and "oratorical flourishes"; it lures its users into the "shallow stream of conversation" where they acquire "a singular fund of superficial knowledge" and sharpen their "wit," but it does not lend itself to "poetry" or "contemplation." It consists in much sound and little substance, and produces a people who are shallow, "all rhetoricians" (*Works*, 6.228): "As a nation, the french are certainly the most eloquent people in the world; their lively feelings giving the warmth of passion to every argument they attempt to support" (*Works*, 6.156). In these passages Wollstonecraft's words recall some of the leading ideas of the *Rights of Woman* just enough to measure the philosophical distance she has come. Her aversion to "moss-covered opinions," her disdain for saccharine sentimentality in the service of the wrong causes, her sensitivity to the power of the word or the carefully turned slogan—all coalesce in this speculative, yet highly provocative, analysis of the discursive habits of a nation.

If her stance towards sensibility seems to be softening, so, too, does her ethics: in *French Revolution* a moderate, Aristotelian code emerges that seeks to elevate the mean and eschew extremes. If she presents the French people as suffering from an excessive refinement (a form of "false sensibility"), she faults their monarchy for laboring under the opposite burden, a deficiency of sensibility. In a rhetorical move that is almost certainly a direct counterstatement to Burke's *Reflections*, she uses the queen of France to illustrate this deficiency. In her case, Wollstonecraft theorizes, absolute power and the "unrestrained indulgence of pleasure" eventually "banish tenderness" from the "female bosom" and "harden" her "heart" (*Works*, 6.84): "It is certain, that education, and the atmosphere of manners in which a character is formed, change the natural laws of humanity; otherwise it would be unaccountable, how the human heart can be so dead to the tender emotions of benevolence, which most forcibly teach us, that real or lasting felicity flows only from a love of virtue, and the practice of sincerity" (*Works*, 6.72). The longer the queen reigned, the more she became "a profound dissembler" (*Works*, 6.73): she could only feign sensibility, or elicit it from others. Finally the semblance of sensibility is not enough to save her, her family, and her class. When disregardful excesses plunge the country into financial crisis, at last the people rebel; and, indulging in their own dark version of their rulers' excesses, they unhouse, imprison, and murder those rulers.

While the account of the queen strives to explain rather than condemn her apparent insensitivity to the plight of her people, Wollstonecraft apparently finds it more difficult to forgive the queen's hardness of heart than the people's lack of judgment. She preaches more when she talks of her, and her tone is stern. She even qualifies her expression of sympathy for her on the night the mob invades her bedroom at Versailles; she provides a cool reminder that Marie Antoinette, too, is merely human: "The laws had been trampled on by a gang of banditti. . . . The altar of humanity had been profaned — The dignity of freedom had been tarnished — The sanctuary of repose, the asylum of care and fatigue, the chaste temple of a woman, I consider the queen only as one . . . was violated with murderous fury" (*Works*, 6.209).

Not surprising considering her view of the French people, Wollstonecraft sees sensibility and its counterfeits at work everywhere in the unfolding events of the French Revolution. It is at the palace and on the streets, in the army and among the Parisian citizens, in the new French Assembly and the mob of ruffians. A guilt-ridden grenadier is led to suicidal despair during a farewell dinner for the royal family's bodyguards, relieved of their duties by the new assembly. He

darted from the midst of his comrades, and accusing himself of having been unfaithful to his prince, endeavoured, several times, to plunge his sword

into his bosom. . . . some blood was permitted to flow — and this theatri-
cal display of sensibility, carried to the highest pitch, produced emotions
almost convulsive in the whole circle, of which an english reader can
scarcely form an idea. (*Works*, 6.195)

Meanwhile, in the provinces, soldiers, sent to shoot villagers who
resisted the new taxes, by "one of those moments of enthusiasm, which
by the most rapid operation of sympathy unites all hearts . . . threw
down their arms, and melting into tears in the embraces of the citizens
whom they came to murder, remembered that they were countrymen
. . . : and, their conduct, quickly applauded with that glow of sensibility which excites imitation, served as an example to the whole army . . .
and might have proved a salutary lesson to any court less depraved and
insensible than that of Versailles" (*Works*, 6.40).

The "ruffians" who invade the royal palace experience a sudden
mood swing when the king announces, shortly thereafter, that he will
move, as requested, from Versailles to Paris: "One sentiment of glad-
ness seemed to animate the whole concourse of people; and their sensibility produced as mad demonstrations of joy as lately had been displayed of ferocity" (*Works*, 6.214). The Parisian citizens, who have
taken to the streets to defend their homes and families from anticipated attack from the court, are transformed by this process into a free and
equal fraternity by "an universal sympathy": "Men of all ranks joining in the throng, those of the first could not be discriminated by any
peculiar decency of demeanor, such public spirited dignity pervaded
the whole mass" (*Works*, 6.88). The new assembly Wollstonecraft
depicts as especially vulnerable to the welling up of both true and false
sensibility. The day of the Tennis Court Oath, their sensibility seems
genuine enough, whether she measures by motive or by effect: "The
benedictions that dropped from every tongue . . . produced an overflow
of sensibility that kindled into a blaze of patriotism every social feeling. . . . in one of those instants of disinterested forgetfulness of private
pursuits, all devoted themselves to the promotion of public happiness,
promising to resist, to the last extremity, all the efforts of such an invet-
erate tyranny" (*Works*, 6.65). Later, however, sensibility leads them
astray more than once, to "predominate," as she claims, "over legisla-
tive dignity" (*Works*, 6.140).

Many of these situations dramatizing sensibility in action seem
deliberately paired, though the pairs are frequently many pages apart.
French military personnel, citizens on the streets, and those in the
Assembly repeatedly offer examples of both true and counterfeit sensibility. What could Wollstonecraft hope to achieve, it seems appropriate to ask, with such a design? Certainly, she seems anxious to

instruct readers in how to tell the difference between look-alikes: one must analyze, she insists, both agents and recipients in order to tell "true" from the "false" sensibility. True sensibility arises in moments of genuine altruism when individuals are consumed by the pure desire to help or work with others. It is "one of those instants of disinterested forgetfulness of private pursuits," "one of those moments of enthusiasm, which by the most rapid operation of sympathy unites all hearts." As these definitions remind us, true sensibility benefits those it enthuses; it galvanizes them into a social unit of equals in some common cause. False sensibility, in contrast, is not grounded in fellow-feeling but flourishes with "ambitious selfishness" (*Works,* 6.143) and "vanity." Representatives of the Assembly, she believes, are particularly prone to feigned sensibility. The effects of false sensibility are rarely beneficial: it deludes and fires people up, impelling them into precipitous and sometimes dangerous decisions and actions:

> Vanity had made every frenchman a theorist, though political aphorisms were never ascertained under the reign of tyranny or caprice. The sagacious part of the nation, it is true, clearly perceived, that the period was arrived, when a revolution was inevitable; but selfishness being incompatible with noble, comprehensive, or laudable views, it is not wonderful, keeping in sight the national foible, that at the meeting of the states-general every deputy had his particular plan to suggest. Few of the leaders embraced the same; and acting, without coalescing, the most violent measures were sure to be the most applauded. We shall find also, that some of the most strenuous advocates for reforming abuses, and establishing a constitution, when their favourite systems were exploded, peevishly retired in disgust: and by afterwards venting it, have hurried into action a race of monsters, the most flagitious that ever alarmed the world by the murder of innocents, and the mockery of justice. (*Works,* 6.143–44)

Her various examples demonstrate Wollstonecraft's now steady awareness that the metonymic signs of sensibility are perfectly ambiguous and cannot be read as sure signs either of wisdom, sincerity, or goodness. In this treatise, sensibility is characterized, in Wollstonecraft's clearest, most impartial manner to date, as a potentially volatile sensitivity to affective stimuli, and that may work either to help or to harm those in its vicinity. Some of her metaphors of light and heat suggest a positive mindscape: sensibility's "glow" can turn enemies into friends or "kindle" "into a blaze of patriotism." Other of her metaphors suggest a mind infected or seduced: it can also lead to "erroneous inferences" and hasty decisions. In her discussion of the French Assembly, for example, she implies that sensibility's operation is best viewed as a "contagion" "excited by a commotion of animal spirits."

Parliamentarians experience, in quick succession, "vivacity of sentiments, the quick transition from a generous emotion to an epigrammatical sensation, . . . the reciprocal mistrust, and the combat of generosity — all diversified by the amiable and seducing enthusiasm" (*Works*, 6.139–40).

Wollstonecraft's presentation of paired instances of sensibility encourages hesitation rather than quick judgment. Readers closing her book are more apt to exercise caution about idealizing sensibility, but they are also much less apt to dismiss it out of hand. Even the ephemeral kind of sensibility most widespread in France, according to Wollstonecraft—sensuality or "transient sympathies of the heart"—may be occasionally beneficial. Although French sensibility is not coupled with sound moral principles, something Wollstonecraft always emphasizes as important, it can nevertheless occasionally regenerate an individual, a group of individuals, or even a nation, because of its potential link to the genuine or "natural feelings of man":

> The natural feelings of man seldom become so contaminated and debased as not sometimes to let escape a gleam of the generous fire, an ethereal spark of the soul; and it is these glowing emotions, in the inmost recesses of the heart, which have continued to feed feelings, that on sudden occasions manifest themselves with all their pristine purity and vigour. But, by the habitual slothfulness of rusty intellects, or the depravity of the heart, lulled into hardness on the lascivious couch of pleasure, those heavenly beams are obscured, and man appears either an hideous monster, a devouring beast; or a spiritless reptile, without dignity or humanity. (*Works*, 6.231–32)

There are several notable things about the metaphors of mind in this passage from the concluding section of *French Revolution*. First of all, although they do not depart dramatically from the mind-as-entity metaphor that dominates the eighteenth century, they modify it sufficiently to make the entity less brittle, less subject to permanent breakage or breakdown. Even in cases where monstrosity prevails, there is always hope for "regeneration." Second, the process of regeneration is attributed to the feelings, here associated with elements that are cleansing (water) and purifying (fire). Third, the myth of Prometheus, too, is linked to the "glowing emotions"—in their "pristine purity and vigor," they are the Greek demigod's "generous fire"—suggesting a returning readiness on Wollstonecraft's part to believe in sensibility's mythic powers.

The role Wollstonecraft grants in *French Revolution* to the feelings in society at large is also equally remarkable for its dynamic qualities. Everywhere she turns, she sees sensibility translating itself into social and political action, much of it positive. She has clearly overcome some barrier in her belief system by crossing the Channel: she has ceased to associate sensibility exclusively with mental or physical enervation or paralysis. It no longer necessarily fosters isolation or passivity; it can also meld and activate. Wollstonecraft breaks out of the introspective, even claustrophobic, mode of much literature of sensibility; and in so doing, she is able to save sensibility for herself, to close the gap so troublesome to her earlier between the ethics of sensibility and an ethics of social activism. Along with her new moral view of the French Revolution, then, she creates a new moral view of sensibility. Her admiration for it is now admittedly more guarded, but, for all that, her belief that it plays a necessary part in the revitalization of individuals and their societies, newly tested by her experiences in France, remains stronger than ever.

As Wollstonecraft retreats from polemics to "moral history," she returns to narrative techniques that allow her to become, for the first time, an original mythmaker of sensibility. At various points in her history, she recounts saving fictions of sensibility—stories designed to demonstrate the social efficacy of sensibility, some set in the present, some in the past, and some in the future. All of them have as an underlying assumption her long-held notion of education as *Bildung*—natural, spontaneous development of the whole individual, head and heart, in interaction with the environment. The fictions about the present, most of them already discussed above, are told by Wollstonecraft as part of the history of the ongoing Revolution: the day sensibility transforms soldiers from murderers to compassionate men, the day it gives birth to equality in the streets of Paris, the day it inspires patriotism at the Tennis Courts. The fictions about the past, however, read more like mythopoeia than actual history. Wollstonecraft labors, in both *Rights of Woman* and *French Revolution*, to demythologize such legendary female figures as Eve and Pandora; but she takes care in *French Revolution* as well to create a new set of myths-of-origins to replace the old.

Time was—she notes in book 3, at a pause in her long look at the effects of the Revolution—when men lived in a savage state of warfare and the hunt. Then the "social feelings" or "sympathy" emerge to transform these savages into civilized citizens, to bring men out of the cave into the city, back from the chase to cultivate fields. The conclusion she draws at the end of this fable is that "friendship" is the "origin of society," the interpersonal force that turns "tribes into nations" (*Works*, 6.146). A variation on the eighteenth-century myth of progress, this fable grants to sensibility, and its offspring sympathy and friendship, the major role in the development of civilization. Fictions of sensibility about the future are much more rare, but at the very end Wollstonecraft does venture one. She predicts that the revolution in France is only temporarily off course—temporarily ailing—and that it will soon right itself (*Works*, 6.235). In many of these fictions, it is worth noting, Wollstonecraft embraces optimism.

A positive side effect of the new sweep of vision in these saving fictions may be to free Wollstonecraft from her worry, aired so often in *Rights of Woman,* that sensibility is just a manipulative masculine euphemism for a feminine weakness. In any event, that worry has disappeared from her text. Sensibility, far from being a male construct here, becomes a universal human attribute, perhaps present excessively in France, but generally also present in all people who have not deadened it by the twin pursuits of getting and spending. She has clearly found a way—through her analysis of the nightmarish events in postrevolutionary France—to synthesize her oldest views and her feminist view into a new worldview. This may account for the new tone audible in this treatise: resonant, as usual, yet balanced—reasonable and compassionate—as well. She is no longer coyly detached, as she is in *Mary*, or furiously biased, as she is in the *Rights of Woman*. The estrangement from sensibility—and herself as woman of sensibility—is over and she is able to admit its presence again in her own voice and to assume her readers will value it, and wish to have it, just as much as they do reason:

> Man may [in the future] contemplate with benevolent complacency and becoming pride, the approaching reign of reason and peace. (*Works*, 6.17)

> Anarchy is . . . fearful . . . and all men of sense and benevolence have been anxiously attentive, to observe what use frenchmen would make of their liberty. (*Works*, 6.47)

> After this account [of the queen's political intrigues], any reflections on the baneful effects of power, or on the unrestrained indulgence of pleasure, that could thus banish tenderness from the female bosom, and harden the human heart, would be an insult to the reader's sensibility. (*Works*, 6.84)

Wollstonecraft has not abandoned her stance as cultural prophet in *French Revolution*, but she has modified that stance to coincide with her new-won peace of mind. In *Rights of Woman* she revels in the role of angry counter-prophet, of moral accuser. She confronts Old Testament and contemporary mythmakers about their cruel "moss-covered opinions" and challenges them to reform those attitudes and themselves, to look into their hearts and rewrite their manuals of conduct. Here, although she faces an actual situation even more nightmarish in France than the imagined "present deplorable state of women" of the *Rights of Woman*, she regains her equanimity, becoming in this case a forgiving prophet who interprets and predicts without condemning, and who clears the way, even in the midst of the Terror, for a new era of reasonable sensibility.

9

A New Page in the History of Her Heart

> To know Mary Wollstonecraft one must read these letters;
> they reveal the whole woman—in all her complexity. It is a
> pity that she wrote only one volume of the kind.
> —Wardle, *Mary Wollstonecraft*, p. 165

In *French Revolution*, Wollstonecraft successfully integrates her long-standing private values with new, hard-won public values, granting sensibility, always embraced as a private enabler, a new active and positive role in effecting social progress. With this to build on, in *Letters in Sweden* (1796) Wollstonecraft liberates sensibility from the inherited fictions that constrain it in her earlier writings—its otherworldliness and passivity; its proclivity to silence, illness, and death; its suspected associations with male tyranny—and then remythologizes it as the parent of imagination and the wellspring of true civilization. Thus transformed, it regains her loyalty and enables her to translate her own habitual behaviors of sensibility, now liberated from reason's judgmental shackles, into innovative and effective narrative techniques. Heightened perceptual awareness turns descriptive passages into evocative poetry; constitutional melancholy infuses unity into traveler and tone; openness to the complex of sentiments she has at the moment enables her to draw on all her previous literary voices and create a narrative persona of depth and mystery; and fellow-feeling enriches the narrator's stance.[1]

While she travels the coasts of the far north as Gilbert Imlay's business agent during the summer of 1795, she also undergoes what is without a doubt the most painful experience of her adult life: the gradual realization that she is not temporarily separated from Imlay but, by his preference, permanently estranged. The travel book, although clearly based on her actual letters to him,[2] softens and diffuses the pain revealed in those letters from her first suspicions of waning affection to the clarity of her final despair: "I am strangely deficient in sagacity.— Uniting myself to you, your tenderness seemed to make me amends for all my former misfortunes.— On this tenderness and affection with that confidence did I rest!—but I leaned on a spear, that has pierced me to the heart.— You have thrown off a faithful friend, to pursue the caprices of the moment" (Hamburg, 27 September 1795, *Collected Letters*, p. 313).

Her business trip is preceded, indeed is precipitated, by an attempt to end her life; and if this trip is Imlay's last attempt to save her,[3] *Letters in Sweden* is her last attempt to save their relationship. Since her eloquent private correspondence to Imlay from France has already failed to dissuade him from his new business and amatory pursuits, she decides to go public, to memorialize both her grievances against him and her love for him, to awaken him from his private reveries to a realization of his moral responsibilities to her and their child. She works to transform him from a captain of commerce into a seer of sensibility, from an irresponsible lover into a caring father. She speaks with urgency and frankness, expressing all that she might say on her subjects, and working to evoke the finer feelings that she still believes lie dormant in him. Her concerns seem all-consuming, seem to override any compunctions she might have about disclosing a private affair, and her own emotional vulnerability, to public scrutiny:

> You know that as a female I am particularly attached to her [their daughter Fanny] — I feel more than a mother's fondness and anxiety, when I reflect on the dependent and oppressed state of her sex. I dread lest she should be forced to sacrifice her heart to her principles, or principles to her heart. With trembling hand I shall cultivate sensibility, and cherish delicacy of sentiment, lest, whilst I lend fresh blushes to the rose, I sharpen the thorns that will wound the breast I would fain guard — I dread to unfold her mind, lest it should render her unfit for the world she is to inhabit — Hapless woman! what a fate is thine!
>
> But whither am I wandering? I only meant to tell you that the . . . kindness of the simple people . . . increased my sensibility to a painful degree. (Letter VI, *Works*, 6.269)

These lines contain familiar Wollstonecraft ideas about education: education as an organic process of the unfolding of inherent potential; the current deplorable state of women's education; and the importance of designing a curriculum for women to train both their heads and their hearts. What makes this passage so distinctive, along with many others like it in *Letters in Sweden*, is its public acknowledgment of feeling and the intense multiplicity of its personal revelation. References to education are made painfully poignant by mentioning her own daughter Fanny; voices from her own past, allegiances lost and refound, return to join in the plea for Fanny's welfare: Wollstonecraft the feminist, absent as recently as *French Revolution*; Wollstonecraft the lover and mother, neither aired so openly before in her public writing; and Wollstonecraft the woman of sensibility, effectively muffled since *Rights of Men*.

Letter VIII in *Letters in Sweden* marks, in addition, Wollstonecraft's complete and newly self-conscious return to the ethics and aesthetics of sensibility.[4] Midway in her journey, she is forced to spend several weeks apart from her daughter Fanny and her maid Marguerite in Tonsberg, Norway; she worries about the separation, but the pause allows her to exercise and reflect, and her health improves. In language that recalls the poetic diction of Gray or Collins she describes the experience of sitting on the cliffs overlooking the water:

> I awoke to follow, with an eye vaguely curious, the white sails, as they turned the cliffs, or seemed to take shelter under the pines which covered the little islands that so gracefully rose to render the terrific ocean beautiful. The fishermen were calmly casting their nets; whilst the seagulls hovered over the unruffled deep. Every thing seemed to harmonize into tranquillity—even the mournful call of the bittern was in cadence with the tinkling bells on the necks of the cows. . . . With what ineffable pleasure have I not gazed—and gazed again, losing my breath through my eyes— my very soul diffused itself in the scene—and, seeming to become all senses, glided in the scarcely-agitated waves, melted in the freshening breeze, or, taking its flight with fairy wing, to the misty mountains which bounded the prospect, fancy tript over new lawns.

This remarkable passage, in which Wollstonecraft, Werther fashion, temporarily loses all sense of self as she becomes all sensibility, is followed by a paragraph declaring her allegiance to the heart:

> You have sometimes wondered, my dear friend, at the extreme affection of my nature.—But such is the temperature of my soul—It is not the vivacity of youth, the hey-day of existence. For years have I endeavoured to calm an impetuous tide—labouring to make my feelings take an orderly course.— It was striving against the stream.—I must love and admire with warmth, or I sink into sadness. Tokens of love which I have received have rapt me in elysium—purifying the heart they enchanted.—My bosom still glows.— Do not saucily ask, repeating Sterne's question, "Maria, is it still so warm?" Sufficiently, O my God! has it been chilled by sorrow and unkindness— still nature will prevail. (Letter VIII, *Works*, 6.279–80)

It might be argued that these are love letters, so all talk of the heart here is simply a functional necessity. Wollstonecraft offers other signs as

well, however, that she is determined to revitalize and reform the creed
of her youth. On the metaphorical level, she presents "feelings" and the
"heart" as natural entities in a coherent, natural landscape of the mind,
and once again grants them positive powers—growth, resilience, integration. She also pays homage to an English predecessor in the ethical
defense of sensibility, another sentimental traveler, Sterne. Indeed, in
Letters in Sweden she seems to entirely forget her recent public quarrels
with male professors of sensibility, even her bitter battle with Burke.[5]
The following defense of a description of a beech-lined avenue in Norway, for an example, buries any reference to her earlier objections to
Burke's masculinist theory of the sublime and the beautiful:

> In these respects my very reason obliges me to permit my feelings to be my
> criterion. Whatever excites emotions has charms for me; though I insist
> that the cultivation of the mind, by warming, nay almost creating the imag-
> ination, produces taste, and an immense variety of sensations and emo-
> tions, partaking of the exquisite pleasure inspired by beauty and sublimi-
> ty. As I know of no end to them, the word infinite, so often misapplied,
> might, on this occasion, be introduced with something like propriety. (Let-
> ter X, *Works*, 6.289)

In *Letters in Sweden*, Wollstonecraft is neither shy, as she is in *Mary*,
nor equivocal, as she is in *Rights of Men*, about her allegiance to sensibility. She declares an end to the war she launches against it in *Rights
of Woman* and emphasizes anew its psychological benefits. It becomes,
for the first time in her literary works, the primary means to her end
and an end, or primary value, in itself, at once medium and message.

Part of her message on the subject, it should be noted, is an emphat-
ic reiteration of the one to be found in *Mary*. She dematerializes[6] sentiment again, redefining it as a "delicacy of feeling and thinking," and
realigning it with qualities of mind: understanding, judgment, taste,
sympathy, tenderness, genius, melancholy, and imagination. She also
builds on this cognitive-emotive characterization of sensibility; she
celebrates the human imagination as the last, best solace for a feeling
heart, and often enters self-soothing fantasies and reveries into the log
of her journey.[7] She terms them "the poetical fictions of sensibility."

One of the most persistent of these poetical fictions in *Letters in Sweden* seeks to mystify, yet naturalize, sensory and emotional suscepti-
bilities, making them mysteriously attractive, if sometimes threatening, forces that spring, despite her reason and against her will, from her
intimate dialogue with nature and human nature:

> Nature is the nurse of sentiment, — the true source of taste; — yet what
> misery, as well as rapture, is produced by a quick perception of the beauti-

ful and sublime, when it is exercised . . . when every beauteous feeling and emotion excites responsive sympathy, and the harmonized soul sinks into melancholy, or rises to extasy [*sic*], just as the chords are touched, like the aeolian harp agitated by the changing wind. (Letter VI, *Works*, 6.271)

During her first wakeful night in Sweden, as she watches her child sleeping, "innocent and sweet as the closing flowers," some memories "attached to the idea of home . . . made 'a tear drop on the rosy cheek [she] had just kissed; and emotions that trembled on the brink of extacy [*sic*] and agony gave a poignancy to [her] sensations, which made [her] feel more alive than usual." She continues with a question that reflects at once her continuing attachment to such feelings and her continuing mystification with them:

What are these imperious sympathies? How frequently has melancholy and even mysanthropy [*sic*] taken possession of me, when the world has disgusted me, and friends have proved unkind. I have then considered myself as a particle broken off from the grand mass of mankind; — I was alone, till some involuntary sympathetic emotion, like the attraction of adhesion, made me feel that I was still a part of a mighty whole, from which I could not sever myself — not, perhaps, for the reflection has been carried very far, by snapping the thread of an existence which loses its charms in proportion as the cruel experience of life stops or poisons the current of the heart. Futurity, what hast thou not to give to those who know that there is such a thing as happiness! I speak not of philosophical contentment, though pain has afforded them the strongest conviction of it. (Letter I, *Works*, 6.248–49)

In this passage Wollstonecraft basks in sensibility's mystification, granting it divine ("imperious") lifesaving powers. Thereafter, throughout these letters, she will cultivate her "imperious sympathies" in order to heal her own wounded spirit: "I am very sick—sick at heart.—" (Letter to Joseph Johnson from London, late 1795, *Collected Letters*, p. 326). At the same time, she will continue to work on the newest among her "poetical fictions of sensibility," begun in *French Revolution*:[8] its vital contribution to the progress of civilization.

In this new saving fiction, Wollstonecraft sees sensibility as the chief protagonist in a general struggle over the human spirit: it nurtures progress, the refinement of manners, the improvement of minds and social institutions. Its antagonist is sensuality, but sensuality now in the specific modern form of middle class commerce. The origins of this new idea are personal and are not hard to trace: her growing conviction that Imlay has prostituted his nobler inclinations (his "revolutionary" commitment and his "affectionate" side) to his new obsession to enjoy life's comforts and get as rich as possible as quickly as possible. Imlay seems not to have acceded to her argument, for she feels compelled to make her point quite personally in Letter XXIII:

> Situation seems to be the mould in which men's characters are formed; so much so, inferring from what I have lately seen, that I mean not to be severe when I add, previously asking why priests are in general cunning, and statesmen false? that men entirely devoted to commerce never acquire, or lose, all taste and greatness of mind. An ostentatious display of wealth without elegance, and a greedy enjoyment of pleasure without sentiment, embrutes them till they term all virtue, of an heroic cast, romantic attempts at something above our nature; and anxiety about the welfare of others, a search after misery, in which we have no concern. But you will say that I am growing bitter, perhaps, personal. Ah! shall I whisper to you — that you — yourself, are strangely altered, since you have entered deeply into commerce — more than you are aware of—never allowing yourself to reflect, and keeping your mind, or rather passions, in a continual state of agitation — Nature has given you talents, which lie dormant, or are wasted in ignoble pursuits. (*Works*, 6.340 – 41)

Wollstonecraft's return to this theme, with increasing frequency, eventually transforms her private campaign against Imlay into a public one, into part of her view of things. Sensibility refines and commerce degrades: "Under whatever point of view I consider society," she insists as she considers the selfishness of propertied citizens of Copenhagen during their recent city fire, "it appears, to me, that an adoration of property is the root of all evil" (Letter XIX, *Works*, 6.325). The prophetic tone suggested here becomes quite pronounced near the end of her letters, where commerce, or, as she sometimes calls it, "trade" or "speculation," becomes the solitary horseman of the apocalypse:

> . . . the more I saw of the manners of Hamburg, the more was I confirmed in my opinion relative to the baleful effect of extensive speculations on the moral character. Men are strange machines; and their whole system of morality is in general held together by one grand principle, which loses its force the moment they allow themselves to break with impunity over the bounds which secured their self-respect. A man ceases to love humanity, and then individuals, as he advances in the chase [*sic*] after wealth; as one clashes with his interest, the other with his pleasures: to business, as it is termed, every thing must give way; nay, is sacrificed; and all the endearing charities of citizen, husband, father, brother, become empty names. But — but what? Why, to snap the chain of thought, I must say farewell. Cassandra was not the only prophetess whose warning voice has been disregarded. How much easier it is to meet with love in the world, than affection! (Letter XXIII, *Works*, 6.342)

The free movement in this passage from commerce to Cassandra, from cause and effect to affect, illustrates the special nature of Wollstonecraft's achievement in this travel book. She has, for once, united private cares and public concerns, feeling heart and restless intellect. Because she presents herself openly here for the first time as a person of sensibility, sensibility as a way of apprehending and dealing with reality can pervade the letters, not only unifying their tone and enhancing their evocative power, but creating a memorable authorial persona.

This is not to suggest that the presence of sensibility alone accounts for the acclaimed success of this book;[9] her choice of genres is crucial as well. The travel book form anchors her in space and time, lending her events a natural progression and her descriptions a storehouse of ready details. The epistolary format allows her at the same time maximum freedom of self-expression. Her description of the palace of Rosembourg in Copenhagen best illustrates the fruits of this happy union of letter, travelogue, and sensibility. Its narrator is so conscious of, and so open to, external as well as internal stimuli that the resulting passage is at once vividly impressionistic and hauntingly evocative. While the travel book quietly lends the passage a natural unity of spatial progression, the letter allows the speaker to weave any sentiments she wishes into her images, to follow her reflections wherever they lead her (in this case, into the past), and to place observations, sentiments, and reflections in whatever order they occur. For an author who, by her own admission, has been plagued with "insensibility to present objects" and who has struggled to make her treatises cohere and move forward clearly, a description like this constitutes a major technical breakthrough:

> This palace, now deserted, displays a gloomy kind of grandeur throughout; for the silence of spacious apartments always makes itself to be felt; I at least feel it; and I listen for the sound of my footsteps, as I have done at midnight to the ticking of the death-watch, encouraging a kind of fanciful superstition. Every object carried me back to past times, and impressed the manners of the age forcibly on my mind. In this point of view the preservation of old palaces, and their tarnished furniture, is useful; for they may be considered as historical documents. . . .
>
> There were cabinets full of baubles, and gems, and swords, which must have been wielded by giant's hand. The coronation ornaments wait quietly here till wanted; and the wardrobe exhibits the vestments which formerly graced these shews. It is a pity they do not lend them to the actors, instead of allowing them to perish ingloriously. (Letter XX, *Works*, 6.328–29)

Wollstonecraft's Advertisement reveals her own recognition that the travel letter format serves her well in *Letters in Sweden*. It lends her narrative a predictable order, but without jeopardizing either the freshness of her impressions or the "unrestrained" flow of her "remarks and reflections" (*Works*, 6.241). It allows her maximum opportunity to trace changes of mind and mood without seeming to interrupt the business of travel; and, in so doing, she reveals a psychological as well as a physical pattern of progression. She conveys gathering disillusionment with the "commercial tribe" of the North and eventually reconsiders the French people in that light. She also conveys gathering gloom about her foundering relationship with Imlay and her constant attempts to adjust her thinking on this subject. In Copenhagen she at last gives up the struggle, admitting personal defeat, but even as she does, she demonstrates the intimate alliance of teller and tale, their successful mutual unfolding: "I . . . view every thing with the jaundiced eye of melancholy — for I am sad — and have cause" (Letter XX, *Works*, 6.331). Her business trip is clearly also a progressive journey into her own evolving mind, a *Bildungsreise* allowing her to integrate subject and object as well as head and heart.

The characteristic tone, as one might expect, is deepening melancholy,[10] a tone struck already in Letter I, then making itself increasingly audible, first at the ends, then also at the beginnings, of letters. It identifies itself as both the mood from which the sensible self wishes to extricate itself and the mood to which it, in the end, again falls victim. Melancholy is at once the alpha and omega of its reflections: Letter II, for example, ends with Wollstonecraft listening to night sounds, the cow's bell, the waters' murmurs:

> Eternity is in these moments: worldly cares melt into the airy stuff that dreams are made of; and reveries, mild and enchanting as the first hopes of love, or the recollection of lost enjoyment, carry the hapless wight into futurity, who, in bustling life, has vainly strove to throw off the grief which lies heavy at the heart. Good night! A crescent hangs out in the vault before, which woos me to stray abroad: — it is not a silvery reflection of the sun, but glows with all its golden splendour. Who fears the falling dew? It only makes the mown grass smell more fragrant. (*Works*, 6.252–53)

In this lyrical passage, in which description of nature intervenes in and substitutes richly for self-expression, the traveler overcomes her sense of grief as she contemplates nature in repose; but that grief nevertheless guides what the traveler sees and records. The natural world itself is seen to have its own equivalent for grief in its "falling dew" and "mown grass." At the same time, it seems to justify the melting of the speaker's "worldly cares" into dreams and hopes; falling dew and mown grass only make, after all, a "sweeter fragrance." The stamp of the sentimental traveler is everywhere in these lines: in their melancholy; in their swift reflective movement from reverie to hope, from

sensitive observation to poetic inference; but especially in their crafted blend of the affective and the cognitive, and in the dialectical relationship between observer and observed that accompanies that blend.
Sensibility, in this instance, creates both variety and unity. There is the
sense of the narrator's mind—emotion and intellection—wholly shared,
yet the sense of a unique psychological identity. The same gentle grief
casts its spell over the first eleven letters, quietly controlling tone and
focus and lending the narrator sympathetic appeal, an identity, and
mystery. It reaches an apotheosis in Letter XI, where the traveler is so
overwhelmed by the sublime landscape in Risor, Norway, that she temporarily forgets her own cares entirely:

> The evening was extremely calm and beautiful. Not being able to walk,
> I requested a boat, as the only means of enjoying free air.
> The view of the town was now extremely fine. A huge rocky mountain
> stood up behind it; and a vast cliff stretched on each side, forming a semi-
> circle. In a recess of the rocks was a clump of pines, amongst which a steeple
> rose picturesquely beautiful.
> The church-yard is almost the only verdant spot in the place. Here,
> indeed, friendship extends beyond the grave; and, to grant a sod of earth,
> is to accord a favour. I should rather chuse, did it admit of a choice, to sleep
> in some of the caves of the rocks; for I am become better reconciled to them
> since I climbed their craggy sides, last night, listening to the finest echoes
> I ever heard. We had a french-horn with us; and there was an enchanting
> wildness in the dying away of the reverberation, that quickly transported
> me to Shakspeare's magic island. Spirits unseen seemed to walk abroad,
> and flit from cliff to cliff, to sooth my soul to peace.
> I reluctantly returned to supper, to be shut up in a warm room, only to
> view the vast shadows of the rocks extending on the slumbering waves. I
> stood at the window some time before a buzz filled the drawing-room; and
> now and then the dashing of a solitary oar rendered the scene still more
> solemn. (*Works*, 6.297)

The melancholy sensibility of the narrator emerges in certain preferences: for the evening, the churchyard, solitude, sublime landscapes,
solemnity and silence, and perhaps, for Shakespeare's late play *The
Tempest*. But any personal sense of loss has been transcended by contemplating Norway's fiords—has been, in effect, sublimated into scenic
description—resulting in a passage of evocative power, yet remarkable
restraint.

Beginning with Wollstonecraft's return to Tonsberg, then her journey to Christiana (modern Oslo), a darker, less disciplined melancholy
displaces this gentle grief, fed, of course, not so much by the changing
images before her as by intensified anxieties about losing her lover.
Occasionally this darker melancholy erupts through the surface of her

narration-description in a solitary cry of despair or pain—"but death," for example, she says as she describes a northern forest, "under every form, appears to me like something getting free" (Letter XV, *Works*, 6.311). More often, however, it surfaces indirectly in her increasingly gloomy descriptions; nothing pleases her as much in the later stages of her trip in Denmark and Germany. Even beautiful landscapes can now "beguile" but can no longer "banish" the "sorrow that had taken up its abode in [her] heart" (Letter XVI, *Works*, 6.315). Her traveler gradually grows insensitive to the beautiful and the sublime, leveling satire not only against the power-hungry aristocrats and the money-hungry businessmen, but even against the indolent, ignorant, pleasure-hungry peasantry:

> Quitting Quistram, I met a number of joyous groups, and though the evening was fresh, many were stretched on the grass like weary cattle; and drunken men had fallen by the road side. On a rock, under the shade of lofty trees, a large party of men and women had lighted a fire, cutting down fuel around to keep it alive all night. They were drinking, smoking, and laughing, with all their might and main. I felt for the trees whose torn branches strewed the ground. — Hapless nymphs! thy haunts I fear were polluted by many an unhallowed flame; the casual burst of the moment!
>
> The horses went on very well; but when we drew near the post-house, the postilion stopt short, and neither threats, nor promises, could prevail on him to go forward. He even began to howl and weep, when I insisted on his keeping his word. Nothing, indeed, can equal the stupid obstinacy of some of these half alive beings, who seem to have been made by Prometheus, when the fire he stole from Heaven was so exhausted, that he could only spare a spark to give life, not animation, to the inert clay. (Letter XVI, *Works*, 6.314)

Wollstonecraft still sees a magical, even a mythic landscape, yet one in which gods and men, and men and nature, have parted ways and are, as a result, devoid of sensibility, insensible to the tragedy of pillaging nature or to the pleas of a suffering fellow human. Her last letter before departure from Europe for Dover concludes with a vision of the behind-the-scenes effect of businessmen so intensely gloomy that it takes on the quality of one of the punishments devised for men by the Old Testament Yahweh:

> During my present journey, and whilst residing in France, I have had an opportunity of peeping behind the scenes of what are vulgarly termed great affairs, only to discover the mean machinery which has directed many transactions of moment. The sword has been merciful, compared with the depredations made on human life by contractors, and by the swarm of locusts who have fattened on the pestilence they spread abroad. These men,

like the owners of negro ships, never smell on their money the blood by which it has been gained, but sleep quietly in their beds, terming such occupations *lawful callings*; yet the lightning marks not their roofs, to thunder conviction on them, "and to justify the ways of God to man."

Why should I weep for myself ? — "Take, O world! thy much indebted tear!"[11]

Adieu!

(Letter XXIV, *Works*, 6.344)

From a biographical perspective, Wollstonecraft's melancholy is a bad sign, and its increase near the end of the journey a worse one, a sign that she has not dealt successfully with her abandonment by Imlay and, in retrospect, a warning of the suicide attempt to follow her return to England. From an aesthetic perspective, however, it is a successful technique, engaging reader sympathies while it lends the traveler-narrator a sense of identity and a convincing illusion of change, both of expanding consciousness and of increasing desperation.

The struggle of the sentimental traveler to maintain some sense of psychological equilibrium in the face of her reluctant correspondent creates the main dramatic tension of these letters. Yet there is another important struggle going on as well: the enlightened female traveler versus the unenlightened foreigners she encounters. In this encounter, as in the other, sensibility repeatedly cuts across former convictions, lending her persona qualities of rich unpredictability, complexity, sympathy, and prophetic power.

In her first days in the Swedish countryside, the traveler finds herself trying to reconcile her own new observation that "here . . . the total want of chastity in the lower class of women frequently renders them very unfit for the trust [of wetnurse]" with her general Jacobin conviction that "amongst the peasantry, there is, however, so much of the simplicity of the golden age in this land of flint — so much overflowing of heart, and fellow-feeling." In attempting to resolve the contradiction, she remembers a favorite maxim of her lover, which suddenly transforms her dialogue with herself into an argument with him: "You have sometimes remarked to me the difference of the manners of the country girls in England and in America; attributing the reserve of the former to the climate — to the absence of genial suns. . . . Who can look at these rocks," she challenges him, "and allow the voluptuousness of nature to be an excuse for gratifying the desires it inspires?" Rather attribute it, she concludes, to "health and idleness."[12]

Generally, Wollstonecraft's close encounters with the third estate in these countries moderates, if it does not reverse, her tendency to idealize them as society's victims. By the time she reaches Norway and sees

the crass greed of the coastal towns, she is revising her earlier plan to
live the remainder of her life in a pastoral setting in the new world. And
changing such passionately held convictions and dreams as these, as
she recognizes herself, signals a general change of life philosophy: she
calls it "turning over" in "solitude" "a new page in the history of [her]
own heart":

> You have probably made similar reflections in America, where the face of
> the country, I suppose, resembles the wilds of Norway. I am delighted with
> the romantic views I daily contemplate, animated by the purest air; and I
> am interested by the simplicity of manners which reigns around me. Still
> nothing so soon wearies out the feelings as unmarked simplicity. I am,
> therefore, half convinced that I could not live very comfortably exiled from
> the countries where mankind are so much further advanced in knowledge,
> imperfect as it is, and unsatisfactory to the thinking mind. Even now I begin
> to long to hear what you are doing in England and France. My thoughts fly
> from this wilderness to the polished circles of the world. (Letter IX, *Works*,
> 6.288–89)

If, in these instances, sensibility in the form of moral sensitivity
seems to dissolve former loyalties, in other instances former antipathies
dissolve in an oceanic flood of sympathy, a gesture of sensibility meta-
morphosed here into an act of intense authorial identification. The foremost object of such sympathy in *Letters in Sweden*, and one familiar to
readers of Wollstonecraft, is the misguided woman of sensibility.
Except for the male sensualist, who is her equivalent, there is no other
character type that so regularly receives uncharitable treatment from
Wollstonecraft in her earlier works. Negative examples include fictional characters at the beginning and end of Wollstonecraft's career
(the nameless female spirit of "Cave of Fancy," Mary's mother and best
friend Ann in *Mary*, and, just possibly, Mary and Maria themselves);
flesh-and-blood women mentioned in Wollstonecraft's private letters
(her own mother, her sister Eliza, her friend Fanny Blood and Fanny's
mother); and the many faceless women she chastises in the *Analytical
Review* or the *Rights of Woman* for succumbing to their culture's notion
of them as "born to please" or "born to feel rather than think." Wollstonecraft's earlier attitudes about such women, excepting a few
instances of fleeting compassion, generally range from mild disdain to
anger; the stories she weaves around them suggest that their mistaken
notions of sensibility render them unfit physically, socially, and intellectually, turning them into invalids, muddle-headed ninnies, or volup-
tuaries, and inept daughters, wives, sisters, mothers, or friends. While
her tales frequently depict women duped into such a condition, as narrator she always maintains some distance from them, as if *she*, a disci-

ple of education and reason, cannot imagine herself in the situation of these victims of miseducation—or no education—at the mercy of every fancy and feeling, hence often victimized by men.

Wollstonecraft's first reference in *Letters in Sweden* to such a woman is her allusion to the unfortunate Maria, abandoned and mad, from Sterne's *Sentimental Journey*; and it is clear from her remark that she not only sympathizes but also empathizes—identifies herself and her own situation—with Maria's situation:

> For years have I endeavoured to calm an impetuous tide — labouring to make my feelings take an orderly course. — It was striving against the stream. — I must love and admire with warmth, or I sink into sadness. Tokens of love which I have received have rapt me in elysium — purifying the heart they enchanted. — My bosom still glows. — Do not saucily ask, repeating Sterne's question, "Maria, is it still so warm?" Sufficiently, O my God! has it been chilled by sorrow and unkindness — still nature will prevail — and if I blush at recollecting past enjoyment, it is the rosy hue of pleasure heightened by modesty; for the blush of modesty and shame are as distinct as the emotions by which they are produced. (Letter VIII, *Works*, 6.280)

Wollstonecraft here places her lover in the role of Yorick, a rhetorical move not nearly so surprising as her assumption of Maria's emotional vulnerability, one so intense that it endangers mental stability. Only once or twice does Wollstonecraft admit to feelings of madness in earlier writings, and then only in the private letters. Here she announces it, along with her passion for Imlay, to the entire reading public.

She next empathizes with a poor, unmarried young woman in Norway, a wet nurse with a child of her own whose lover has "run away to get clear of the expence [*sic*]." From her remarks it is clear that Wollstonecraft sees many connections between her own situation and the young woman's:

> There was something in this most painful state of widowhood which excited my compassion, and led me to reflections on the instability of the most flattering plans of happiness . . . till I was ready to ask whether this world was not created to exhibit every possible combination of wretchedness. I asked these questions of a heart writhing with anguish, whilst I listened to a melancholy ditty sung by this poor girl. It was too early for thee to be abandoned, thought I, and I hastened out of the house, to take my solitary evening's walk — And here I am again, to talk of any thing, but the pangs arising from the discovery of estranged affection, and the lonely sadness of a deserted heart. (Letter VIII, *Works*, 6.283)

So overwhelming is the temptation to empathize with women made unfortunate by love that it finally even overcomes Wollstonecraft's usual antipathy to the rich. While she is in Copenhagen, she recalls (or is told) the story of the late queen of Denmark, Matilda. She was sister to George III of England, married to the "depraved" Christian VII of Denmark at age fifteen, discovered later in the embraces of his court physician, then exiled to Celle in Hanover and dead by the age of twenty-four. Wollstonecraft is appalled by the Danes' invectives against the dead queen, whom she characterizes as a model, modern mother and a devoted social reformer: "Poor Matilda!" Wollstonecraft concludes, "thou hast haunted me ever since my arrival; and the view I have had of the manners of the country, exciting my sympathy, has increased my respect for thy memory!" (Letter XVIII, *Works*, 6.321–22). And Wollstonecraft continues to be, as she says here, "haunted" by Matilda when, shortly thereafter, she visits the palace gardens where she lived: "As they are in the modern and english style, I thought I was following the footsteps of Matilda, who wished to multiply around her the images of her beloved country" (Letter XX, *Works*, 6.329).

A final female figure whom Wollstonecraft closely identifies with in these letters is the tragic poet-prophet Cassandra. Deprived first of country and countrymen, in this sense doubly abandoned just as Wollstonecraft must have felt herself abandoned in postrevolutionary Paris, and then again in Scandinavia, Cassandra is not so much mad as maddened by the deafness of her captors (by Apollo's decree) to her stunning prophecies. Seer in a strange land, Cassandra sees and describes but is powerless to prevent the unfolding of the last dark events in the history of the House of Atreus. At last even her lover-abducter, whose betrayal of a daughter will lead to his betrayal by his own wife, abandons her and she is left to mourn and reflect on her losses, then be killed by that same wife: "To business, as it is termed, every thing must give way; nay, is sacrificed; and all the endearing charities of citizen, husband, father, brother, become empty names. But — but what? Why, to snap the chain of thought, I must say farewell. Cassandra was not the only prophetess whose warning voice has been disregarded. How much easier it is to meet with love in the world, than affection!" (Letter XXIII, *Works*, 6.342).

This is the first time that Wollstonecraft ever refers to herself explicitly in her works as a "prophetess," although from her *Rights of Men* on she occasionally assumes the role. Cassandra might not have been her choice in earlier days when she envisioned an idyllic future to result from improvements in education. She continues to hope in *Letters in Sweden* that people and their nations will progress; but any picture of an idyllic future is conspicuously absent. The future looks threatening to her, a world in which taste and sentiment will be choked out by the desires to consume or to keep, a world in which even the best and brightest women will remain, like Cassandra, captives, still deprived of developing most of their potential, still little more than hostages to the pleasures of men. Why go on seeing and speaking under such circumstances? her final terse remarks on landing in Dover seem to ask:

> Adieu! My spirit of observation seems to be fled — and I have been wandering round this dirty place, literally speaking, to kill time; though the thoughts, I would fain fly from, lie too close to my heart to be easily shook off, or even beguiled, by any employment, except that of preparing for my journey to London. — God bless you! (Letter XXV, *Works*, 6.345)

It would be a mistake to call *Letters in Sweden* a personal triumph for Wollstonecraft. Like the German hero of sensibility, Werther, whose melancholy response to misfortune in love so closely resembles hers, Wollstonecraft feels herself defeated by circumstances; *Letters in Sweden* fails, as all her attempts fail, to bring Imlay back to her; and, in that knowledge, she tries suicide again just a few months after she returns to England. Yet very few protagonists of literature build structures of achievement so visibly on the ruins of self-defeat as Werther and Wollstonecraft, and that success has to do with the thoroughness with which they embrace and espouse the notion of sensibility. They do not simply, like dilettantes, entertain its ideas; they live them, and they translate them into successful narrative techniques. They fuse sensibility's primary characteristics—keenness of observation, quickness of feeling, self-awareness, and melancholy reflection—into their narratives, as they do their favorite preoccupations: nature, art, love, and friendship. If their openness to stimuli sometimes blurs the edges of their characters, jeopardizes their identities and makes them far too vulnerable to hurt, at the same time it lends their characters greater depth, dynamism, and mystery.

Brissenden's *Virtue in Distress* places *Werther* at the end of the sentimental novel tradition but at the beginning of another: out of the "chrysalis of the novel of sentiment" Goethe creates in *Werther* a "modern novel, with its emphasis on the psychological life of the individual."[13] If *Letters in Sweden* were a novel, it would be just such a novel; as it is, it represents a new kind of travel literature in which the evolving subject virtually dominates, even constitutes, the landscape being traversed.[14] It is easy to see why her book enjoyed such resonance among the Romantics, for it especially, of all her works, demonstrates sufficient theoretical and practical understanding of the operations of imagination to earn her a place among them.[15] For Wollstonecraft this is the triumph—if she does not conquer her tragic sensitivity, then in any event in articulating it she forges a new literary persona: alive to both external and internal worlds, poignantly melancholy, sympathetic because empathetic, capable of changing and perceiving change. The internalized is at last externalized in her most remarkable literary achievement.

10
One Last Fiction:
Sensibility Imprisoned

By allowing women but one way of rising in the world, the
fostering the libertinism of men, society makes monsters of
them, and then their ignoble vices are brought forward as a
proof of inferiority of intellect.   —*Maria* (*Works,* 1.8.133)

Having taken a long break from novel writing, Wollstonecraft pours her
radical ideas into fictional form once more in *Maria* (1796–98), very
possibly in order to reach a larger audience,[1] but death overtakes her
before she can finish her task. Even as a fragment, however, *Maria* nearly achieves the same fusion of personal and political belief systems that
Letters in Sweden achieves in a nonfictional medium.[2] To accomplish
this, Wollstonecraft spins two stories—more precisely, reweaves two
paradigmatic fictions of sensibility—into one. The first, a heroic narrative of women's emancipation, reenvisions the brave new fiction of
feminine sensibility that Wollstonecraft first offers her readers in *Mary.*
The second, a potentially tragic narrative of the socially sanctioned
restraint of women, reformulates the darker *Werther*-like fictions of sensibility that haunt the margins of nearly all Wollstonecraft's works.

In this case, the darker fiction is *Maria*'s title story—and the one
advertised in the opening lines of the author's preface: "The Wrongs
of Woman, like the wrongs of the oppressed part of mankind, may be
deemed necessary by their oppressors: but surely there are a few, who
will dare to advance before the improvement of the age, and grant that
my sketches are not the abortion of a distempered fancy, or the strong
delineations of a wounded heart" (*Works,* 1.83). In announcing the
inflammatory story as the cover story, Wollstonecraft may be bowing
to her most sympathetic readers, who would expect as much from the
author of *Rights of Woman,* even though she anticipates in the same

breath the negative reception this story will get from most readers. Interestingly, however, the cover story of the preface does not become the lead story in the text but must be pieced together from various interpolated tales of men's tyranny, relegated by Wollstonecraft to the heroine's past. The narrative of emancipation, not mentioned at all in the preface, constitutes the frame and main story of the text. In it, women bond together to combat men's tyranny, transforming mutual sympathy into a redemptive sisterhood so committed that it occasionally leads to civil disobedience, and changing the declamation of sentimental self-absorption into the rhetoric of radical social protest. In the process they undergo a metamorphosis from victims to victors. This structure may well mirror the tale's intent, for *Maria* conveys a sense of guarded optimism about woman's—and sensibility's—future prospects.

Contrasting the book with *Mary* best reveals the extent to which Wollstonecraft fashions a new feminist program in *Maria* out of the hand-me-down ethic of sensibility. Mary's distinguishing characteristic, her enslavement to compassion, involves her in two interesting, sometimes educational, relationships, but does very little else for her except give her a temporary sense of purpose in life. At the same time, it traps her in self-defeating situations; it consumes her with service to people doomed to die young. The idea of social activism never occurs to Mary; rather than reform the tainted world, she works to present a morally inviolate self to the next one. In consonance with this goal, the virtues Mary cultivates are self-sacrificial and intensely self-directed. The last glimpse of Mary is of a woman whose life has contracted to a kind of living death: revulsed by her husband and still in love with her dead lover, her only comforts are her acts of charity and her thoughts of heaven: "In moments of solitary sadness, a gleam of joy would dart across her mind — She thought she was hastening to that world *where there is neither marrying*, nor giving in marriage" (*Works*, 1.31.73).

Wollstonecraft presents Maria, too, as a heroine of sensibility; in fact, her physical description in chapter 4 quietly announces Wollstonecraft's returning interest in the entire lexicon of sensibility. Terms from the ethics, aesthetics, and physiology of sensibility (and a touch of Lavater's physiognomy) all unite to characterize Maria as a woman of extraordinary feeling and understanding:

Time had only given to her *countenance the character of her mind.* Revolving thought, and exercised *affections* had banished some of the playful graces of innocence, producing insensibly that *irregularity of features* which the struggles of the understanding to trace or govern the *strong emotions of the heart,* are wont to *imprint on the yielding mass.* Grief and care had mellowed, without obscuring, the bright tints of youth, and the thoughtfulness

which resided on her brow did not take from the *feminine softness of her fea-*
tures; nay, such was the *sensibility* which often mantled over it, that she frequently appeared, like a large proportion of her sex, only *born to feel*; and
the activity of her well-proportioned, and even almost *voluptuous* figure,
inspired the idea of *strength of mind*, rather than of body. There was a *sim-*
plicity sometimes indeed in her manner, which bordered on *infantine* ingenuousness, that led people of common discernment to underrate her talents,
and smile at the flights of her *imagination*. But those who could not comprehend the *delicacy of her sentiments*, were attached by her *unfailing sym-*
pathy, so that she was very *generally beloved* by characters of very different descriptions; still, she was *too much under the influence of an ardent*
imagination to adhere to common rules. (*Works*, 1.4.104; emphasis mine)

Maria combines many character traits Wollstonecraft embraces as a
young woman, then disowns as a young militant (impressionability,
feminine softness, voluptuousness, infantine ingenuousness, delicacy
of feeling) with other character traits she applauds all her life (affections and strong emotions, strength of mind, simplicity, sympathy, and
ardent imagination). Even as a compendium of Wollstonecraft's ideal
virtues, however, neither Maria nor her eventual friend Jemima can be
praised, like Mary, as "slaves of compassion." Maria, whose profligate
husband George Venables humiliates her, then has her confined to an
asylum and deprived of her child, is far too overwhelmed by her own
griefs as the story opens to be cognizant of anyone else's; and Jemima, to begin with simply her attendant in the asylum, has long since
moved beyond pain or grief to the "misanthropy of despair" (*Works*,
1.2.91). The self-absorption of each is shattered by the story of the
other; but—and here they differ markedly from Wollstonecraft's first
heroine Mary—their response moves very swiftly from passive sympathy to empathy, and from there to hard-won mutual respect and mutual support in their campaign to eradicate injustice in their world, each
for the other's sake. Jemima, a poor woman brutalized by a series of
men and then cast out by society, at first only concerns herself with
doing, and keeping, her attendant's job, which does not, needless to say,
include collusion with the inmates; but Maria's story of her husband's
exquisite cruelty moves the cynical Jemima first to compassion, next
to admiration for her abilities, and then to active resistance to tyranny:

Jemima . . . could patiently hear of Maria's confinement on false pretences;
she had felt the crushing hand of power, hardened by the exercise of injustice, and ceased to wonder at the perversions of the understanding, which
systematize oppression; but, when told that her child, only four months old,
had been torn from her, even while she was discharging the tenderest maternal office, the woman awoke in a bosom long estranged from feminine emo-

tions, and Jemima determined to alleviate all in her power, without haz-
arding the loss of her place, the sufferings of a wretched mother, apparently injured, and certainly unhappy. A sense of right seems to result from the
simplest act of reason, and to preside over the faculties of the mind, like the
master-sense of feeling, to rectify the rest; but (for the comparison may be
carried still farther) how often is the exquisite sensibility of both weakened
or destroyed by the vulgar occupations, and ignoble pleasures of life?
(*Works*, 1.1.88–89)

Similarly, Maria, at first rendered apathetic by the loss of her infant
daughter, after hearing Jemima's life story begins to see her search for
her daughter, her survival, and her escape for her daughter's sake as
part of a campaign to change the system that brutalizes orphans like
Jemima:

> Thinking of Jemima's peculiar fate and her own, she was led to consider the
> oppressed state of woman, and to lament that she had given birth to a daugh-
> ter. Sleep fled from her eyelids, while she dwelt on the wretchedness of
> unprotected infancy, till sympathy with Jemima changed to agony, when it
> seemed probable that her own babe might even now be in the very state she
> so forcibly described. (*Works*, 1.6.120)

In each case, the infant daughter is the catalyst to personal transformation and female bonding; for Maria and Jemima she becomes an
emblem both of the present vulnerability of woman and of their common cause—the improvement of the lot of the next generation of women.
At last the two women, with suffering, sympathy, and a cause in common, forget their past in their struggle for liberation. When Maria wishes to break her isolation by having books and writing tools, Jemima
agrees to break the prison rules and provide them. Later a fellow prisoner asks to visit Maria in her cell, and again, Jemima agrees to break
prison rules to bring them together. Finally, when Maria decides she
must escape, Jemima not only aids her in her flight but discovers and
steals her child to keep her company in hiding. Their dramatic progress
from self-absorption to sisterhood,[3] from despair to solidarity and civil
disobedience, provides a positive counterpoint to the novel's title story:
society's many crimes against ("the wrongs of") women.

Mary differs as much from Maria in her words as in her actions.
Made bookish and reclusive by acute sensibility and childhood neglect,
she speaks very seldom; more often, when people or events disturb her,
she turns to her journal, pouring out her thoughts to no one in particular. Her journal, for much of the tale her only confidante, serves its
proper homeostatic purpose in the psychology of classic sensibility: it
eases her heart. Yet it fails to alter either her unhappiness or the things

that cause it. The abrupt conclusion to her "rhapsody on sensibility" underlines the impotence of such effusions: "Sensibility is indeed the foundation of all our happiness," she muses, "but it is only to be felt; it escapes discussion" (*Works*, 1.24.59–60).

In contrast to Mary, Maria is careful to direct her much more pointed reflections to someone quite particular, and often to someone who might be in a position to change things as they are. She shares with Jemima and Darnford her longings for freedom; she addresses her worries about her daughter in her Memoirs; and she casts her ruminations on divorce into the form of a protest brief to the court. Contrast Mary's intensely introspective, non-assertive, and diffuse reflections in the face of her unhappy marriage to the self-conscious and trenchant protest of Maria:

> *Mary*: Every cause in nature produces an effect; and am I an exception to general rule? have I desires implanted in me only to make me miserable? will they never be gratified? shall I never be happy? My feelings do not accord with the notion of solitary happiness. In a state of bliss, it will be the society of beings we can love, without the alloy that earthly infirmities mix with our best affections, that will constitute great part of our happiness. (*Works*, 1.18.46)

> *Maria*: I will not enlarge on those provocations which only the individual can estimate; but will bring forward such charges only, the truth of which is an insult upon humanity. In order to promote destructive speculations, Mr Venables prevailed on me to borrow certain sums of a wealthy relation; and, when I refused further compliance, he thought of bartering my person; and not only allowed opportunities to, but urged, a friend from whom he borrowed money, to seduce me. On the discovery of this act of atrocity, I determined to leave him, and in the most decided manner, for ever. I consider all obligations as made void by his conduct; and hold, that schisms which proceed from want of principles, can never be healed. (*Works*, 1.17.179)

Maria's words suggest a third difference between her and Mary, probably their point of widest divergence. Emotionally and intellectually, Maria has broken free. She has, as she remarks in her memoirs, an "emancipated mind" (*Works*, 1.11.153) no longer shackled to any of the outworn creeds, customs or opinions on women's essence, duties, or rights that block Mary from attaining adequate freedom either for her head or her heart. It could scarcely be an accident, considering Wollstonecraft's lifelong interest in Locke's epistemology and political philosophy, that she has Maria apply the principles of his social contract to her domestic contract: breach of faith by one party constitutes the other party's release from obligation. Acts of tyranny justify refusal to cooperate, resistance, even rebellion. The fact that this little drama of resistance plays itself out in a narrow sphere does not seem to diminish its importance for Wollstonecraft; on the contrary, she seems to believe that in the area of domestic reform, private actions may be as effective in bringing about change as shifts in public policy.

Maria's intellectual liberation helps to explain her willingness to take a whole series of risks that Mary would never dare to take: becoming a prison escapee, stealing her child, renouncing her marriage, living with Darnford (her lover) out of wedlock, suing for divorce, and contemplating suicide. In one way the judge at the end of the novel assesses Maria correctly; she does "plead her feelings" frequently to justify her action. In *Mary*, *Education of Daughters*, and *Rights of Woman*, Wollstonecraft argues incessantly for woman's right to develop her full potential; in *Maria* she focuses much of the time on a woman's right to command her own heart:

> When novelists or moralists praise as a virtue, a woman's coldness of constitution, and want of passion; and make her yield to the ardour of her lover out of sheer compassion, or to promote a frigid plan of future comfort, I am disgusted. They may be good women, in the ordinary acceptation of the phrase, and do no harm; but they appear to me not to have those "finely fashioned nerves," which render the senses exquisite. They may possess tenderness; but they want that fire of the imagination, which produces *active* sensibility, and *positive* virtue. (*Works*, 1.10.144; emphasis hers)

Maria learns how to stand up for her rights like this before the reader's eyes; she begins as a heroine without much more backbone than Mary, but, as Wollstonecraft promises in *Education of Daughters*, adversity makes one thoughtful, and as she suggests in *French Revolution*, tyranny renders one daring. And so it is with Maria. Nor does her sense of autonomy depend, as it does for Mary and for the oppressed women described in *Rights of Woman*, on ideal circumstances. She acts like a free agent in her marital bedroom, in her prison cell, or in hiding; one's thoughts and one's conscience alone, she has realized, make one free: "While no command of a husband can prevent a woman from suffering for certain crimes, she must be allowed to consult her conscience, and regulate her conduct, in some degree, by her own sense of right. The respect I owe to myself, demanded my strict adherence to my determination of never viewing Mr Venables in the light of a husband, nor could it forbid me from encouraging another" (*Works*, 1.17.180).

Even in fragmentary form, *Maria* illustrates clearly Wollstonecraft's agenda for women of sensibility in 1797. They should not abandon that sensibility but rather save it for its capacity to emancipate women: they should make it both a primary reason for and one of the tools of social change. Its presence in the novel signals hope for personal and social improvements; it is repeatedly represented as the first mover in any change of attitude, although Jemima's redemption by sensibility is the most dramatic one in the book: " 'Four years have I been attendant on many wretches, and' — she lowered her voice, — 'the witness of many enormities. . . . Still what should induce me to be the champion for suffering humanity? — Who ever risked any thing for me? — Who ever acknowledged me to be a fellow-creature?' — Maria took her hand, and Jemima, more overcome by kindness than she had ever been by cruelty, hastened out of the room to conceal her emotions" (*Works*, 1.5.119). Her metamorphosis from being a craven servant as brutal as her many brutal masters to being Maria's fiercely loyal and loving friend highlights Wollstonecraft's trust that sensibility can be woman's last, most saving, grace, a capacity that can not only solace her in, but also extricate her from, any psychological oppression perpetuated by misogyny. Her message to women through *Maria* seems clear enough: they should sympathize with each other, unite and protest, unless they prefer, as she fears they will in *Rights of Woman*, to hug their chains.

Talk of sisterhood, redemption, and social protest notwithstanding, there is a dark story told in *Maria* as well. Maria's experience of some of the joys of sensibility, especially literature and sympathetic affection, is intense and nearly absolute. At the same time, the world she inhabits is generally much crasser for women than the world of Mary. Each of the many interpolated tales of abused women she hears drives home the same point—the selfish brutality of men, a brutality epitomized in the portrait of the detestable Venables. The system of justice is exposed as an instrument designed to maintain a very unjust status quo, an instrument whose reactionary spirit the story captures in the judge's speech; and the world itself is equated with a prison-madhouse where the cruelest and greediest generally prevail. Even friends of feeling in this gloomy, nearly absurdist, world Wollstonecraft creates are highly unreliable. This side of the novel seems Wollstonecraft's equivalent to Werther's final nightmare vision of his beloved Nature as an open pit of predation. The parallel is worth pursuing, because Maria and Werther have a major weakness in common: both are quixotes of sensibility, initially enthralled by sensibility and eventually impugned as mad thralls to it by their unsympathetic societies.

On the evening of 29 August, 1797, Mary Wollstonecraft and William Godwin spent the final hours before the onset of her labor pains reading aloud from Goethe's *Werther*.[4] Their choice of books may have been an idle one; she asks Godwin more than once in the latter days of her pregnancy to bring her a novel "or some book of sheer amusement"; and interest in Werther runs high in England in the late 1790s.[5] Yet they also may have intentionally chosen Goethe's controversial "catechism of sensibility" to serve them in the program of mutual reform documented in their letters, William striving to convince Mary that she should moderate her sensibility and command her emotions, Mary encouraging him to exercise his feelings more. At the end of his *Memoirs* of her life, he credits her for having fostered his sensitivities; and in the same *Memoirs* he draws a parallel between her and Werther that has been controversial ever since: both, he maintains, are persons "endowed with the most exquisite and delicious sensibility, whose minds seem almost of too fine a texture to encounter the vicissitudes of human affairs, to whom pleasure is a transport, and disappointment is agony indescribable. This character is finely pourtrayed by the author of the Sorrows of Werter. Mary was in this respect a female Werter."[6]

Still another possibility, of course, is that Wollstonecraft's work *Maria* brings *Werther* to mind. Born, very much like *Werther*, out of its author's simultaneous attraction to and resistance of Rousseau's eroticized sensibility in the *Nouvelle Héloïse*,[7] *Maria* is Wollstonecraft's tragic female Quixote. Like Werther, she depends upon literature to stimulate and soothe her passions, and this dependency both frees and circumscribes her personality, demonstrates the genius of sensibility, but also its literariness, its fragile artificiality, its constitutional incompatibility with the world-at-large. Such a female character has long been in the wings waiting to be developed by Wollstonecraft. She sketches out vignettes of her in various works: the mother of her first heroine, Mary; young ladies in the pedagogical treatises; women in the *Analytical* reviews and *Rights of Woman*. All learn false sensibility through their reading and are thereby rendered unfit for life; self-centered, shatterbrained, and ridiculously sentimental about odd things—lap dogs, for example—they make those around them miserable by indulging themselves. It is not simply what these Quixotes of sensibility read, however, but how they read, that causes them difficulty.

Literature is Werther's main accomplice in his ill-fated struggle for self-realization through love or art. He sees it as his only comfort in a comfortless world; he reads to steady his overwrought heart: "I want strains to lull me," he tells his friend Wilhelm, "and I find them abundantly in my Homer."[8] Unfortunately, the books Werther finds most comforting offer him impossible, even harmful, role models. Even though he knows that Charlotte is engaged, for example, he lingers near home, imagining himself to be one of the proud, "illustrious suitors of Penelope," and reveling in his capacity to weave the threads of this archaic literary world into the tapestry of his own life.[9] He fails to realize that this same capacity blocks his ability to deal with the reality of losing Charlotte and prevents him from growing in ways that might save his life. Even more disabling are the later literary crutches he gathers around himself. His gleanings from Ossian, the New Testament, and *Emilia Galotti* allow him to rationalize suicide as heroic action, Christlike martyrdom, or political victimization.

Werther's trouble as a reader springs from his failure to resist the sirens of aesthetic experience. Most readers maintain a balance between subject and object that allows them to absorb a text, yet to reflect on it as well. Werther, in contrast, loses himself either in subjective enjoyment or object adoration—in either case, a kind of prereflective emotional meltdown. In this state, he permits art to impose its form, meaning, and purpose upon his external and internal reality, a way of reading that reception theorist Hans-Robert Jauss describes as "the pathological reverse side of the aesthetic experience."[10] Before Charlotte's marriage, Homer is Werther's Bible, Odysseus his mentor. He recasts his experiences, especially somewhat painful ones he wishes were otherwise, into the shape of episodes from the *Odyssey*; he views himself in the heroic role of Odysseus; and he basks in Odysseus's emotional well-being. After Charlotte's marriage, Werther turns to Ossian, a poet whose dark, emotionally charged text magnifies his unhappiness:

> Ossian has superseded Homer in my heart. What a world into which that magnificent poet carries me! . . . I meet the grey bard as he wanders on the heath seeking the footsteps of his fathers; alas! he finds only their tombstones. . . . When I read the deep sorrow in his countenance. . . . O friend, I would, like a true and noble knight, draw my sword, and deliver my lord from the long and painful languor of a living death, and dismiss my own soul to follow the demigod whom my hand had set free![11]

Werther's reactions clearly demonstrate that the oldest apology for literary sensibility—its capacity to foster identification with others—needs to be qualified. Werther's habit of empathizing with his literary analogues tyrannizes him. His self raises no protective barriers, and what his admired fictional characters do, he assumes he must do. Their actions become for him questionable, sometimes dangerous, personal imperatives.

Such responses, when shared with others, become what Jauss identifies as "cultic participation," another reader behavior closely associated with characters of sensibility, in which two or more people develop a strong emotional bond based on mutual identification with particular literary characters, authors, or texts. The texts are then allowed to serve as catalysts for communal—and often sexually charged—emotional experience; as sufficient legitimation of such emotions; and as sufficient proof of the existence of a special emotional elite. The thunderstorm scene in *Werther* provides a striking instance of such cultic participation. The experience seems innocent enough at the time but nevertheless unlocks oceanic feelings in Werther that will ultimately annihilate him. As Charlotte watches rainclouds retreat from the pavilion area where she and Werther have been dancing, she is reminded suddenly of a German poet of sensibility:

> Charlotte leaned on her elbow; her eyes wandered over the scene; she looked up to the sky, and then turned to me; her eyes were filled with tears; she put her hand on mine and said "Klopstock!" I ... felt overcome by the flood of emotion. ... It was more than I could bear. I bent over her hand, kissed it in a stream of ecstatic tears, and again looked into her eyes. Divine Klopstock! If only you could have seen your apotheosis in those eyes![12]

In true cultlike—or, in the words of the linguist Halliday, antisociety—fashion,[13] a literary allusion, here simply the name of an author, becomes a secret code word for entry into an imaginary utopian sphere, a literary republic of free and equal gentle hearts where these reader-lovers may enjoy, on the seemingly neutral ground of shared literary experience, wishes, fears, and passions otherwise forbidden by their situation or by society. This thunderstorm scene foreshadows the later, more sinister Ossian scene on the eve of Werther's suicide[14] in which cultic participation becomes dystopic, driving the lovers to mutually destructive deeds and words. When Werther comes to visit Charlotte against her wishes while Albert is away, she suggests that he read to her from his translation of Ossian. She intends to divert Werther's attention from his unhappy state of mind and from her; but the passages he has chosen unfortunately have the opposite effect. They strike a tone of wild, melancholy mourning as they tell of the deaths of heroes and doomed lovers. After several pages, Werther and Charlotte are forced to stop by their "fearful agitation," and the editor adds that "they felt their own fate in the misfortunes of Ossian's heroes—felt this together, and merged their tears." A few short sentences later the emotions Ossian has released in them overwhelm them, and cultic participation explodes into personal desire. "They lost sight of everything. The world vanished before them. He clasped her in his arms tightly, and covered her trembling, stammering lips with furious kisses."[15] Here all natural or social divisions between them, including marriage bonds, dissolve in an all-engrossing emotional experience that, ironically enough, will permanently tear them apart. Their hearts may "beat in unison,"[16] something Werther is very proud of, but that puts them tragically out of harmony with themselves and their world.

Wollstonecraft's Maria and her admirer Darnford are two more such sensitive and sympathetic readers. Like Charlotte and Werther, they are swept away by a radical empathy and cultic participation that provide them with vital emotional sustenance, yet place them at odds with society's moral imperatives. The heroine differs most markedly from Goethe's hero in that she is presented as a normative rather than a pathological character of sensibility, a feat all the more remarkable because most of the action in *Maria* takes place in a madhouse. Wollstonecraft manages to make the prison-madhouse where Maria's husband has confined her reflect on the world around her rather than on her. It becomes an emblem of woman's situation in a brutal society that sanctions "matrimonial despotism" (*Works*, 1.84), a point Maria reinforces in describing her unhappy life with her Mr. Venables: "Marriage had bastilled me for life" (*Works*, 1.10.146). In such a fictional context, the Werther syndrome necessarily becomes more than a psychological state. It gains clear-cut psychosexual and social implications as well; and the resulting novel fragment is not just another study of the dangers of reading with sensibility but rather an analysis of the particular dangers involved in being a woman reader of sensibility, dangers which can come from outside as well as from inside the individual woman.

Maria reads to escape from her literal prison, as Werther does to flee from his metaphoric one; she devours books (*Works*, 1.2.90) to comfort her aching heart. Yet her reading complicates her situation, and never more so than when it seduces her into a bittersweet friendship with a fellow prisoner. One day Jemima enters her cell with a "fresh parcel of books" acquired from "a gentleman confined in the opposite corner of the gallery." As Maria takes up the books, her heart throbs with "sympathetic alarm," betraying, as Werther so often does, the special vulnerability of a character of sensibility. She rushes to empathize at the expense of her own peace of mind, to draw analogies at the expense of protecting the boundaries of the self. "They come," she says of the books, "from a wretch condemned, like me, to reason on the nature of madness, by having wrecked minds continually under his eye" (*Works*, 1.2.93). Although Maria envisions the invisible donor as a perfect counterpart to herself, however, her experience is actually significantly different from his and, for that matter, also from Werther's; for unlike them, she is not free to choose the books she reads. They are books written by men and selected by an unknown man. Her literary experience, in other words, is twice mediated by men.

As she looks through her "mine of treasure," Maria discovers "some marginal notes": "They were written with force and taste . . . containing various observations on the present state of society and government, with a comparative view of the politics of Europe and America," and "with a degree of generous warmth . . . perfectly in unison with Maria's mode of thinking." These notes[17] pique Maria's interest, arouse her emotions, and cause her to bond emotionally with the marginal author. In a variant kind of cultic participation, she reads these marginal notes "over and over again"; and "fancy, treacherous fancy" begins "to sketch a character, congenial with her own, from these shadowy outlines." She next tries to read a "book on the powers of the human mind," but in her state of emotional arousal can only concentrate on books that speak to her heart: "Her attention strayed from cold arguments on the nature of what she felt, while she was feeling, and she snapped the chain of theory to read Dryden's Guiscard and Sigismunda." Maria now hurries to return the books in the hope "of getting others — and more marginal notes" (*Works*, 1.2.93–94).

With the "poor maniac's strain" of a young woman in a neighboring cell, also the victim of parental and marital tyranny, "sinking into her very soul," Maria begins to read the next book the gentleman sends her, Rousseau's *Nouvelle Héloïse*. Under such circumstances, Maria's immediate and complete immersion in the book seems understandable: Héloïse's story "seemed to open a new world to her — the only one worth inhabiting." In a manner reminiscent of Werther's longing for Homeric lullabies, Maria now gleans from Rousseau's novel only "feelings, culled to gratify her own." She weaves together art and life in her imagination, as Werther had, although her fancies have a much more convincing air of inevitability about them than his do. What else could she do with a single book, on loan from a mysterious donor (known to her only as the inhabitant of the book's margins), and an intolerable external reality, the narrator suggests, but blend Rousseau's hero and her own mysterious stranger, lending St. Preux his form, and lending him "all St Preux's sentiments and feelings"? (*Works*, 1.2.95–96).

After Maria jots down a few marginal notes of her own in one of his books, the mysterious stranger sends her an importunate concealed note: "Whoever you are, who partake of my fate, accept my sincere commiseration. . . . I will enquire, *why* you are so mysteriously detained — and I *will* have an answer" (*Works*, 1.3.98). Thus it is that Maria learns the name of Henry Darnford, whose sometimes literary, sometimes epistolary friendship will become her chief occupation in succeeding weeks. A relationship becomes central to the two of them that has been literally marginal and, because of Maria's married state, will remain virtually marginal, as fragile as the literary texts and contexts it depends on. Their conversations, the narrator admits, are generally reserved, "excepting, when discussing some literary subject, flashes of sentiment, inforced by each relaxing feature, seemed to remind them that their minds were already acquainted" (*Works*, 1.3.100). Imprisoned in an asylum, they have little else to fill their time but books and conversations; excluded from a life of action, they choose a reasonable alternative, a life of reflection. Their obsessive cultivation of the sentimental in this circumstance is understandable, but if they must read, why not read books that will encourage them to exert themselves to change their lot or themselves? How can it help them to remain lost in literary utopias or reveries?

Yet more than exclusion from society or reading preferences ultimately threatens Maria and Darnford's relationship. The tale makes us aware of three problematic male responses to feminine sensibility that much more immediately jeopardize their friendship: some men ignore sensibility; others acknowledge it, but only as a sign of woman's inferiority; and still others cultivate it themselves, but in a dangerous, exploitative form. Maria's husband, Mr. Venables, the most heavily satirical portrait in the book, is a self-indulgent tyrant very much like Maria's father and brother (and a number of other male figures in Wollstonecraft's works) so "embruted" by his pursuit of pleasures of the flesh, so habitually intoxicated, that he is blind to Maria's refined sensibility. He pillages her fortune, tries to sell her sexual favors to a friend, and separates her from her child, all with the same indifference, upbraiding her for her "romantic sentiments," and presenting himself as the real ideal man: "He asserted, 'that all the world were governed by their own interests; those who pretended to be actuated by different motives, were only deeper knaves, or fools crazed by books, who took for gospel all the rodomantade nonsense written by men who knew nothing of the world . . .'" (*Works*, 1.12.156). In the environment created by this insensitive, libertine husband, Maria realizes that her sensibility is worse than useless; it is good for nothing but to recoil on her, to render her a more perfect victim.

The judge who denies Maria's plea for a divorce at the end of the story acknowledges women's propensity for feelings but only to reinforce his own contempt for them:

> The judge, in summing up the evidence, alluded to "the fallacy of letting women plead their feelings, as an excuse for the violation of the marriage–vow. . . . We did not want French principles in public or private life — and, if women were allowed to plead their feelings, as an excuse or palliation of infidelity, it was opening a flood-gate for immorality. What virtuous woman thought of her feelings? —" (*Works*, 1.17.181)

The judge's comments reveal Wollstonecraft's awareness of the amazing extent of English paranoia at the time of the French Revolution— even women's behavior, it seems, needs to be regulated to prevent the spread of the infection to English shores—but also, more to the point in this context, her familiarity with the double-bind argument about women and feelings. On the one hand, the judge assumes that women have an abundance of feelings. At the same time, however, he assumes that to plead on the basis of those feelings, or even to think of them at all, is to be "French" and "immoral." As Wollstonecraft protests in her *Rights of Woman*, men often catch women in this impossible paradox, leaving women of sensibility "exalted by their inferiority" (*Works*, 5.4.124). Darnford may adore Maria's sensibility, but Venables scoffs at her feelings as "romantic sentiments" and labels the anger he rouses in her "madness." The judge, too, interprets Maria's emotionality as probable madness ("indeed the conduct of the lady did not appear that of a person of sane mind," *Works*, 1.17.181).

Unfortunately, not just reactionary judges but even well-read men of sensibility do not make women's lives appreciably better in *Maria*. Maria's uncle and benefactor is so kind and benevolent that she thinks immediately of him as she defines "true sensibility" in her memoirs:

> The sensibility which is the auxiliary of virtue, and the soul of genius, is in society so occupied with the feelings of others, as scarcely to regard its own sensations. With what reverence have I looked up at my uncle, the dear parent of my mind! when I have seen the sense of his own sufferings, of mind and body, absorbed in a desire to comfort those, whose misfortunes were comparatively trivial. (*Works*, 1.13.163)

His solicitude renders him a passionate champion of the downtrodden, especially of women like Maria, trapped in states of unholy matrimony: "I must repeat his own words; they made an indelible impression on my mind: 'The marriage state is certainly that in which women, generally speaking, can be most useful; but I am far from thinking that a woman, once married, ought to consider the engagement as indissoluble . . . in case her husband merits neither her love, nor esteem" (*Works*, 1.10.147). Unfortunately, this champion is, like Mary's Henry, physically frail and dies in the midst of Maria's trials. With the veil of his affectionate protection torn away, Maria sees the cruel truth about women's position in her society. Venables "pillages" her modest inheritance from the uncle, but she has no legal means of fighting back:

> But a wife being as much a man's property as his horse, or his ass, she has nothing she can call her own. . . . The tender mother cannot *lawfully* snatch from the gripe of the gambling spendthrift, or beastly drunkard, unmindful of his offspring, the fortune which falls to her by chance; or (so flagrant is the injustice) what she earns by her own exertions. No; he can rob her with impunity, even to waste publicly on a courtezan; and the laws of her country — if women have a country — afford her no protection or redress from the oppressor, unless she have the plea of bodily fear.(*Works*, 1.11.149)

Maria's lover Darnford, a self-professed man of feeling, also holds views much more sympathetic to women than the judge's on the questions of love, marriage, and divorce. Employing the vocabulary of sentiment, he writes Maria supportively about "the absurdity of the laws respecting matrimony, which, till divorces could be more easily obtained, was . . . the most insufferable bondage. . . . Delicacy, as well as reason, forbade her ever to think of returning to her husband: was she then to restrain her charming sensibility through mere prejudice?" (*Works*, 1.15.172).

Despite his generous views, however, he fails to make Maria happy, primarily because his own sense of sensibility is tragically incompatible with hers. He has not been taught, the narrator informs us, to restrain that sensibility: "Accustomed to submit to every impulse of passion," to Darnford "every desire became a torrent that bore down all opposition" (*Works*, 1.3.99). His feelings for Maria, however closely they may seem to correspond to the sanctioned feelings of sensibility—pity, sympathy, and affection—become a threat because they seek immediate, and, under the circumstances, dangerous physical expression: "The tear which glistened in his eye, when he respectfully pressed her to his bosom, rendered him peculiarly dear to the unfortunate mother. . . . In former interviews, Darnford had contrived, by a hundred little pretexts, to sit near her, to take her hand, or to meet her eyes . . ." (*Works*, 1.15.172). Once she escapes from confinement and begins to live with him, Maria discovers that he is volatile, self-centered, and only seemingly sympathetic (in Wollstonecraft's terms, that his sensibility is false): "A fondness for the sex often gives an appearance of humanity to the behaviour of men, who have small pretensions to the reality; and they seem to love others, when they are only pursuing their own gratification" (*Works*, 1.16.176). This is also the charge Wollstonecraft levels at Rousseau and his admirers in chapter 5 of *Rights of Woman*: they are sensualists in sentimental clothing, and their pretense to disinterested sympathy endangers not only women of true sensibility but also the very idea of sensibility itself. Darnford may help Maria to escape from the asylum, but his sympathy seems to end, in several of the elliptical conclusions at the end of the novel, in physical seduction and abandonment, a fiction of sensibility very possibly based in Wollstonecraft's actual experience with Gilbert Imlay:

> Darnford's letters were affectionate; but circumstances occasioned delays, and the miscarriage of some letters rendered the reception of wished-for answers doubtful: his return was necessary to calm Maria's mind.

> A prosecution for adultery commenced — Trial — Darnford sets out for France — Letters — Once more pregnant — He returns — Mysterious behaviour — Visit — Expectation — Discovery — Interview — Consequence.

Sued by her husband — Damages awarded to him — Separation from bed
and board — Darnford goes abroad — Maria into the country — Provides
for her father — is shunned — Returns to London — Expects to see her lover
— The rack of expectation — Finds herself again with child — Delighted
—A discovery—A visit—A miscarriage—Conclusion.

Divorced by her husband — Her lover unfaithful — Pregnancy — Miscarriage — Suicide. (*Works*, 1.182–83)

The narrator does not condemn Darnford irrevocably here; perhaps
Wollstonecraft's inability to do so, in the light of her own experiences
and convictions, even forces her to break off the novel. In any event,
she might have had Maria anticipate the outcome. Darnford tells her
of his youthful selfishness and extravagance, but his sympathy, coupled with his taste for the literature of sensibility, blinds her. As his
emissary, Rousseau's text prepares the way well, awakening Maria's
desires and convincing her, with her own complicity, that Darnford
shares with St. Preux all manner of noble qualities of mind. She completes the transference shortly after she first meets him: "Having had
to struggle incessantly with the vices of mankind, Maria's imagination
found repose in pourtraying the possible virtues the world might contain. Pygmalion formed an ivory maid, and longed for an informing
soul. She, on the contrary, combined all the qualities of a hero's mind,
and fate presented a statue in which she might enshrine them" (*Works*,
1.4.105). Wollstonecraft distrusts the feminine version of this Pygmalion reader reflex not, however, as her earlier works tend to suggest,
because the literature of sensibility is inherently enervating, but
because women are still so seldom free.

What renders Maria—and woman—especially vulnerable in Wollstonecraft's mind is her radical delimitation to a sphere in which she
can exercise only her emotions. Her incarceration in the madhouse—
that is to say, her strict confinement to the realm of the nonrational and
possibly criminal—prevents her from engaging in any useful physical,
intellectual, or social activities; and it is this situation that causes her
to be preyed upon by her feelings: "What chance . . . had Maria of escap-
ing, when pity, sorrow, and solitude all conspired to soften her mind,
and nourish romantic wishes, and, from a natural progress, romantic
expectations?" (*Works*, 1.4.104). It is prison life, then (or more precisely, prison = life), that cripples women: it makes them far too dependent upon male mediation, and far too open to male predation.

Wollstonecraft has aired these ideas before, most memorably in
Rights of Woman, but there they are abstractions. In *Maria*, her abstractions become emotionally charged plots, and her metaphors of confinement become the memorable asylum setting. *Maria* transforms

implausible polemic into a plausible and moving narrative.[18] This part of Wollstonecraft's final fiction of the wrongs of woman, of "things as they are," is bleak and labyrinthine. Just possibly *Maria* is a fragment because Wollstonecraft could conceive of no resolution for her final fiction of sensibility, in which a refined, intelligent woman is placed, like Kafka's Joseph K, "under arrest." She is then arbitrarily countermanded, redefined, and harassed until, little by little, she is reduced to a nearly fatal apathy.

Despite its pessimism and its fragmentary state, however, *Maria* remains a courageous[19] and guardedly optimistic book. Broaching topics some people still became pale when they mention, its experimental structure as a collection of confessions makes it read like a gripping, behind-the-scenes documentary exposing all the seamy undersides of eighteenth-century marriage: addiction to gambling, prostitutes, and alcohol, lovelessness, wife-selling, child stealing, imprisonment. In all, it contains portraits of over a half-dozen women from various stations in life, all "wronged" by men. Maria frequently acknowledges in passing a kind of fierce pity for these women victims of the oppression perpetuated by misogyny; but she concentrates at all times on anatomizing that misogyny in the strongest possible terms:

> Are not . . . the despots for ever stigmatized, who, in the wantonness of power, commanded even the most atrocious criminals to be chained to dead bodies? though surely those laws are much more inhuman, which forge adamantine fetters to bind minds together, that never can mingle in social communion! What indeed can equal the wretchedness of that state, in which there is no alternative, but to extinguish the affections, or encounter infamy? (*Works*, 1.11.154)

The optimism implicit in *Maria* is moderate; signs of hope, nonetheless, are present in both characters and plot, although they are subtle enough to be best appreciated in contrast to her other fictions of sensibility. Unlike the Vindications, in which all men threaten to become the enemy, some men in *Maria* are sympathetic, even occasionally helpful, to women in oppressive situations. Unlike nearly all the women in *Mary*, the *Analytical Review*, and the *Rights of Woman*, who are depicted as mere ciphers bereft of understanding, passion, and physical stamina, and hence incapable of uniting to better their lives, the heroines in Maria are capable of reflection, passion,[20] and compassion for their sisters and act autonomously, whenever possible, in accordance with their own ethics and values. In contrast to Mary, Maria faces her troubles boldly: renouncing her marriage, suing for divorce, living in adultery, "pleading her feelings" in the court, and nearly taking her own life.

Liberation of this sort is possible for her, and for Jemima, because they have discovered what Mary never does: that freedom is finally a state of mind. As a prison attendant, Jemima makes a whole series of independent decisions about how to treat Maria; once her sympathies are engaged, she refuses to be bound by the rules of the warden. Just after Maria discovers Venables's worst villainy and declares herself released from her marriage vows, she exults in her new-found freedom even though she knows he has just locked her in her room: " 'Was it possible? Was I, indeed, free?' — Yes, free I termed myself, when I decidedly perceived the conduct I ought to adopt. How had I panted for liberty — liberty, that I would have purchased at any price, but that of my own esteem! I rose, and shook myself; opened the window, and methought the air never smelled so sweet. The face of heaven grew fairer as I viewed it, and the clouds seemed to flit away obedient to my wishes, to give my soul room to expand. I was all soul" (*Works*, 1.11.152). If liberation is possible for these heroines of feeling, early death—or living death—is not (as it seems to be in *Mary* and "Cave of Fancy") inevitable. There are frequently compelling reasons to live, a lesson that Jemima brings home to Maria in the longest of Wollstonecraft's optional conclusions:

> She swallowed the laudanum; her soul was calm — the tempest had subsided — and nothing remained but an eager longing to forget herself — to fly from the anguish she endured to escape from thought—from this hell of disappointment. . . .
>
> A new vision swam before her. Jemima seemed to enter — leading a little creature, that, with tottering footsteps, approached the bed. The voice of Jemima sounding as at a distance, called her — she tried to listen, to speak, to look!
>
> "Behold your child!" exclaimed Jemima. Maria started off the bed, and fainted. — Violent vomiting followed. . . .
>
> Maria gazed wildly at her, her whole frame was convulsed with emotion; when the child, whom Jemima had been tutoring all the journey, uttered the word "Mamma!" She caught her to her bosom. . . . She remained silent for five minutes, crossing her arms over her bosom, and reclining her head, — then exclaimed: "The conflict is over! I will live for my child!" (*Works*, 1.183–184)

However tentatively, in *Maria* Wollstonecraft presents a society moving toward transition, toward the restitution of some modicum of power to women over their bodies and minds, even over their childrens' lives and their fortunes. And sensibility, as ever in Wollstonecraft's works, instigates and fosters those changes. *Maria* also offers its readers a strikingly new fiction of sensibility as an "active," heroic virtue.

It now inspires social involvement as well as self-improvement; in this instance, a resistance movement among several women under the banner of liberty and justice.[21] As symbolic action, *Maria* is an especially significant step forward; for in it Wollstonecraft concretizes and conquers the prison-house of sensibility that earlier often holds her and her heroines in captivity.[22] Its continuing existence as a male construct is acknowledged, but Wollstonecraft no longer grants it the power to "bastille" women. Jemima and Maria, both literally and symbolically, break out of the prison of false or self-centered sensibility to participate in life on their own terms. For them, and for Darnford and Maria's daughter, the old regime with its hierarchies, petty monarchs, and moss-covered opinions, is permanently over, even if the men in charge of their society—who often have no understanding whatsoever of the nuanced, subversive antilanguage of sensibility—have not yet noticed.

II

Conclusion: An Ending
Without a Resolution

Wollstonecraft's attitudes toward sensibility undergo the paradigmatic shifts of a disciple during her lifetime: naïve acceptance, critical rejection, mature return. In her youth she demonstrates a willingness to believe many of its myths, and uses its metaphors and discourses without much self-consciousness. The medical discourse of sensibility may enjoy a slight ascendancy over the moral and the aesthetic in her early private letters, but Richardson's ethical discourse dominates her early fictions. Her early heroines are variations on his Clarissa, that paradoxical combination of physical fragility and indomitable spiritual superiority. Midcareer Wollstonecraft turns a new critical, feminist eye on sensibility. The medical discourse she favors in early writings she now deploys against the notion: she insists that the cultivation of sensibility creates women who are intellectual, psychological, and physical cripples. In attitudes that align her closely with satirists of sensibility like Austen and Peacock, she recommends its rejection to all thinking women and repudiates its metonyms and myths. The last active years before her death mark Wollstonecraft's measured return to the creed of sensibility; she rehabilitates it in a form compatible to her own political beliefs. At this stage, the moral and aesthetic discourses of sensibility take precedence for her over the medical, but she also begins to fashion her own myths of sensibility. She grants it regenerative powers in society as well as in the individual, and she preaches her creed to her lovers, and to the world, in *Letters in Sweden* and *Maria*. At the last, her early enthusiasm about the genius, virtue, ecstasy, and benevolence sensibility could foster in its practitioners is much subdued; but despite recurring bouts of pessimism and suspicion, she persists in a certain dogged idealism about people of extraordinary sensitivity. Limited change is possible for them, and through them, in the world.

In this intellectual odyssey, Wollstonecraft enjoys many small triumphs, even if she fails to achieve any final, larger victory. She redefines sensibility to adapt it to new revolutionary contexts, including political upheaval and feminism, then transforms its by then familiar behaviors into innovative forms and literary techniques. Susceptibility and quickness of feeling and understanding inspire, in *Mary*, the creation of her own female *Bildungsroman*; melancholy informs the unique character of the governess Mrs. Mason; keen powers of introspection and observation yield, in "Cave of Fancy," an original allegory of the mind, a new myth celebrating sensibility's interiority; impassioned self-expression translates, in the Vindications and *Maria*, into biting, epigrammatic social and political protest; and, in *Maria* and *French Revolution,* fellow-feeling, the noblest of the social virtues, inspires a new myth about civilization and its potential for progress. Late in her career, she succeeds in integrating the two dominant concerns of her adult life—social reform and women's rights—with her favorite tenets of sensibility. She achieves the best fusion of all these forces in *Letters in Sweden*; in this, most certainly her best literary production, affective blends with cognitive, private concerns with public, to create a three-dimensional female traveler with considerable stature and evocative power.

In her ever-more-subtle understanding of the implications of the notion of sensibility for women, Wollstonecraft has no rivals but Austen. Her persistent worries about its misuses, its effects on women's minds and bodies, its seductive literature, its counterfeits, and its antisocial behaviors form a long, cautionary tale in all her works from *Mary* to *Maria*; each new work represents a new chapter in that tale. *Letters in Sweden* dramatizes the life-threatening dangers as well as the poignant pleasures of cultivating the aesthetic melancholy that "Cave of Fancy" celebrates; as a cautious positive postscript to her Vindications, *French Revolution* points up the possible benefits that men of sensibility might bring to their societies; and in *Maria* the prison-madhouse becomes the stark emblem of the mind-numbing isolation of a life lived, like her original heroine Mary's, too exclusively according to dictates of sensibility.

At the same time, Wollstonecraft never gains enough detachment from the language of sensibility to achieve genuine clarity about its severe limitations as a language of the self. If she is not waxing enthusiastic about it, she is furious about it or its abuses—both signs of the tenacity of its grip on her. History remembers her primarily for her resistance to it in her middle years; but, despite that resistance, like many of her contemporaries, she never finds an alternate language to use for the affective part of her experience that demands, as the turn of the century approaches, ever-increasing attention. The discourses of sensibility at least seem to offer new secular, scientifically verifiable descriptions of the mysterious workings of the mind, the connections between mind and body, and the warfare between reason and the lower faculties. They also offer the lower faculties new stature: senses, imagination, passions, sympathy, all contribute to knowledge, even genius, and virtue. Even the tough-minded in the century occasionally succumb to sensibility's seductive metaphors and myths, and Wollstonecraft is only sometimes to be counted among the tough-minded.

Finally, sensibility does not serve Wollstonecraft so well as she serves it. It does not translate as well into a feminist ethic as it does, for the Romantics, into an aesthetic one. Her struggles to reshape her heroines with the tools of this language do more to demonstrate needs: the need for a new psychology, new literary genres, and new social, economic, and political alternatives for women. Modern feminism continues to work to fill those needs and has, with understandable skepticism, roundly rejected the creed of sensibility and its pale Victorian legacy of sentimentalism. This may explain why twentieth-century students of Wollstonecraft prefer to emphasize her rationalist leanings; their own views of sensibility sometimes bear an uncanny resemblance to Wollstonecraft's most satiric vision of it in her *Rights of Woman*.

In the literature on Wollstonecraft, both feminist and non-feminist, the two charges most frequently brought against her are lack of imagination and lack of control; and her steady reliance on the language of sensibility is almost certainly complicitous in those failures. Its metaphors blind Wollstonecraft to attractive alternative habits of mind or occupations for women. From beginning to end her heroines only rarely do more than emote and empathize, their talents squandered on the like-minded or the ungrateful poor, their protests muffled by circumstance or circumspection or buried in journals. Moreover, sensibility's language skepticism and its predilection for spontaneous utterance over crafted message lull Wollstonecraft into writing habits that jeopardize her authority, hence her message. She indulges her belief that spontaneity, sincerity, and genius are one and the same, boasting she will not shape her sentences or chisel her paragraphs into inauthenticity; but this turns out to be a self-defeating habit that often leaves her work unread and herself relegated to the ranks of fascinating personalities of lesser literary talent.

All the same, her story deserves telling, for it says a great deal about how it felt to be an intelligent woman with literary ambitions at the end of the eighteenth century. Competing doctrines and revolutionary ideas of her day meet and collide in her works: reason and passion; self-interest and compassion; rights of men and women; divine right and social contract; expanding commerce and endangered sensibility; decorum and confessional self-expression. There can be little wonder that she fails to synthesize all these polarities; the wonder is that she brazens it out so memorably, leaving behind her a legacy of literary encounters with her enemies.

Notes

Preface

1. The five major works are: *Vindication of the Rights of Men* (1790), *Vindication of the Rights of Woman* (1792), *An Historical and Moral View of the French Revolution* (1794), *Letters in Sweden* (1796), and *The Wrongs of Woman*, also known as *Maria* (1798). Janet Todd and Marilyn Butler have edited *The Works of Mary Wollstonecraft*, 7 vols. (New York: New York University Press, 1989); it will be hereafter cited as *Works* (see Abbreviations). Three noteworthy extended studies are Gary Kelly, *Revolutionary Feminism: The Mind and Career of Mary Wollstonecraft* (London: Macmillan, 1992); Jennifer Lorch, *Mary Wollstonecraft: The Making of a Radical Feminist* (New York: Berg, 1990); and Mary Poovey, *The Proper Lady and the Woman Writer: Ideology as Style in the Works of Mary Wollstonecraft, Mary Shelley, and Jane Austen* (Chicago: University of Chicago Press, 1984).

2. William Godwin saw Wollstonecraft as a "female Werter," *Memoirs of Mary Wollstonecraft* (1798; New York: Greenberg Press; London: Constable, 1927), p. 73. An influential twentieth-century biographer, Ralph M. Wardle, presents her as a disciple of reason in *Mary Wollstonecraft: A Critical Biography* (Lincoln: University of Nebraska Press, 1951), pp. 90, 95, 166 – 68, 211. Much of the best recent criticism has seen her trying to balance reason and passion: Kelly, "Mary Wollstonecraft: Texts and Contexts," *Eighteenth-Century Life* 2.2 (1975): 38 – 40 and *Revolutionary Feminism*, p. 40; Mitzi Myers, "Unfinished Business: Wollstonecraft's *Maria*," *Wordsworth Circle* 11 (1980): 107–14; Catherine N. Parke, "What Kind of Heroine Is Mary Wollstonecraft?" in *Sensibility in Transformation: Creative Resistance to Sentiment from the Augustans to the Romantics. Essays in Honor of Jean H. Hagstrum*, ed. Syndy M. Conger (Rutherford, N.J.: Fairleigh Dickenson University Press, 1990), pp. 103–19; Mary Poovey, "Mary Wollstonecraft: The Gender of Genres in Late Eighteenth-Century England," *Novel* 15.2 (1982): 111–26; Janet Todd, *Women's Friendship in Literature* (New York: Columbia University Press, 1980), pp. 191–226.

3. Most adamant on the subject of the imprisoning effects of the language of sensibility are S. D. Harasym, "Ideology and Self: A Theoretical Discussion of the 'Self' in Mary Wollstonecraft's Fiction," *English Studies in Canada* 12.2 (1986): 163–77; Mary Poovey, *The Proper Lady*, pp. 48–113; Janet Todd, " 'The Unsex'd Females': Mary Wollstonecraft and Mary Hays," in *The Sign of Angellica: Women, Writing and Fiction, 1660–1800*, pp. 236 –52 (New York: Columbia University Press, 1989); and Anna Wilson, "Mary Wollstonecraft and the Search for the Radical Woman," *Genders* 6 (1989): 88–101.

4. For a general overview and extensive bibliography of the scholarship on sensibility, see Conger, *Sensibility in Transformation*, pp. 208–29. John Mullan, *Sentiment and Sociability: The Language of Feeling in the Eighteenth Century* (Oxford: Clarendon Press, 1988) offers an original discussion of the discourse of sensibility; and Janet Todd has prepared a handbook, *Sensibility: An Introduction* (London: Methuen, 1986). For a recent overview of current skeptical criticisms, see, for example, K. M. Newton, *Interpreting the Text: A Critical Introduction to the Theory and Practice of Literary Interpretation* (New York: St. Martin's Press, 1990). This skepticism can offer a bracing challenge to the idea of an Author: "Subjectivity is only a 'deceptive plenitude . . . merely the wake of all the codes which constitute me'" (Newton, *Interpreting the Text*, p. 82, quoting Roland Barthes, *S/Z*). Anglo-American scholarship devoted to the recovery or rehabilitation and interpretation of women writers has tended to resist the view that the author is little more than an archaic organizing principle for literary historians and critics. Such feminists would answer Michel Foucault's question, "What difference does it make who is speaking?" with "A great deal!" (Foucault, "What is an Author?" in *Textual Strategies: Perspectives in Post-Structuralist Criticism*, ed. Josué V. Harari [Ithaca, N.Y.: Cornell University Press, 1979], pp. 141–60). Both Jonathan Culler, "Literary Theory," and Naomi Schor, "Feminist and Gender Studies," offer very cogent explorations of the recent developing tensions between modern feminist and poststructuralist studies (*Introduction to Scholarship in Modern Languages and Literatures*, 2d ed., ed. Joseph Gibaldi [New York: Modern Language Association, 1992], pp. 219–22, 272–75). The present study operates on the interrelated assumptions that, first, the Wollstonecraft discussed is not the real (irrecoverable) historical individual but a transdiscursive construct or textual inhabitant, who, written about and writing, leaves traces of an identity behind her; and that, second, a textual study can, like a good archaeological dig, recover some of those traces.

5. This thesis dominates chap. 5, "Animadversions on Some of the Writers Who Have Rendered Women Objects of Pity, Bordering on Contempt."

6. Butler, introduction to *Works*, 1.7–28, emphasizes Wollstonecraft's rhetorical flexibility, as does Elissa S. Guralnick, "Rhetorical Strategy in Mary Wollstonecraft's *A Vindication of the Rights of Woman*," *Humanities Association Review* 30 (1979): 174–85.

7. M. A. K. Halliday, "Anti-Languages," *American Anthropologist* 78 (1976): 570–84.

8. H. C. Finsen, "Empfindsamkeit als Raum der Alternative," *Deutschunterricht* 29.4 (1977): 27–38.

9. Roman Jakobson, "The Speech Event and the Functions of Language," in *On Language*, ed. Linda R. Waugh and Monique Monville-Bursten (Cambridge: Harvard University Press, 1990), pp. 69–79.

10. For excellent treatments of the derivatives, connotations, and evolution of the terms "sentiment" and "sensibility," see William Empson, *The Structure of Complex Words* (London: New Directions, 1951), pp. 250–69, 306–10; Eric Erämetsä, *A Study of the Word "Sentimental" and of Other Linguistic Characteristics of the Eighteenth-Century Sentimentalism in English Literature* (Helsinki: Helsingen Liike Kinjapaino Oy, 1951); Jean H. Hagstrum, *Sex and Sensibility: Ideal and Erotic Love from Milton to Mozart* (Chicago: University of Chicago Press, 1980), pp. 1–23; and Raymond Williams, *Keywords: A Vocabulary of Culture and Society* (New York: Oxford University Press, 1976), pp. 235–38.

11. Murray Cohen, *Sensible Words: Linguistic Practice in England 1640–1785* (Baltimore: Johns Hopkins University Press, 1977), p. xxiv.

12. Alan T. McKenzie, *Certain, Lively Episodes: The Articulation of Passion in Eighteenth-Century Prose* (Athens: University of Georgia Press, 1990), chaps. 2 and

3. McKenzie believes that despite terminological confusion, "by 1700 the passions were better understood, better regarded, and more effectively articulated than ever before" (p. 55).

13. Magda B. Arnold, ed., *Feelings and Emotions* (New York: Academic Press, 1970), p. 123, is sure that "while behavior theory is still supreme in such fields as learning, where at first glance cognition seems equally important, there is hardly a rival in sight for cognitive theory in the field of emotion."

14. Robert Gordon, *The Structure of Emotions* (New York: Cambridge University Press, 1987), p. 23 and chaps. 3–4; Silvano Arieti, "Cognition and Feeling," in *Feelings and Emotions*, ed. Arnold, pp. 135–43.

15. Wardle, *Mary Wollstonecraft*, p. 37.

16. Gilbert Ryle, *The Concept of Mind* (London: Hutchinson, 1949; reprint Chicago: University of Chicago Press, 1984), pp. 43, 94–99. (Page citations are to the reprint edition.)

17. George Lakoff and Mark Johnson, *Metaphors We Live By* (Chicago: University of Chicago Press, 1980), p. 15.

18. Eva Feder Kittay, *Metaphor: Its Cognitive Force and Linguistic Structure* (Oxford: Clarendon Press, 1987; reprint Oxford: Clarendon Press, 1989), p. 90 (Page citations are to the reprint edition.); Lakoff and Johnson, *Metaphors We Live By*, p. 39.

19. Lakoff and Johnson, *Metaphors We Live By*, p. 57; Michael Kearns, *Metaphors of Mind in Fiction and Psychology* (Lexington: University Press of Kentucky, 1987), pp. 36, 63.

20. Lakoff and Johnson, *Metaphors We Live By*, p. 10.

21. Kittay, *Metaphor*, pp. 90, 13–14, 120.

22. The phrase is from Laurence Sterne, "The Bourbonnais," in *A Sentimental Journey through France and Italy*, ed. Ian Jack (New York: Oxford University Press, 1984). Nancy Armstrong, "The Rise of Feminine Authority in the Novel," *Novel* 15.2 (1982): 127–45; Terry Eagleton, *The Rape of Clarissa: Writing, Sexuality, and Class Struggle in Samuel Richardson* (Minneapolis: University of Minnesota Press, 1982), p. 4; Katharine M. Rogers, *Feminism in Eighteenth-Century England* (Urbana: University of Illinois Press, 1982), chap. 4; and Janet Todd, "The Fantasy of Sensibility: Frances Brooke and Susannah Gunning," in *The Sign of Angellica*, pp. 161–91—all provide a moderately positive view of the literature of sensibility as an empowerment, however limited, of women in the eighteenth century.

23. Kearns, *Metaphors of Mind*, p. 42.

24. Roland Barthes, "Myth Today," in *Mythologies*, trans. Annette Lavers (1957; New York: Hill and Wang, 1972), pp. 109–59; Kittay, *Metaphor*, p. 42.

25. Colin Murray Turbayne, *Metaphors for the Mind: The Creative Mind and Its Origins* (Columbia: University of South Carolina Press, 1991), pp. 3–4.

26. Kearns, *Metaphors of Mind*, p. 42, talks of philosophers' linguistic assumptions in the century; John Mullan, "Hypochondria and Hysteria: Sensibility and the Physicians," chap. 5 of *Sentiment and Sociability*, pp. 201–40, talks of physicians. J. H. Plumb, *England in the Eighteenth Century (1714–1815)*, vol. 7 of *The Pelican History of England*, 9 vols. (Baltimore: Penguin, 1969), pp. 91–97, talks of the rise of Methodism; and Lawrence Stone, *The Family, Sex, and Marriage 1500–1800* (New York: Harper & Row, 1977) talks of the increase in affectionate relationships. Williams, *Keywords*, p. 237, believes the word "sentimental" was damaged during and after the French Revolution. Donald Greene, "Latitudinarianism and Sensibility: The Genealogy of the 'Man of Feeling' Reconsidered," *Modern Philology* 75.2 (1977): 159–83 challenges R. S. Crane's theory of sensibility's origins in "Suggestions Toward a Genealogy of the 'Man of Feeling,'" *ELH* 1.3 (1934): 205–30 and also the

general assumption of many scholars that its influence pervades the latter part of the century.

27. Victor Lange, ed., introduction to *The Sorrows of Young Werther, The New Melusina, Novelle* by Johann Wolfgang von Goethe (New York: Holt, Rinehart and Winston, 1949), p. xi. The epithet for Goethe's novel is from Hans-Robert Jauss, "Rousseaus 'Nouvelle Héloïse' und Goethes 'Werther' im Horizontwandel zwischen französischer Aufklärung und deutschem Idealismus," in *Ästhetische Erfahrung und literarische Hermeneutik* (Frankfurt am Main: Suhrkamp, 1982), 2.588.

28. Goethe, *Werther*, pp. 120–21.

29. Ibid., pp. 127–28.

30. Lange, introduction to *Werther*, p. x.

31. Godwin, *Memoirs*, p. 73.

32. Sandra Gilbert and Susan M. Gubar, "Sexual Linguistics: Gender, Language, and Sexuality," *NLH* 16.3 (1985): 515–43 and Elaine Showalter, "Feminist Criticism in the Wilderness," *Critical Inquiry* 8.2 (1981): 179–205 are germinal essays. Deborah Cameron's "Introduction: why is language a feminist issue?" in *The Feminist Critique of Language: A Reader*, ed. Cameron (New York: Routledge, 1990), pp. 1–28, and Mary Eagleton's introduction to *Feminist Literary Criticism*, ed. Eagleton (New York: Longman, 1991), pp. 1–23, are very useful overviews of the subject.

33. The extreme position is taken by Hélène Cixous, "The Laugh of the Medusa," in *Literary Criticism and Theory: The Greeks to the Present*, ed. Robert Con Davis and Laurie Finke (1975; New York: Longman, 1989), pp. 732–47. The specific citation can be found on p. 746.

34. Robin Lakoff, *Language and Woman's Place* (New York: Harper and Row, 1975), pp. 53–56, 61–62, 82. Janet M. Todd, "The Language of Sex in *A Vindication of the Rights of Woman*," *Mary Wollstonecraft Newsletter* 1.2 (April 1973): 10–17, points out evidence of Wollstonecraft's keen awareness of linguistic markers for sexual difference.

35. Couze Venn, trans., "Women's Exile: Interview with Luce Irigaray," in *Feminist Critique*, ed. Cameron, pp. 80–96.

Introduction

1. For presentations of Wollstonecraft as an apologist for reason, see Harriet Blodgett, "Emily Vindicated: Ann Radcliffe and Mary Wollstonecraft," *Weber Studies* 7.2 (1990): 48–61, and Guralnick, "Rhetorical Strategy," pp. 174–85. For an overview of Wollstonecraft's reception, see her biographers Kelly, *Revolutionary Feminism*; Wardle, *Mary Wollstonecraft*; and Claire Tomalin, *The Life and Death of Mary Wollstonecraft* (New York: New American Library, 1974). See also Janet Todd's *Mary Wollstonecraft: An Annotated Bibliography* (New York: Garland, 1976).

2. Williams, *Keywords*, p. 235; Empson, *The Structure of Complex Words*, p. 269. See Preface nn. 4 and 10 for studies of the language of sensibility. Indispensable general discussions of the development and manifestations of sensibility as a literary and cultural phenomenon are Louis Bredvold, *The Natural History of Sensibility* (Detroit: Wayne State University Press, 1962); R. F. Brissenden, *Virtue in Distress: Studies in the Novel of Sentiment from Richardson to Sade* (New York: Harper & Row, 1974); Stephen D. Cox, *"The Stranger Within Thee": Concepts of the Self in Late-Eighteenth-Century Literature* (Pittsburgh: University of Pittsburgh Press, 1980); the previously cited Crane, "Suggestions Toward a Genealogy of the 'Man of Feeling'"; Northrop

Frye, "Towards Defining an Age of Sensibility," in *Eighteenth-Century English Literature: Essays in Modern Criticism*, ed. James L. Clifford, 3d ed. (New York: Oxford University Press, 1959), pp. 311–18; Greene, "Latitudinarianism and Sensibility: The Genealogy of the 'Man of Feeling' Reconsidered"; Hagstrum, *Sex and Sensibility*; Mullan, *Sentiment and Sociability*; George S. Rousseau, "Nerves, Spirits, and Fibres: Towards Defining the Organs of Sensibility—with a Postscript 1976," *The Blue Guitar* 2 (1976): 125–53; and J. M. S. Tompkins, *The Popular Novel in England 1770–1800* (1932; Lincoln: University of Nebraska Press, 1961).

3. On the reception of *Werther* in England, see Stuart P. Atkins, *The Testament of Werther in Poetry and Drama* (Cambridge: Harvard University Press, 1949); John Boening, ed., *The Reception of Classical German Literature in England, 1760–1860*, 10 vols. (New York: Garland, 1977); and Syndy M. Conger, "The Sorrows of Young Charlotte: Werther's English Sisters 1785–1805," *Goethe Yearbook* 3 (1986): 21–56. On the controversy over *Werther* in Germany, see Gunter H. Hertling, "Die *Werther*-Kritik im Meinungsstreit der Spätaufklärer," *German Quarterly* 36 (1963): 403–13; Hans-Robert Jauss, "Rousseaus 'Nouvelle Héloïse' and Goethes 'Werther' im Horizontwandel"; and Klaus R. Scherpe, *Werther und Wertherwirkung: Zum Syndrom bürgerlicher Gesellschaftsordnung im 18. Jahrhundert* (Bad Homburg: Gehlen, 1970).

4. Goethe, *Werther*, pp. 76–77.

5. Gordon, *The Structure of Emotions*, p. 21, notes that the term "emotion" is a metaphor; Empson, *The Structure of Complex Words*, p. 257, mentions that in the eighteenth century sensibility becomes a "stock metaphor."

6. Kearns, *Metaphors of Mind*, p. 21.

7. Lakoff and Johnson, *Metaphors We Live By*, pp. 39, 61, 26, 116, 85.

8. Goethe, *Werther*, p. 32.

9. "Consciousness," in *The Oxford Companion to the Mind*, ed. Richard L. Gregory (New York: Oxford University Press, 1987), p. 161.

10. Goethe, *Werther*, p. 22.

11. Jauss, *Ästhetische Erfahrung* 1.227–31.

12. John Locke, *An Essay Concerning Human Understanding*, ed. Alexander Campbell Fraser, 2 vols. (1690; London: Constable, 1959), 1.1.15.48–49 (citations are to book, chapter, section, and page number).

13. Ibid., 2.3.1.142–43. Kearns, *Metaphors of Mind*, pp. 48, 58–59, 61, offers insight into the implications of Locke's mind-as-entity metaphor.

14. Locke, *Essay*, 2.21.54.350. On the faculties as powers of the mind, not discrete "real beings," see 2.21.5 to 2.21.6.14.

15. Ibid., 2.7.10.164–65. Locke's mind model, according to *The Oxford Companion to the Mind*, emphasizes "transparency," pp. 162, 439–40.

16. Fraser, *Essay*, p. xi.

17. Locke, *Essay*, 2.1.7.126.

18. Kearns, *Metaphors of Mind*, pp. 63–64.

19. Sympathy, like sensibility, became a generalized term used both for interpersonal and intracorporal experience. See Mullan, *Sentiment and Sociability*, pp. 25–27; and James Rodgers, "Sensibility, Sympathy, Benevolence: Physiology and Moral Philosophy in *Tristram Shandy*," in *Languages of Nature: Critical Essays on Science and Literature*, ed. L. J. Jordanova (New Brunswick, N.J.: Rutgers University Press, 1986), pp. 117–58.

20. Sterne, *Sentimental Journey*, p. 5. Sensibility's presentation of human subjectivity, at least in Sterne's case, is designed to challenge the scientific materialist's view; see John A. Dussinger, "The Sensorium in the World of *A Sentimental Journey*," *Ariel E* 13.2 (1982): 3–16.

21. Jean H. Hagstrum, "Towards a Profile of the Word *Conscious* in Eighteenth-Century Literature," in *Psychology and Literature in the Eighteenth Century*, ed. Christopher Fox (New York: AMS Press, 1987), pp. 23–50.

22. Sterne, *Sentimental Journey*, p. 34.

23. Goethe, *Werther*, pp. 35, 3.

24. Ibid., p. 74.

25. "Sentiment": "feelings which involve an intellectual element"; "a thought or reflection coloured by or proceeding from emotion" (*Oxford English Dictionary*).

26. Goethe, *Werther*, p. 77. Mullan presents Richardson's stories as "parables" in "Richardson: Sentiment and the Construction of Femininity," *Sentiment and Sociability*, pp. 57–113; Peter J. Stanlis illuminates Rousseau's sensibility in "Burke and the Sensibility of Rousseau," *Thought* (1961): 246–76, as does Hagstrum, *Sex and Sensibility*, pp. 219–46; Jauss reads *Werther* as Goethe's resistant response to Rousseau's *Nouvelle Héloïse* in *Ästhetische Erfahrung*, 2.585–653.

27. See Tompkins, *Popular Novel*, pp. 34–37; cf. R. P. Utter and Gwendolyn B. Needham, *Pamela's Daughters* (New York: Macmillan, 1936).

28. Bredvold, "The Ethics of Feeling," in *Natural History of Sensibility*, pp. 1–26; Brissenden, "Sentimentalism: An Attempt at Definition," in *Virtue in Distress*, pp. 11–55; Mullan, "Sympathy and the Production of Society," in *Sentiment and Sociability*, pp. 18–56; and *British Moralists*, ed. L. A. Selby-Bigge, with a new introduction by Bernard H. Baumrin, vol. 1 (1897; New York: Bobbs-Merrill, 1964).

29. Adam Smith, *The Theory of Moral Sentiments*, ed. D. D. Raphael and A. L. MacFie (1976; Indianapolis: Liberty Press, 1982), pp. 306–7, 220, 9. Brissenden, *Virtue in Distress*, believes Smith's work on sympathy is "paradigmatic," p. 39.

30. Cox, "Self and the Aesthetics of Sensibility," in *"The Stranger Within,"* pp. 35–58.

31. Edward Young, "Conjectures on Original Composition in a Letter to the Author of *Sir Charles Grandison*" (1755), in *Enlightened England*, ed. Wylie Sypher, rev. ed. (New York: Norton, 1942), pp. 607–8.

32. Michel Foucault, *The Care of the Self*, vol. 3 of *The History of Sexuality*, trans. Robert Hurley, 3 vols. (New York: Random House, 1988), pp. 54–58. See also McKenzie, "Quickening Forces: Theoretical and Physical Modifications of the Traditional Components," in *Certain, Lively Episodes*, pp. 55–88, and Mullan, "Hypochondria and Hysteria: Sensibility and the Physicians," in *Sentiment and Sociability*, pp. 201–40. Several other sources provide invaluable background on the subject of medicine and sensibility: Karl M. Figlio, "Theories of Perception and the Physiology of Mind in the Late Eighteenth Century," *History of Science* 13 (1975): 177–212; Sergio Moravia, "The Enlightenment and the Sciences of Man," *History of Science* 18 (1980): 247–68; L. J. Rather, *Mind and Body in Eighteenth-Century Medicine: A Study Based on Jerome Gaub's De regimine mentis* (Berkeley: University of California Press, 1965); and G. S. Rousseau, "Nerves, Spirits, and Fibres."

33. G. J. Barker-Benfield, *The Culture of Sensibility: Sex and Society in Eighteenth-Century Britain* (Chicago: University of Chicago Press, 1992), pp. xxvii, 27; Tompkins, *Popular Novel in England*, p. 148.

34. Barker-Benfield, *Culture of Sensibility*, understands the implications of gendering sensibility both for men and for Wollstonecraft, pp. xxvii, 2, 104–53. See also ch. 6 n. 14.

35. Cox, "The Self as Stranger," in *"The Stranger Within,"* pp. 3–12; see also pp. 4, 37.

36. Williams, *Keywords*, p. 236.

37. Ibid., p. 237.
38. Hagstrum, *Sex and Sensibility*, p. 252.
39. Lakoff and Johnson, *Metaphors We Live By*, p. 72. Chris Jones, "Godwin to Mary: The First Letter," *Keats-Shelley Review* 1 (1986): 61–74, also believes that Wollstonecraft tried to "take sensibility into more challenging territory" (p. 71).
40. Wollstonecraft criticizes Madame de Staël for "blind homage" to Rousseau, then later criticizes one of Rousseau's biographers for "cold" reading; see *Analytical Review* 4 (July 1789) and 6 (April 1790) in *Works*, 7.136, 228.
41. Wollstonecraft compares the experience of pure or unmixed feelings to the supposed "bliss of paradisiacal days" in *Mary*, chap. 24, *Works*, 1.59.

Chapter 1. Epistolary Revelations

1. This is the impression sometimes given by Wollstonecraft's American biographer Wardle, pp. 81–82, 105–6, and editor Butler in her introduction to *Works*, pp. 7–28.
2. G. S. Rousseau, "Nerves, Spirits, and Fibers," p. 154, believes that the language of sensibility had no rivals in the area of psychological analysis but rather formed a common "substratum of uttered thought" shared by all interested parties in the age.
3. These are qualities ascribed to the literature of sensibility by Northrop Frye, "Towards Defining an Age of Sensibility," pp. 311–18.
4. Wardle, *Mary Wollstonecraft*, p. 53.
5. Paul Parnell, "The Sentimental Mask," *PMLA* 78 (1963): 529–35.
6. Wardle, *Mary Wollstonecraft*, pp. 73–81.
7. This portrait by Opie appears on the frontispiece of Helene Simon, *William Godwin und Mary Wollstonecraft: Eine biographische Studie* (Munich: Beck, 1909).
8. Wollstonecrafts's letters on pp. 6–7 and 10 are cited by permission of The Carl H. Pforzheimer Collection of Shelley and His Circle; The New York Public Library; and the Astor, Lenox, and Tilden foundations. The letters discussed on pp. 12 and 14–15 are quoted by permission of Lord Abinger and the Bodleian Library.
9. Janet Todd anatomizes Wollstonecraft's unhealthy early view of friendship in her *Women's Friendship in Literature*, pp. 191–216.
10. Wardle, "Return to Bondage (1786–87)," in *Mary Wollstonecraft*, pp. 60–82; Tomalin, *Life and Death*, pp. 40–60.
11. Wardle notes Wollstonecraft's interest in Paley in his introduction to the *Collected Letters*, pp. 33–34; see also her letter to Eliza of 27 June 1787, pp. 154–56, and Wardle's note on p. 156.
12. See Preface, p. xvi.
13. Tomalin, *Life and Death*, p. 145.
14. See Preface, pp. xxiv–xxv.
15. Goethe, *Werther*, pp. 10–11, 36.
16. Tomalin, *Life and Death*, p. 145.
17. Ibid., p. 178.
18. Ibid., pp. 163–180.
19. Goethe, *Werther*, pp. 45–46.
20. Hagstrum, *Sex and Sensibility*, pp. 24–49, emphasizes the importance of Milton's mythic couple in the articulation of affectionate relationships in the eighteenth century; Wollstonecraft evokes this same scene from Milton in a love letter to Imlay,

suggesting that she idealized both lovers, and both relationships, in a similar fashion (see August 1793, *Collected Letters*, p. 235).

21. *Collected Letters*, p. 263.

Chapter 2. *Mary: A Fiction*

1. See *Works*, 1.4.

2. Wollstonecraft's letters on pp. 35 and 52 are cited by permission of The Carl H. Pforzheimer Collection of Shelley and His Circle; The New York Public Library; and the Astor, Lenox, and Tilden foundations.

3. For an explication of the structuralist distinction between "story" and "narration," see Shlomith Rimmon-Kenan, *Narrative Fiction: Contemporary Poetics* (New York: Methuen, 1983), pp. 3–4. Marcia Tillotson, "Recent Wollstonecraft," *Blake Illustrated Quarterly* 12 (1978): 58–64, reads the equivocal treatment of sensibility in *Mary* as Wollstonecraft trying and failing to patch up the split between mind and heart (p. 58).

4. See Introduction.

5. This hypothesis is best articulated by Hagstrum, " 'Such, Such Were the Joys': The Boyhood of the Man of Feeling," in *Changing Taste in Eighteenth-Century Art and Literature* (Los Angeles: William Andrews Clark Memorial Library, 1972), pp. 41–62; and George A. Starr, "Sentimental De-education," in *Augustan Studies: Essays in Honor of Irvin Ehrenpreis*, ed. Douglas Lane Patey and Timothy Keegan (Newark: University of Delaware Press, 1985), pp. 253–62.

6. For the intellectual influences on *Mary*, see Butler, introduction to *Works* 1.8; Kelly, "Godwin, Wollstonecraft, and Rousseau," *Women and Literature* 3.2 (1975): 21–26; introduction to *Mary and the Wrongs of Woman* (1976; New York: Oxford University Press, World's Classics 1983), pp. ix–xii, and *Revolutionary Feminism*, pp. 23–54; and Parke, "What Kind of Heroine Is Mary Wollstonecraft?" in *Sensibility in Transformation*, pp. 106–7, 110–13.

7. The *Bildungsroman* is best defined as a novel that traces the development of a coherent self as both an unfolding from within and a shaping from without. See Giro von Wilpert, *Sachwörterbuch der Literatur* (Stuttgart: Kröner, 1964), p. 73.

8. Kearns, *Metaphors of Mind*, pp. 45–59.

9. Moira Ferguson and Janet Todd, *Mary Wollstonecraft* (Boston: Twayne, 1984), p. 31, see *Mary* as a story of "sentimental education."

10. Tompkins, *The Popular Novel in England*, p. 148. Kelly, *Revolutionary Feminism*, p. 41, emphasizes the revolutionary appeal of sensibility to Wollstonecraft and her contemporaries; Kelly sees class and gender consciousness even in the youthful Wollstonecraft (see especially chaps. 1, 2, and 3).

11. Kelly, introduction to *Mary*, pp. xi–xii.

12. See also, in *Works*, 1.8.25, 1.13.34, 1.18.45, 1.25.63, 1.30.72.

13. Rimmon-Kenan's discussion of FID is very helpful, *Narrative Fiction*, pp. 110–16.

14. Early novels by all three of these authors stimulated naïve readings of two kinds: reading as if the story were true, and reading as if the story were a program for imitative action. See Jauss, *Ästhetische Erfahrung*, 1.212–13 and 2.585–89.

15. Myers, "Pedagogy as Self-Expression in Mary Wollstonecraft: Exorcising the Past, Finding a Voice," in *The Private Self: Theory and Practice of Women's Autobiographical Writings*, ed. Shari Benstock (Chapel Hill: University of North Carolina Press, 1988), pp. 192–210, notices the "merging" of Mary and the narrator, resulting,

she believes, in a shift in the novel to "raw unmediated feeling" and "imprisoning sensibility" (p. 200).

16. Rimmon-Kenan, *Narrative Fiction*, p. 81.

Chapter 3. "Cave of Fancy"

1. Samuel Johnson, *The History of Rasselas, Prince of Abyssinia*, in *Samuel Johnson*, ed. Donald Greene, Oxford Authors (New York: Oxford University Press, 1984), p. 335.

2. See Preface, pp. xix–xx.

3. John Graham, "Lavater's *Physiognomy* in England," *Journal of the History of Ideas* 22 (1961): 561–72.

4. Wollstonecraft also divides people into those with and without sensibility (see chap. 1).

5. Wollstonecraft reiterates her belief that sensibility builds character in *Rights of Woman, Works*, 5.5.183.

6. Mullan, *Sentiment and Sociability*: "This sensibility [in Richardson's novels] is not so much spoken as displayed. Its instrument is a massively sensitized, feminine body; its vocabulary is that of gestures and palpitations, sighs and tears. The vocabulary is powerful because it is not spoken (but only spoken of); it is everything that punctures or interrupts speech" (p. 61).

7. *Collected Letters*, p. 263.

Chapter 4. Early Thoughts on Education

1. Poovey, *The Proper Lady*, sees *Mary* and *Education of Daughters* as poles apart, p. 55. She suggests that Wollstonecraft advocates "self control and submission" in the latter and "romantic expectations" in the former.

2. For Wollstonecraft's familiarity with Rousseau, see Butler, *Works*, 4.9; Kelly, *Mary*, p. 206n, notes her "allegiance to the empirical psychology of Locke and Hartley as adapted by Richard Price and Rousseau."

3. See "Locke" and "Rousseau" in "History of the Philosophy of Education," in *The Encyclopedia of Philosophy* (New York: Macmillan, 1967), 6.234–35.

4. Kearns, *Metaphors of Mind*, pp. 88–134.

5. Alexander Pope, "Epistle II To a Lady," in *Poetry and Prose of Alexander Pope*, ed. Aubrey Williams (Boston: Houghton Mifflin, 1969), p. 167:

> Nothing so true as what you once let fall,
> "Most Women have no Characters at all."
> Matter too soft a lasting mark to bear,
> And best distinguish'd by black, brown, or fair.
>
> (ll. 1–4)

6. Wardle, *Mary Wollstonecraft*, p. 88. Myers, "Pedagogy as Self-Expression in Mary Wollstonecraft: Exorcising the Past, Finding a Voice," offers a much more extensive analysis and positive view of Mason's role in *Original Stories* as a mentor and enabler guiding the girls toward "rational and affective awakening," "self-command and psychic self-sufficiency": "Mary is a metaphor for female selfhood embattled against a hostile world; the *Original Stories* offer an enabling myth" (p. 202).

Chapter 5. The Fictions of Sensibility under Analysis

1. Butler, *Works*, vol. 7, in her Prefatory Note to Wollstonecraft's contributions to the *Analytical Review*, summarizes the controversy surrounding the attribution of articles signed "M," "W," and "T," to Wollstonecraft (pp. 14–18). The key participators in this controversy are Wardle, "Mary Wollstonecraft, *Analytical Reviewer*," *PMLA* 62.4 (1947): 1000–1009; Derek Roper, "Mary Wollstonecraft's Reviews," *Notes and Queries*, n.s. 5 (1958): 37–38; and Sally N. Stewart, "Mary Wollstonecraft's Contributions to the *Analytical Review*," *Essays in Literature* 11.2 (1984): 187–99. Myers, "Sensibility and the 'Walk of Reason': Mary Wollstonecraft's Literary Reviews as Cultural Critique," in *Sensibility in Transformation*, pp. 120–44, also provides a valuable discussion of the controversy and, in addition, an invaluable analysis of Wollstonecraft's reviews as documentation of the "emergent feminist's" new models of reading, female selfhood, and aesthetics, pp. 130–31.

2. The page in this case refers directly to the *Analytical Review*, as this particular passage is not included in Butler, *Works*. Citations elsewhere are also to the original page numbers, which are listed in the top corner margins of volume 7 of *Works*. Cf. *Education of Daughters*, *Works*, 4.20. Wollstonecraft reiterates this point by excerpting the passage for the *Female Reader*, *Works*, 4.73.

3. Myers, "Sensibility," p. 135.

4. Myers points out Wollstonecraft's vigorous criticism of women novelists who "write *like* woman," "for serving as passive channels, through which linguistic and cultural codes flow without resistance" (ibid., p. 125).

5. Myers believes Wollstonecraft resists sensibility primarily as "literary and behavioral cliché" (ibid., p. 133).

6. Conger, "The Sorrows of Young Charlotte," provides a list of those admirers, pp. 51–52 n. 4.

7. Parke, "What Kind of Heroine," in *Sensibility in Transformation*, traces the evolution of Wollstonecraft's attitude toward Rousseau, pp. 110–13.

8. See Roy Pascal, "The Creative Personality," in *The German Sturm und Drang* (Manchester: Manchester University Press, 1953), pp. 133–69.

9. Myers, "Sensibility," concludes from the values Wollstonecraft endorses here and elsewhere—individual protest, passion, perception, personal growth, self-definition, and self-realization—that she is a romantic, p. 135.

10. Myers notes Wollstonecraft's "preoccupation with style, a conviction that style, substance and consciousness indivisibly interconnect" (ibid., p. 132).

Chapter 6. Private and Public Revolutions: Burke as Catalyst

1. This information was culled from two sources: Todd, *Mary Wollstonecraft: An Annotated Bibliography*, pp. 8, 14, 18, 20; and Wardle, *Mary Wollstonecraft*, pp. 110, 121.

2. Patricia Yaeger, *Honey-Mad Women: Emancipatory Strategies in Women's Writing* (New York: Columbia University Press, 1988), p. 151, believes this charge is precipitous. See also Poovey, *The Proper Lady*, pp. 67–68.

3. Kelly, "Mary Wollstonecraft as *Vir Bonus*," *English Studies in Canada* 5 (1979): 275–91: "Her polemical passion did not, however, come out of the intellectual blue. It was fuelled by a passion of quite a different kind, for Henry Fuseli, painter,

poet, critic, corresponding member of the *Sturm und Drang*, self-confessed genius, . . . admirer of Rousseau . . . " (p. 276).

4. Wollstonecraft reviews Macaulay Graham's *Letters on Education* for the *Analytical Review* in November, the same month in which she writes her reply to Burke (Wardle, *Mary Wollstonecraft*, p. 110).

5. Butler, introduction to *Works*, 1.9–15.

6. In their rush to defend the rights of the heart, proponents of sensibility frequently attack—either indirectly or directly—repressive social institutions. English writers of sensibility are generally more conciliatory and conservative than their continental counterparts, especially the writers of the so-called German Storm and Stress. Friedrich Schiller first notices the affinity between sentiment and satire in his justly famous *Über naïve und sentimentalische Dichtung* (1795–96). See Syndy M. Conger, "The Sentimental Logic of Wollstonecraft's Prose," *Prose Studies* 10.2 (1987): 143–58.

7. The *Analytical Review*'s actual review of Burke's *Reflections* also appears in November (8 [November 1790]: 295–307, 408–14) and contains several points of agreement with Wollstonecraft's. It cannot, however, be attributed to Wollstonecraft with any certainty.

8. Wardle, *Mary Wollstonecraft*, p. 118.

9. Poovey offers the hypothesis in *The Proper Lady* that Wollstonecraft lashes out in *Rights of Men* against "her old enemy, feeling" (p. 59).

10. *Works*, 5.10, 9, 29, 13–15, 26–28, 17, 60, 7, 18.

11. *Works*, 5.9, 30–34, 48, 12, 9.

12. Guralnick, "Rhetorical Strategy," p. 179, develops this thesis for *Rights of Woman* but, given her premises, it should apply as well to *Rights of Men*.

13. Cox, "Sensibility as Argument," in *Sensibility in Transformation*, analyzes the slippery adaptibility of the language of sensibility, pp. 64–66.

14. Conger, "Sensibility Restored: Radcliffe's Answer to Lewis's *The Monk*," in *Gothic Fictions: Prohibition/Transgression*, ed. Kenneth W. Graham (New York: AMS Press, 1989), pp. 113–49, discusses the gendrification of the language of sensibility, pp. 114–19.

15. Tompkins, *The Popular Novel*, pp. 97, 148. Terry Castle elaborates this thesis in "The Female Thermometer," *Representations* 17 (1987): 1–27: "In the eighteenth century, the cult of sensibility was an early sign of the weakening of sexual polarities . . . " (p. 13).

16. Both quotations in this passage are appropriated and defamiliarized by Wollstonecraft from Burke's *Reflections*; see *Works*, 5.31 nn. a and b.

17. Bernard H. Baumrin, new introduction to *British Moralists*, pp. lxix–lxxiii.

18. Butler, *Works*, 1.16, detects sexual puritanism in Wollstonecraft's attitudes.

19. Poovey, *The Proper Lady*, makes much of the contradictions in *Rights of Men* spawned by Wollstonecraft's ambivalence, pp. 58, 64.

20. Wilson, "Mary Wollstonecraft and the Search for Radical Woman," develops this thesis for *Rights of Woman*, which she calls "an attempt to subordinate sensibility to sense" that "reveals a repressed awareness both of the impossibility of her project of the insertion of female subject into the rational code and of the possible value of sensibility for women's expression" (p. 89).

21. Yaeger, *Honey-Mad Women*, pp. 150–51, 155, 161, 170–76.

22. Wardle, *Mary Wollstonecraft*, p. 120, names rhetorical power as the greatest strength of *Rights of Men*.

Chapter 7. The Rights of Woman and the Wrongs of Sensibility

1. Poovey, *The Proper Lady*, pp. 69–81; Wilson, "Mary Wollstonecraft and . . . Radical Woman," pp. 88–101.

2. The phrase is Wardle's, *Mary Wollstonecraft*, pp. 156, 168; cf. Guralnick, "Rhetorical Strategy," p. 174.

3. See Introduction, pp. xlii–xlviii.

4. Mullan, *Sentiment and Sociability*, pp. 201–40; cf. Fox, introduction to *Psychology and Literature in the Eighteenth Century*, pp. 1–22.

5. This is a citation from Pope's *Essay on Man* 2.136; see Butler 5.186 n. a.

6. Irigaray, "Women's Exile," in *The Feminist Critique of Language*, pp. 91, 94–96. Janet Todd's "The Language of Sex in *A Vindication of the Rights of Woman*," sheds light on Wollstonecraft's language sensitivity to sexual terms in her treatise.

7. On Rousseau, in addition to John Cleary, "Madame de Staël, Rousseau, and Mary Wollstonecraft," *Romance Notes* 21.3 (1981): 329–33, see the following previously cited essays: Parke, "What Kind of Heroine Is Mary Wollstonecraft?"; Guralnick, "Rhetorical Strategy"; and Kelly, "Godwin, Wollstonecraft, and Rousseau."

8. The Wollstonecraft letter discussed on p. 124 is cited by permission of Lord Abinger and the Bodleian Library.

9. Two essays offer especially insightful and evenhanded discussions of Wollstonecraft's shifting tone: Wilson, "Mary Wollstonecraft and . . . Radical Woman," and Anna Vlasapolos, "Mary Wollstonecraft's Mask of Reason in *A Vindication of the Rights of Woman*," *Dalhousie Review* 60.3 (1980): 462–71. Kelly sees stylistic unevenness as evidence of Wollstonecraft's radical subject matter: a "transgressive style" for transgressive material, pp. 111–12, 120, 138–38.

10. Todd, *Mary Wollstonecraft: An Annotated Bibliography*, pp. 12, 14, 21.

11. Laurie A. Finke, " 'A Philosophic Wanton': Language and Authority in Wollstonecraft's *A Vindication of the Rights of Woman*," in *The Philosopher as Writer: The Eighteenth Century*, ed. Robert Ginsberg (Toronto: Associated University Presses, 1987), pp. 155–76, discovers "masculine" (objective, assertive) and "feminine" (subjective) styles in the treatise as well as a synthesis of the two, a third new "truly philosophical style, one which, in effect, subsumes the differences between masculine and feminine in its pursuit of general truths" (p. 165).

12. Conger, "The Sentimental Logic of . . . Wollstonecraft's Prose," interprets the *Rights of Woman* in the light of Schiller's definition of the sentimental mode.

13. Julie Ellison, "Redoubled Feeling: Politics, Sentiment, and the Sublime in Williams and Wollstonecraft," *Studies in Eighteenth-Century Culture* 20 (1990): 197–215.

14. Kelly, "Mary Wollstonecraft as *Vir Bonus*," pp. 278–83.

15. Mary Wilson Carpenter, "Sibylline Apocalyptics: Mary Wollstonecraft's *A Vindication of the Rights of Woman* and Job's Mother's Womb," *Literature and History* 12.2 (1986): 215–28.

Chapter 8. The Test of the Revolution

1. Butler, introduction to *Works* 1.17–19; Wardle, *Mary Wollstonecraft*, pp. 206–13.

2. Todd, *Mary Wollstonecraft: An Annotated Bibliography*, pp. 11, 13, 19, 21.

3. "*French Revolution* may be used as an important, if bulky guide to the confrontation of two very different kinds of Jacobinism, English and French" (Kelly, "Mary Wollstonecraft: Texts and Contexts," p. 40).

Chapter 9. A New Page in the History of Her Heart

1. Carol Poston, introduction to *Letters Written During a Short Residence in Sweden, Norway, and Denmark*, by Mary Wollstonecraft (Lincoln: University of Nebraska Press, 1976), pp. vii-xx, also sees the book as a moment of creative synthesis for Wollstonecraft.

2. It is instructive to compare Wollstonecraft's actual letters to Imlay during this period to the published ones. This can be done either by consulting vol. 6 of the *Works*, which contains selected letters to Johnson and Imlay as well as *Letters in Sweden*, or by reading the *Collected Letters*, pp. 230–330.

3. Cf. chap. 1, pp. 18–31. For various speculations on Imlay's motives, see Poston, "Introduction" to *Letters in Sweden*, p. xi; Tomalin, *Life and Death*, p. 175; and Wardle, *Mary Wollstonecraft*, p. 225.

4. Cf. Introduction, pp. xlii–xlix.

5. Cf. chap. 6, pp. 97–111, and chap. 7, pp. 118–22.

6. Cf. chap. 7, pp. 115–16.

7. Letter II, *Works*, 6.251; Letter X, *Works*, 6.293–94; Letter XIII, *Works*, 6.300–301; Letter XVI, *Works*, 6.312.

8. Cf. chap. 8, pp. 143–44.

9. The book was widely acclaimed, generously reviewed, and frequently translated (Butler, introduction to the *Works*, 1.23–24; Wardle, *Mary Wollstonecraft*, pp. 256–57).

10. Butler, introduction to the *Works*, reminds readers that Wollstonecraft's creation of a melancholy traveling persona precedes Byron's Childe Harold. She believes that *Letters in Sweden* is "historically a more important book than has properly been acknowledged" (p. 23).

11. She cites Milton's *Paradise Lost* I.26 and Edward Young's *Night Thoughts* I.304 (Butler, *Works*, 6.344nn).

12. Letter IV, *Works*, 6.258; Letter I, *Works*, 6.246.

13. Brissenden, *Virtue in Distress*: "Werther . . . is . . . a three-dimensional, vital individual with depths and mysteries"; "And in the story of his sufferings it is possible to see the modern novel, with its emphasis on the psychological life of the individual rather than on story, emerging from the chrysalis of the novel of sentiment" (p. 267).

14. She is one of the new, late-century "egotic" travelers described by Charles L. Batten, Jr. in his *Pleasurable Instruction: Form and Convention in Eighteenth-Century Travel Literature* (Berkeley: University of California Press, 1978), p. 80.

15. In her many fine articles on Mary Wollstonecraft, Myers tends to view her as a romantic artist (see especially Myers, "Mary Wollstonecraft's *Letters Written in Sweden*: Toward Romantic Autobiography," *Studies in Eighteenth-Century Culture* 8, [1979]: 165–85), as do Kelly and Meena Alexander, *Women in Romanticism* (Savage, Md.: Barnes and Noble, 1989), pp. 36, 43.

Chapter 10. One Last Fiction: Sensibility Imprisoned

1. Butler, introduction to *Works*, 1.24–26.

2. Cf. Myers, "Unfinished Business: Wollstonecraft's *Maria*": "It [*Maria*] gropes toward reconciliation of the tension between a rational, radical philosophy and a passionate personal need. . . . the problem of integrating a rational feminist program with one woman's subjective feminine vision" (p. 107). Janet Todd, "Reason and Sensibility in Mary Wollstonecraft's *The Wrongs of Woman*," *Frontiers* 5.3 (1980): 17–20,

develops a similar thesis, that Wollstonecraft's ideal is "androgynous, a judicious mingling of male reason and female sensibility" (p. 17).

3. Todd traces the progress of Jemima and Maria's relationship in *Women's Friendship*, pp. 218–26.

4. Tomalin, *Life and Death*, p. 214.

5. Wollstonecraft to Godwin, 30 August 1797; cf. 26 June 1797, *Godwin and Mary*, pp. 119, 109. For information on the English Werther mania, see Atkins, *The Testament of Werther in Poetry and Drama*.

6. Godwin, *Memoirs*, p. 73.

7. This is Jauss's thesis in his "Rousseaus 'Nouvelle Héloïse' und Goethe's 'Werther' im Horizontwandel. . . . "

8. Goethe, *Werther*, p. 4.

9. Ibid., p. 24.

10. Jauss, *Ästhetische Erfahrung*, 1.29.

11. Goethe, *Werther*, pp. 83–84.

12. Ibid., p. 22.

13. See the discussion of Halliday's essay, "Anti-Languages," in the Preface, pp. xiii–xiv.

14. Goethe, *Werther*, pp. 109–19.

15. Ibid., pp. 117–18.

16. Ibid., p. 76.

17. The Darnford-Maria relationship bears occasional resemblances to the Imlay-Wollstonecraft friendship. Darnford's comments here are reminiscent of Imlay's ideas in his *Topographical Description of the Western Territories of North America*.

18. Wardle, *Mary Wollstonecraft*, believes Wollstonecraft's preoccupation with her thesis dominates and mars *Maria*, pp. 298–99.

19. Tomalin, *Life and Death*, notes the boldness of the subject matter in *Maria*, p. 197, as does Moira Ferguson, introduction to *Maria or The Wrongs of Woman* (New York: Norton, 1975), pp. 5–16. Ferguson calls it the "most militant" of Wollstonecraft's fictions, p.12, and suggests that it "offers a unique exposé of eighteenth-century oppressed womanhood" (p. 16).

20. "But the most striking thing about *Maria* was probably its outspoken assertion that women had sexual feelings and rights" (Tomalin, *Life and Death*, p. 196).

21. Parke, "What Kind of Heroine Is Mary Wollstonecraft?" in *Sensibility in Transformation*, pp. 112–113.

22. "Mary is a prisoner of her sex's sensibility" (Kelly, introduction to *Mary*, p. xi); cf. Harasym, "Ideology and Self," for a similar perspective on both *Mary* and *Maria*.

Works Cited

Alexander, Meena. *Women in Romanticism*. Savage, Md.: Barnes and Noble, 1989.

Arieti, Silvano. "Cognition and Feeling." In *Feelings and Emotions*, edited by Magda B. Arnold, 135–43. New York: Academic Press, 1970.

Arnold, Magda B., ed. *Feelings and Emotions*. New York: Academic Press, 1970.

Armstrong, Nancy. "The Rise of Feminine Authority in the Novel." *Novel* 15.2 (1982): 127–45.

Atkins, Stuart P. *The Testament of Werther in Poetry and Drama*. Cambridge: Harvard University Press, 1949.

Barker-Benfield, G. J. *The Culture of Sensibility: Sex and Society in Eighteenth-Century Britain*. Chicago: University of Chicago Press, 1992.

Barthes, Roland. *Mythologies* (1957). Translated by Annette Lavers. New York: Hill and Wang, 1975.

Batten, Charles L., Jr. *Pleasurable Instruction: Form and Convention in Eighteenth-Century Travel Literature*. Berkeley: University of California Press, 1978.

Blodgett, Harriet. "Emily Vindicated: Ann Radcliffe and Mary Wollstonecraft." *Weber Studies* 7.2 (1990): 48–61.

Boening, John, ed. *The Reception of Classical German Literature in England, 1760–1860*. 10 vols. New York: Garland, 1977.

Bredvold, Louis. *The Natural History of Sensibility*. Detroit: Wayne State University Press, 1962.

Brissenden, R. F. *Virtue in Distress: Studies in the Novel of Sentiment from Richardson to Sade*. New York: Harper & Row, 1974.

Cameron, Deborah, ed. "Introduction: why is language a feminist issue?" to *The Feminist Critique of Language: A Reader*. New York: Routledge, 1990.

Carpenter, Mary Wilson. "Sibylline Apocalyptics: Mary Wollstonecraft's *A Vindication of the Rights of Woman* and Job's Mother's Womb." *Literature and History* 12.2 (1986): 215–28.

Castle, Terry. "The Female Thermometer." *Representations* 17 (1987): 1–27.

Cixous, Hélène. "The Laugh of Medusa." 1975. In *Literary Criticism and Theory: The Greeks to the Present*, edited by Robert Con Davis and Laurie Finke, 732–47. New York: Longman, 1989.

Cleary, John. "Madame de Staël, Rousseau, and Mary Wollstonecraft." *Romance Notes* 21.3 (1981): 329–33.

Cohen, Murray. *Sensible Words: Linguistic Practice in England 1640–1785*. Baltimore: Johns Hopkins University Press, 1977.

Conger, Syndy M., ed. *Sensibility in Transformation: Creative Resistance to Sentiment from the Augustans to the Romantics*. Essays in Honor of Jean H. Hagstrum. Rutherford, N.J.: Fairleigh Dickenson University Press, 1990.

———. "Sensibility Restored: Radcliffe's Answer to Lewis's *The Monk*." In *Gothic Fictions: Prohibition/Transgression*, edited by Kenneth W. Graham, 113–49. New York: AMS Press, 1989.

———. "The Sentimental Logic of Wollstonecraft's Prose." *Prose Studies* 10.2 (1987): 143–58.

———. "The Sorrows of Young Charlotte: Werther's English Sisters 1785–1805." *Goethe Yearbook* 3 (1986): 21–56.

Cox, Stephen D. "Sensibility as Argument." In *Sensibility in Transformation: Creative Resistance to Sentiment from the Augustans to the Romantics*, edited by Syndy M. Conger, 63–82. Rutherford, N.J.: Fairleigh Dickenson University Press, 1990.

———. *"The Stranger Within Thee": Concepts of the Self in Late-Eighteenth-Century Literature*. Pittsburgh: University of Pittsburgh Press, 1980.

Crane, R. S. "Suggestions Toward a Genealogy of the 'Man of Feeling.'" *ELH* 1.3 (1934): 205–30.

Culler, Jonathan. "Literary Theory." In *Introduction to Scholarship in Modern Languages and Literatures*, 2d ed., edited by Joseph Gibaldi, 201–35. New York: Modern Language Association, 1992.

Dussinger, John A. "The Sensorium in the World of *A Sentimental Journey*." *Ariel E* 13.2 (1982): 3–16.

Eagleton, Mary, ed. Introduction to *Feminist Literary Criticism*. New York: Longman, 1991.

Eagleton, Terry. *The Rape of Clarissa: Writing, Sexuality, and Class Struggle in Samuel Richardson*. Minneapolis: University of Minnesota Press, 1982.

Ellison, Julie. "Redoubled Feeling: Politics, Sentiment, and the Sublime in Williams and Wollstonecraft." *Studies in Eighteenth-Century Culture* 20 (1990): 197–215.

Empson, William. *The Structure of Complex Words*. London: New Directions, 1951.

The Encyclopedia of Philosophy. New York: Macmillan, 1967.

Erämetsä, Eric. *A Study of the Word "Sentimental" and of Other Linguistic Characteristics of the Eighteenth-Century Sentimentalism in English Literature*. Helsinki: Helsingen Liike Kinjapaino Oy, 1951.

Ferguson, Moira. Introduction to *Maria or The Wrongs of Woman*. New York: Norton, 1975.

Ferguson, Moira, and Janet Todd. *Mary Wollstonecraft*. Boston: Twayne, 1984.

Figlio, Karl M. "Theories of Perception and the Physiology of Mind in the Late Eighteenth Century." *History of Science* 13 (1975): 177–212.

Finke, Laurie A. " 'A Philosophic Wanton': Language and Authority in Wollstonecraft's *A Vindication of the Rights of Woman*." In *The Philosopher as Writer: The Eighteenth Century*, edited by Robert Ginsberg, 155–76. Toronto: Associated University Presses, 1987.

Finsen, H. C. "Empfindsamkeit als Raum der Alternative." *Deutschunterricht* 29.4 (1977): 27–38.

Flavin, Louise. "*Mansfield Park*: Free Indirect Discourse and the Psychological Novel." *Studies in the Novel* 19.2 (1987): 137–59.

Foucault, Michel. *The Care of the Self.* Vol. 3 of *The History of Sexuality.* Translated by Robert Hurley. 3 vols. New York: Random House, 1988.

———. "What is an Author?" In *Textual Strategies: Perspectives in Post-Structuralist Criticism,* edited by Josué V. Harari, 141–60. Ithaca, N.Y.: Cornell University Press, 1979.

Fox, Christopher, ed. *Psychology and Literature in the Eighteenth Century.* New York: AMS Press, 1987.

Frye, Northrop. "Towards Defining an Age of Sensibility." In *Eighteenth-Century English Literature: Essays in Modern Criticism,* 3d ed., edited by James L. Clifford, 311–18. New York: Oxford University Press, 1959.

Gilbert, Sandra, and Susan M. Gubar. "Sexual Linguistics: Gender, Language, and Sexuality." *NLH* 16.3 (1985): 515–43.

Godwin, William. *Memoirs of Mary Wollstonecraft.* New York: Greenberg; London: Constable, 1927.

Goethe, Johann Wolfgang von. *The Sorrows of Young Werther. The New Melusine. Novelle,* introduction by Victor Lange. New York: Holt, Rinehart, and Winston, 1949.

Gordon, Robert. *The Structure of Emotions.* New York: Cambridge University Press, 1987.

Graham, John. "Lavater's *Physiognomy* in England." *Journal of the History of Ideas* 22 (1961): 561–72.

Greene, Donald. "Latitudinarianism and Sensibility: The Genealogy of the 'Man of Feeling' Reconsidered." *Modern Philology* 75.2 (1977): 159–83.

Gregory, Richard L., ed. *Oxford Compenion to the Mind.* New York: Oxford University Press, 1987.

Guralnick, Elissa S. "Rhetorical Strategy in Mary Wollstonecraft's *A Vindication of the Rights of Woman.*" *Humanities Association Review* 30 (1979): 174–85.

Hagstrum, Jean H. *Sex and Sensibility: Ideal and Erotic Love from Milton to Mozart.* Chicago: University of Chicago Press, 1980.

———. " 'Such, Such Were the Joys': The Boyhood of the Man of Feeling." In *Changing Taste in Eighteenth-Century Art and Literature,* 41–62. Los Angeles: William Andrews Clark Memorial Library, 1972.

———. "Towards a Profile of the Word *Conscious* in Eighteenth-Century Literature." In *Psychology and Literature in the Eighteenth Century,* edited by Christopher Fox, 23–50. New York: AMS Press, 1987.

Halliday, M. A. K. "Anti-Languages." *American Anthropologist* 78 (1976): 570–84.

Harasym, S. D. "Ideology and Self: A Theoretical Discussion of the 'Self' in Mary Wollstonecraft's Fiction." *English Studies in Canada* 12.2 (1986): 163–77.

Hertling, Gunter H. "Die *Werther*-Kritik im Meinungsstreit der Spätaufklärer." *German Quarterly* 36 (1963): 403–13.

Irigaray, Luce. "Women's Exile. Interview with Luce Irigaray." Translated by Couze Venn. In *The Feminist Critique of Language,* edited by Deborah Cameron, 80–96. New York: Routledge, 1990.

Jakobson, Roman. "The Speech Event and the Function of Language." In *On Language,* edited by Linda R. Waugh and Monique Monville-Bursten, 69–79. Cambridge: Harvard University Press, 1990.

Jauss, Hans-Robert. *Ästhetische Erfahrung und literarische Hermeneutik.* Vol. 1. Munich: Wilhelm Fink, 1977.

———. "Rousseau's 'Nouvelle Héloïse' und Goethe's 'Werther' im Horizontwandel zwischen französischer Aufklärung und deutschem Idealismus." In *Ästhetische Erfahrung und literarische Hermeneutik,* vol. 2, pp. 585–653. Frankfurt am Main: Suhrkamp, 1982.

Johnson, Samuel. *The History of Rasselas, Prince of Abyssinia.* In *Samuel Johnson,* edited by Donald Greene, 335–418. Oxford Authors Series. New York: Oxford University Press, 1984.

Jones, Chris. "Godwin to Mary: The First Letter." *Keats-Shelley Review* 1 (1986): 61–74.

Kearns, Michael. *Metaphors of Mind in Fiction and Psychology.* Lexington: University Press of Kentucky, 1987.

Kelly, Gary. "Godwin, Wollstonecraft, and Rousseau." *Women and Literature* 3.2 (1975): 21–26.

———. "Mary Wollstonecraft as *Vir Bonus.*" *English Studies in Canada* 5 (1979): 275–91.

———. "Mary Wollstonecraft: Texts and Contexts." *Eighteenth-Century Life* 2.2 (1975): 38–40.

———. *Revolutionary Feminism: The Mind and Career of Mary Wollstonecraft.* London: Macmillan, 1992.

———, ed. Introduction to *Mary and The Wrongs of Woman.* New York: Oxford University Press, 1976. Reprint. New York: Oxford University Press, World's Classics, 1983.

Kittay, Eva Feder. *Metaphor: Its Cognitive Force and Linguistic Structure.* Oxford: Clarendon Press, 1987. Reprint, Oxford: Clarendon Press, 1989.

Lakoff, George, and Mark Johnson. *Metaphors We Live By.* Chicago: University of Chicago Press, 1980.

Lakoff, Robin. *Language and Woman's Place.* New York: Harper & Row, 1975.

Locke, John. *An Essay Concerning Human Understanding,* edited by Alexander Campbell Fraser. 2 vols. 1690. Reprint. London: Constable, 1959.

Lorch, Jennifer. *Mary Wollstonecraft: The Making of a Radical Feminist.* New York: Berg, 1990.

McKenzie, Alan T. *Certain, Lively Episodes: The Articulation of Passion in Eighteenth-Century Prose.* Athens: University of Georgia Press, 1990.

Moravia, Sergio. "The Enlightenment and the Sciences of Man." *History of Science* 18 (1980): 247–68.

Mullan, John. *Sentiment and Sociability: The Language of Feeling in the Eighteenth Century.* Oxford: Clarendon Press, 1988.

Myers, Mitzi. "Mary Wollstonecraft's *Letters Written . . . in Sweden*: Toward Romantic Aubiography." In *Studies in Eighteenth-Century Culture* 8 (1979): 165–85.

———. "Pedagogy as Self-Expression in Mary Wollstonecraft: Exorcising the Past, Finding a Voice." In *The Private Self: Theory and Practice of Women's Autobiographical Writings,* edited by Shari Benstock, 192–210. Chapel Hill: University of North Carolina Press, 1988.

———. "Sensibility and the 'Walk of Reason': Mary Wollstonecraft's Literary Reviews as Cultural Critique." In *Sensibility in Transformation: Creative Resistance to Sentiment from the Augustans to the Romantics,* edited by Syndy M. Conger, 120–44. Rutherford, N.J.: Fairleigh Dickenson University Press, 1990.

———. "Unfinished Business: Wollstonecraft's *Maria.*" *Wordsworth Circle* 11 (1980): 107–14.

Newton, K. M. *Interpreting the Text: A Critical Introduction to the Theory and Practice of Literary Interpretation.* New York: St. Martin's Press, 1990.

Parke, Catherine N. "What Kind of Heroine Is Mary Wollstonecraft?" In *Sensibility in Transformation: Creative Resistance to Sentiment from the Augustans to the Romantics,* edited by Syndy M. Conger, 103–19. Rutherford, N.J.: Fairleigh Dickenson University Press, 1990.

Parnell, Paul. "The Sentimental Mask." *PMLA* 78 (1963): 529–35.

Pascal, Roy. *The German Sturm und Drang.* Manchester: Manchester University Press, 1953.

Plumb, J. H. *England in the Eighteenth Century (1714–1815).* Vol. 7 of *The Pelican History of England.* 9 vols. Baltimore: Penguin, 1969.

Pope, Alexander. "Epistle II To a Lady." In *Poetry and Prose of Alexander Pope,* edited by Aubrey Williams. Boston: Houghton Mifflin, 1969.

Poovey, Mary. "Mary Wollstonecraft: The Gender of Genres in Later Eighteenth-Century England." *Novel* 15.2 (1982): 111–26.

———. *The Proper Lady and the Woman Writer: Ideology as Style in the Works of Mary Wollstonecraft, Mary Shelley, and Jane Austen.* Chicago: University of Chicago Press, 1984.

Poston, Carol H. Introduction to *Letters Written During a Short Residence in Sweden, Norway, and Denmark,* by Mary Wollstonecraft. Lincoln: University of Nebraska Press, 1976.

Rather, L. J. *Mind and Body in Eighteenth-Century Medicine: A Study Based on Jerome Gaub's De regimine mentis.* Berkeley: University of California Press, 1965.

Rimmon-Kenan, Shlomith. *Narrative Fiction: Contemporary Poetics.* New York: Methuen, 1983.

Rodgers, James. "Sensibility, Sympathy, Benevolence: Physiology and Moral Philosophy in *Tristram Shandy.*" In *Language of Nature: Critical Essays on Science and Literature,* edited by L. J. Jordanova, 117–58. New Brunswick, N.J.: Rutgers University Press, 1986.

Rogers, Katharine M. *Feminism in Eighteenth-Century England.* Urbana: University of Illinois Press, 1982.

Roper, Derek. "Mary Wollstonecraft's Reviews." *Notes and Queries,* n.s. 5 (1958): 37–38.

Rousseau, George S. "Nerves, Spirits, and Fibres: Towards Defining the Organs of Sensibility—with a Postscript 1976." *The Blue Guitar* 2 (1976): 125–53.

Ryle, Gilbert. *The Concept of Mind.* 1949. Reprint. Chicago: University of Chicago Press, 1984.

Scherpe, Klaus R. *Werther und Wertherwirkung: Zum Syndrom bürgerlicher Gesellschaftsordnung im 18. Jahrhundert.* Bad Homburg: Gehlen, 1970.

Schor, Naomi. "Feminist and Gender Studies." *Introduction to Scholarship in Modern Languages and Literatures,* edited by Joseph Gibaldi, 262–87. New York: Modern Language Association, 1992.

Selby-Bigge, L. A., ed. *British Moralists.* 2 vols. 1897. Reprint. New introduction by Bernard H. Baumrin. New York: Bobbs-Merrill, 1964.

Showalter, Elaine. "Feminist Criticism in the Wilderness." *Critical Inquiry* 8.2 (1981): 179–205.

Simon, Helene. *William Godwin und Mary Wollstonecraft: Eine biographische Studie.*. Munich: Beck, 1909.

Smith, Adam. *The Theory of Moral Sentiments*, edited by D. D. Raphael and A. L. Macfie. 1976. Reprint. Indianapolis: Liberty Press, 1982.

Stanlis, Peter. "Burke and the Sensibility of Rousseau." *Thought* (1961): 246 –76.

Starr, George A. "Sentimental De-education." In *Augustan Studies: Essays in Honor of Irvin Ehrenpreis*, edited by Douglas Lane Patey and Timothy Keegan, 253– 62. Newark: University of Delaware Press, 1985.

Sterne, Laurence. *A Sentimental Journey through France and Italy.* Edited by Ian Jack. New York: Oxford University Press, 1984.

Stewart, Sally N. "Mary Wollstonecraft's Contributions to the *Analytical Review*." *Essays in Literature* 11.2 (1984): 187– 99.

Stone, Lawrence. *The Family, Sex, and Marriage 1500–1800.* New York: Harper & Row, 1977.

Tillotson, Marcia. "Recent Wollstonecraft." *Blake Illustrated Quarterly* 12 (1978): 58– 64.

Tomalin, Claire. *The Life and Death of Mary Wollstonecraft.* New York: New American Library, 1974.

Tompkins, J. M. S. *The Popular Novel in England 1770–1800.* 1932. Reprint. Lincoln: University of Nebraska Press, 1961.

Todd, Janet. "The Language of Sex in *A Vindication of the Rights of Woman*." *Mary Wollstonecraft Newsletter* 1.2 (1973): 10 –17.

———. *Mary Wollstonecraft: An Annotated Bibliography.* New York: Garland, 1976.

———. "Reason and Sensibility in Mary Wollstonecraft's *The Wrongs of Woman*." *Frontiers* 5.3 (1980): 17–20.

———. *Sensibility: An Introduction.* London: Methuen, 1986.

———. *The Sign of Angellica: Women, Writing and Fiction, 1660–1800.* New York: Columbia University Press, 1989.

———. *Women's Friendship in Literature.* New York: Columbia University Press, 1980.

Turbayne, Colin Murray. *Metaphors for the Mind: The Creative Mind and Its Origins.* Columbia: University of South Carolina Press, 1991.

Utter, R. P., and Gwendolyn B. Needham. *Pamela's Daughters.* New York: Macmillan, 1936.

Vlasopolos, Anna. "Mary Wollstonecraft's Mask of Reason in *A Vindication of the Rights of Woman*." *Dalhousie Review* 60.3 (1980): 462–71.

von Wilpert, Giro. *Sachwörterbuch der Literatur.* Stuttgart: Kröner, 1964.

Wardle, Ralph M. "Mary Wollstonecraft, *Analytical* Reviewer." *PMLA* 62.4 (1947): 1000 –1009.

———. *Mary Wollstonecraft: A Critical Biography.* Lincoln: University of Nebraska Press, 1951.

———, ed. *Collected Letters of Mary Wollstonecraft.* Ithaca: Cornell University Press, 1979.

———, ed. *Godwin & Mary: Letters of William Godwin and Mary Wollstonecraft.* Lincoln: University of Nebraska Press, 1966.

Williams, Raymond. *Keywords: A Vocabulary of Culture and Society.* New York: Oxford University Press, 1976.

Wilson, Anna. "Mary Wollstonecraft and the Search for the Radical Woman." *Genders* 6 (1989): 88–101.

Wollstonecraft, Mary. *The Works of Mary Wollstonecraft*, edited by Janet Todd and Marilyn Butler. 7 vols. New York: New York University Press, 1989.

Yaeger, Patricia. *Honey-Mad Women: Emancipatory Strategies in Women's Writing.* New York: Columbia University Press, 1988.

Young, Edward. "Conjectures on Original Composition in a Letter to the Author of *Sir Charles Grandison*" (1755). In *Enlightened England*, edited by Wylie Sypher, 601–8. New York: Norton, 1942.

Index

Addison, Joseph, and Richard Steele, xlviii
"Address to the Deity, An" (James Thomson), 81
Adventurer, The, 71, 81
Agathon (Christoph Martin Wieland), 37
Aikin, A[nna] L[aetitia] [Barbauld], 81
Albert de Nordenshild, 92
Analogy: and verification of sensibility, xxxiv
Analytical Review (Wollstonecraft's contributions), xlviii–xlix, 8, 85–96, 136, 167; on abduction of sensibility by mediocre writers, 87–90; aesthetic of sensibility in, 92–96; on cliché-ridden sentimental novels, 85–90; compared to "Cave of Fancy," 93; —*French Revolution*, 136; —*Maria*, 167, 176; —*Rights of Men*, 98; —*Rights of Woman*, 85, 88, 94; contrasted to *Letters in Sweden*, 156; criticism of eroticization of sensibility in, 87–90, 93; easy to misconstrue, 85–86; ethic of sensibility in, 90, 95–96; on excess sensibility as "sickly," 93; as the last stage in Wollstonecraft's self-education, 85–86; on myths of sensibility, 87–88; reviews of *Rights of Men*, 97; —Rousseau, 90–92; —*Sorrows of Werther*, 88–90, 95; sensitivity to style in, 93–94; tone, 88, 98; voice of sensibility audible in, 95–96; and Wollstonecraft's sense of the ridiculous, 86–87, 89–90

Anatomy of Melancholy (Robert Burton), xliv
Anti-language, vii–xiv
Arden, Jane, 6–8, 10–12, 125
Arieti, Silvano, xv
Arundel, 93
Austen, Jane, xliii, xlv–xlvi, 37, 60, 88, 179–80

Barker-Benfield, G. J., xlv
Barthes, Roland, xix–xx, xxii, xli–xliii, 61
Bible, the, xli, 81, 114, 118–19, 138, 143–44, 168
Bildung and *Bildungsroman*, 37, 39–52, 143, 152, 180
Bishop, Meredith, 12–14
Blood, Fanny, 13–15, 156
Blood, George, 124
Brissenden, R. F., 159
British Critic, 133
Brontës, the, xlvi
Burke, Edmund, xxii, xxiv, xliii, xlv, xlviii–xlix, 9, 111, 114, 116, 119, 133, 139, 148; as challenge to Wollstonecraft's belief system, 97–111
Burney, Fanny, xlvi

Carpenter, Mary Wilson, 129
"Cave of Fancy" (Wollstonecraft), xvi, 61–68, 106, 156, 180; allegory in, 67; as anti-mimetic, 61, 67; cautionary tale in, 61, 63, 66–67; compared to *Analytical Review*, 93; —*Maria*, 177;

Wardle, Ralph, 6, 8, 77, 112, 145
Williams, Raymond, xxx, xlvii
Wollstonecraft, Everina, 124
Wollstonecraft, Eliza, 12–14, 106, 156
Wollstonecraft, Mary: assessing herself,
5, 10–12, 14–16, 33–34;
authoritative personae in the works
of, xiii, 69, 95, 97–98, 128, 144,
146–47; central contradiction in her
life and works, xi–xii; and
contradictions in the belief system of
sensibility, xxix–xxx, 15–18, 22–23,
28–29, 35, 67–68, 76–80, 90–92,
101–2, 105–8, 124–25, 135–41, 160,
179–80; and creative resistance to
sensibility, xxvi, xxix, xlvi–xlix; —in
Analytical Review, 86–93; —in
"Cave of Fancy," 68; —in
correspondence, 16–18, 34; —in
education treatises, 82; —in Letters
in Sweden, 145, 179–80; —in Mary,
35, 39, 56, 60; —in Rights of Men and
Rights of Woman, 97–129; as
daughter of the Enlightenment, xi,
xxix, 70; as demythologizer, xxii; —
in Analytical Review, 87–88; —in
education treatises, 82; —in French
Revolution, 143; —in Letters in
Sweden, 145, 149–51, 154–58; —in
Mary, 35, 45–46, 53–56; —in Rights
of Men, 100–108; —in Rights of
Woman, 114–16, 118–19; as "female
Werther," xxii–xxiii, xxix, 8, 12, 16,
23–24, 27, 31, 33; as Feminist, xi, 35,
94–95, 100, 112–29, 146–47, 154,
156–58, 160–78; in France, 18–26,
133–44; on friendship, 6–8, 10–12,
43–53, 126–27, 162–66; as heir to
the myths of sensibility, xxvi,
xxxiii–xxxiv, xl–xlii, 8, 13–14,
20–21, 31–34, 61–68, 71–72, 88,
100–101, 123–27, 158; as historian
of sensibility, 133–44; as
impassioned polemicist in the name
of reason, 97–129; in Ireland, 14–17,
80; as language conscious, xiv, xvi,
xxiii–xxiv; —in Analytical Review,
93–95; —in correspondence, 6–8,
23, 29–34; —in French Revolution,
135–38; —in Maria, 164, 169–72; —
in Mary, 45–47, 53–54; —in Rights

of Men, 100, 104–7, 111; —in Rights
of Woman, 116–17, 120–22, 125;
and the literature of sensibility,
xxii–xxiii, xxx, xli–xlii, xlviii–xlix;
—in correspondence, 6–8, 21, 31,
34; —in Analytical Review, 86–96;
—in Letters in Sweden, 147, 157; —in
Maria, 160, 166–71, 175; —in Mary,
35, 37–38, 42; —in Rights of Men,
97–111; —in Rights of Woman,
115–16, 119–23; and melancholy,
xvi, xxi; —in Analytical Review,
86–89, 95–96; —in "Cave of
Fancy," 61–68; —in correspondence,
14–16, 19–22, 25–34; —in
education treatises, 73, 78–80; —in
French Revolution, 134–35; —in
Letters in Sweden, 149, 152–55,
157–59; —in Maria, 162; —in Mary,
38–39, 46–47, 54; —in Rights of
Woman, 112, 124, 127–29; as
mythmaker of sensibility in her own
right: —in "Cave of Fancy," 61–68;
—in correspondence, 5, 11, 23,
27–28; —in French Revolution, 136,
138, 142–44; —in Letters in Sweden,
145, 148–51, 154–55, 158–59; —in
Mary, 35; —in Rights of Men, 108; as
novelist of sensibility, 35–60,
160–78; and preference for
spontaneous, unadorned style, xxxiv,
7–12, 33–34, 93–94, 99–101, 104–7,
116, 120–21, 125, 138; her private
correspondence and sensibility, 5–34;
as reviewer of fiction, 85–96; and
Romanticism, xi, 94, 159; on
sensibility and civilization, 136,
138–45, 149–50; —and its
counterfeits, 72, 75, 87, 89–90,
93–94, 97–103, 136, 173; —and
education, 36–41, 43, 63, 66–82,
71–72, 75, 90, 105, 112–13, 117–23,
125–27, 138–39, 143, 146, 150, 152,
159, 174; —and joy, xix, xl, 27, 60,
166; —and gender, 13–15, 48–49,
65–66, 73, 86–87, 100–102,
112–29, 144–45, 148, 150, 156–58,
160, 165–66; —and genius, 16–17,
23, 27–28, 35–36, 39–40, 47–48, 62,
65–66, 90–91, 103–5, 161–62; —
and illness, 13–16, 35, 38, 66–68,